WHAT THE FACH?!

WHAT THE FACH?!

THE DEFINITIVE GUIDE FOR OPERA SINGERS AUDITIONING AND WORKING IN GERMANY, AUSTRIA AND SWITZERLAND

SECOND EDITION

(VIS MÄNI MEHR INFORMATIONS TO MAKE WERY GUT EXPERIENCES)

Philip Shepard

WHAT THE FACH?! PRESS

WHAT THE FACH?!

The Definitive Guide for Opera Singers Auditioning and Working in Germany, Austria and Switzerland

© 2010 by What The FACH?! Press

Previous edition published under Philip Shepard Press, 2007

What The FACH?! Press: Kansas City, Missouri

Published by What-The-Fach.com Press

2010 Edition

ISBN 1451577028

EAN-13: 9781451577020

Library of Congress Control Number: 2010927854

All Rights Reserved. No part of this publication may be reproduced or transmitted in any form or by any means, electronic or mechanical, including photocopying and recording, or by any information storage retrieval system, without permission in writing from the publisher.

Additional paperback, eBook, iPad, iPhone, iTouch, eReader, and Amazon Kindle copies of *What The FACH?!* may be purchased from any bookstore and at **www.what-the-fach.com**. Follow us on Twitter at **@WhatTheFACHbook**.

CONTENTS

PREFACE TO SECOND EDITION	11
2010 ~ Somewhere in Europe	
DEDICATION	14
AUTHOR'S ACKNOWLEDGMENTS	14
EINS: How Good Are Your Goods?	15
Is a Fest contract right for you?	15
Can you really live over here? Do you really want to live here?	17
How old are you? Are you hot? How much do you weigh?	21
Am I at an advantage or disadvantage because I am a native English speaker?	23
ZWEI: It's All in the Preparation	24
Alles auf Deutsch, Ami.	24
How about learning Some German before you come?	25
How about learning some German in Germany before your audition tour?	26
The work climate	26
Let's talk Fach. Ohhhhh yeaaah.	28
Operetta	31
Theater sizes	32
When should I come? How long do I gotta stay?	33
DREI: Me Write Agents and Theaters Real Good With Real Neat Publicity Materials in German	36
Writing agents	37
Writing theaters	38
Publicity materials: cover letter, résumé, and biography	39
CDs	40
Web sites, e-mail, and fax	41
When to send your materials	41
VIER: I'm Gonna Need a Sugar Daddy	42

Passports and visas	43
Finding a home base	45
Finding an apartment	46
Hotels. No, I didn't say hostels.	47
Audition fees	48
Coaches	48
Food	48
Cash machines, banking, and travelers checks	50
Health/Travel insurance	50
What to pack	51

FÜNF: Planes, Trains, and Automobiles (and Buses and Bicycles and S-Bahns) — 52

Getting to Europe	52
Before you choose an American-based airline...	53
Getting around Europe by train	54
Public city transportation (bus/U-Bahn/S-Bahn)	58
Ride sharing	59
Air travel within Europe	59
Auto rental	60
Buy a used bike	61

SECHS: Your Trip Over and Arrival to the Mother Continent — 62

Pre-Audition Tour Checklist	62
Handy/Mobile phone	63
Üben/Practicing	65
Internet and your laptop	65
Internet telephoning	66
So, you're krank/sick	66

SIEBEN: Agents and Theaters: They Love You, They Hate You, They Love You... — 69

What to expect at agent auditions	69
A note on what to wear and what not to wear	70
Repertoire to bring	71

Contents

Forms, etc. — 72
The agent wants to work with you! — 73
When will they send me to theater auditions? — 73
Follow-up and nurturing the singer-agent relationship — 74
So the agent does not want to work with you — 75
Theater auditions — 76
A typical theater audition — 76

ACHT: You're Hired (You Like Me, You Really Like Me!) — 79
What do you do now? — 79
1. Negotiate the contract/Verhandeln — 80
    Fach classification and specific roles — 82
    Duration of contract, salary, and per performance/broadcast fees — 82
    Agent commission — 83
    Pay — 83
    Plane tickets — 84
2. Find an apartment/Wohnung suchen — 85
3. Registration/Anmelden — 86
4. Residence permit and work permit/ Aufenthaltserlaubnis/ Aufenthaltsbewilligung and Arbeitserlaubnis — 86
    In Germany — 87
    In Austria — 88
5. Income tax classification card/Lohnsteuerkarte — 91
6. You have to put all that money somewhere. Get a bank account and learn how to transfer money back home for free./Bankkonto — 92
7. Choose your health insurance/Krankenkasse and Krankenversicherung — 94
8. Get a driver's license / Der Führerschein — 95

NEUN: Taxes and Kindergeld (Money for the Kids) — 96
Taxes in Germany — 96
Taxes in Germany when you are guesting — 99
    Foreigner's Tax/Ausländersteuer — 99
    Income tax for guest performances — 100
    Einspringen taxes — 100

WHAT THE FACH?!

Lodging	100
Taxes in Austria	101
Doing your taxes/Steuererklärung	102
Kindergeld	102

ZEHN: Pot Luck Dinner — **104**

Festing and guesting	104
Künstlersozialkasse / KSK	105
Jumping in/Einspringen	106
Tipping with festing, guesting, and einspringen	107
Renegotiating your Fest contract	109
Teaching English during your audition tour	109
Opera studios and young artist programs	112
Chorus work	113

ELF: INTERVIEWS: You Think I'm Full of Crap? Then Read What My Colleagues Have to Say. — **113**

INTERVIEW 1 ~ Ellen Rissinger, American coach	114
INTERVIEW 2 ~ Angela Fout, American soprano	120
INTERVIEW 3 ~ Christine Graham, American soprano	123
INTERVIEW 4 ~ Thomas Schmidt (not his real name), European conductor	126
INTERVIEW 5 ~ Damon Nestor Ploumis, American/British/Greek buffo bass-baritone	130
INTERVIEW 6 ~ Robert Tannenbaum, American stage director and Oberspielleiter (Chief Producer of Opera) of Badisches Staatstheater Karlsruhe	135
INTERVIEW 7 ~ Helene von Orlowsky, Swedish Künstlerische Betriebsdirektorin (Director of Artistic Administration) for Austria's Landestheater Linz	153
INTERVIEW 8 ~ Alma Wagner (not her real name), German mezzo-soprano	161

ZWÖLF: NYIOPS: Never Heard of Them? Where Have You Been? — **169**

Interview with David Blackburn, CEO, founder of NYIOP, Artistic Consultant for Teatro Communale Bologna, and (as of 2010) Director of Artistic Operations for Palm Beach Opera	170

CONTENTS

DREIZEHN: All in the Family: Life in an Ensemble — **177**
Intendant, colleagues, and atmosphere — 177
Where to start festing and when to jump ship? — 180
Da du da Sie — 181
Illness and vacation — 182
Musical preparation and stage rehearsals — 183
Plays well with others — 185
Stability — 186

CONCLUSION: Veni, Vidi, Vici — **187**

PHRASE BOOK AND DICTIONARY — **188**
The Very Basic — 188
Publicity — 188
For the Résumé — 189
Musical Terminology — 190
In the Theater — 191
    Places in the Theater — 191
    Places on Stage — 192
    People in the Theater — 193
    Activities in the Theater — 194
    Miscellaneous in the Theater — 195
    Phrases to use before your audition — 196
    Phrases to use during your audition — 197
On the Telephone — 198
In Sickness and in Health — 199
Contracts — 200
Bureaucracy: Permits, Money, and Taxes — 200
Transportation — 202
Finding an Apartment — 204
Miscellaneous — 205

WEB SITES AND DOCUMENTS — **206**
Embassies and Consulates General — 206

Germany	206
Austria	206
Switzerland	206
Foreign Embassies in Germany	207
Foreign Embassies in Austria	207
Foreign Embassies in Switzerland	207
Visa Applications and Essential Documents	208
Opera Studios / Young Artist Programs	208
Recommended Reading, Publications, and Documents	209
Transportation Websites	210
Airline Search Sites	211
European Airline/Discount Airline Search Sites	211
Discount European Airlines	211
Traditional European Airlines	213
Eurailpasses, Train Travel, Hotels, and Travel/Health Insurance	213
Local Public Transportation Web Sites	214
Apartments	214
Mobile Phone/Handy Providers	214
Practice Spaces	215
Audition Websites	216
German Language Schools	216
Banks and Money Transfer Service	217
Internet	217
Taxes and Finance	217
Social Services ~ Retirement, Health Insurance, and Kindergeld	218
Miscellaneous Websites	219

RESOURCES   **221**

Prescription and Nonprescription Medication	221
National Holidays	228
Sample Résumé	230
Form Letters	231
Form E-Mails	233
ZAV Audition Invitation E-Mail	235

Contents

Opera and Concert Agents	236
Agents in Germany	236
Agents in Austria	245
Agents in Switzerland	248
Seven Ways to Soak in the Language	250
Ten Things I Love about Germany and Austria	250

PREFACE TO THE SECOND EDITION

2010 ~ Somewhere in Europe

So much has changed in the world since I wrote the First Edition of *What The FACH?!* in 2007. We have had a near-complete global economic meltdown and the arts are going through precarious times. Fun, fun, fun. But don't quit reading.

While most of what I originally wrote is still accurate, I felt that now would be the perfect time to revisit this book and make some important revisions and expand on what I began back in the pre-Potts/Boyle/Bieber/Snookie years. I have made the predictable changes that come with updates (i.e. re-checking facts and numbers, etc.) and have also expanded the Second Edition to include additional interviews and extra sections. Naturally, my opinions have evolved, as well, due to four more seasons of experience in this crazy opera world. I have tried my utmost to keep the sardonic and optimistic tone in this book, but I have also tempered it with the pragmatic optimism one settles into after four more seasons here. I have thrown away my last pair of rainbow colored sunglasses and am here to give you, as I did in the First Edition, a first-hand, honest look into the German-speaking opera world.

This book began as a Thursday evening project, stretching into an all night project, and growing steadily into an insatiable obsession to create the definitive guide for opera professionals in German-speaking Europe. I could not have done this alone. *What The FACH*?! (www.what-the-fach.com) is the definitive resource for opera singers planning to audition and work in Germany, Austria, and Switzerland. This book is filled with my personal experiences as a full-time, working American opera singer in Europe. I have included advice about what you need to do in preparation for a successful audition trip, information about negotiating your first contract, and plenty of thoughts on how to make a smooth and painless transition to a working singer, making a living in Europe.

I am not shy about expressing my opinion and you are, of course, welcome to take it or leave it. However, this book presents you with accurate, factual information from numerous sources that will save you countless hours of searching, mental anguish, and all-too-frequent frustration.

Many sources were used in compiling information for this book: official publications from the German, Austrian, and Swiss governments;

PREFACE

publications from professional organizations; interviews with numerous colleagues; Rudolf Kloiber's *Handbuch der Oper; Deutsches Bühnen Jahrbuch*; and also plenty of personal experience. Because my German-speaking European performing experience is mostly in Austria and Germany, I have chosen to include Switzerland only when I can confidently present accurate information. Although I am American, I have made a concerted effort to keep citizens of other nations in mind while writing this book, particularly the fine people of Canada, Australia, New Zealand, Great Britain, and South Africa. Occasionally, the information I have provided may be slanted towards the American reader, and I hope that it does not diminish the usefulness of this publication for singers of other nationalities and with other mother languages besides English. For this, I ask your understanding.

For the sake of clarification, whenever I mention *Fest*, the *Festsystem* and auditioning in Europe, I am referring to the same entity: being a full-time employed singer in a German, Austrian or Swiss opera house. Throughout the book, I have included German translations in both the masculine and feminine (e.g., *Intendant/–in*) that are useful words for your German vocabulary. A comprehensive phrasebook and dictionary may be found beginning on p. 188.

I have chosen to remain anonymous (writing under a pseudonym) as have some subjects of my interviews; anonymity affords me the luxury of expressing my uncensored opinions, and it's just the way I prefer it. With that said, what I write is true and unembellished, the people I have interviewed are real, working professionals, and I have double-checked my facts to insure that I present you with accurate information.

Here is the *Reader's Digest* version of who I am and the path I took to my present career in Europe, where I have been living and working for seven seasons. In December a few years ago after completing the New York City main stage audition season, I was faced with two months free before my next engagement. I had recently earned my Master's degree from a top program in America and had just completed my distinguished (and perhaps too lengthy) young artist program career. I was working with an artist manager in New York and was just beginning to do main stage work in America. I had around twenty roles—big and small—on my résumé and two small engagements in my future, but I wanted to gain experience one can only find in Europe.

I decided to come to Germany for five weeks in January and

WHAT THE FACH?!

February for an impromptu audition tour. In preparation, I lined up one German house audition through a generous friend and then sent my materials semi-randomly to about forty agents and ten theaters in the German-speaking world. I really had no idea at all how to go about an audition tour. To my amazement, within a week of sending my materials away, I began receiving invitations to audition from both agents and theaters. Before I left America, I already had six auditions arranged.

After three weeks in Europe and a few auditions, I had a stroke of incredibly good fortune when an agent (for whom I had not yet auditioned, strangely enough) called me at 11:30 AM. He asked me if I was available to jump immediately into rehearsals of a leading role in an opera (that I had already performed twice). "Yes, of course," was my answer. At 6 PM that same day, after stopping briefly at the music store for the piano/vocal score and then taking a three-hour train trip, I was rehearsing on the stage of a reputable regional German house. I was hired as a guest for the production, which paid for my next few months in Germany. Just like those bad diet pill commercials say, results may vary, and my results were an enormous stroke of good fortune combined with preparation.

A few months later and with another stroke of great fortune, I replaced a singer at the last minute as a guest in a production that also led to my first *Fest* contract with a "B" House. The rest is history, and many seasons later—full of both *Fest* and guest work—I am now a freelance opera singer living in Germany, with work in both Europe and America.

So there you go. I have been here for a while, I have a healthy international career, and I have some worthwhile tips to pass along. Living and working in Europe is exciting, interesting, frustrating, exhausting, invigorating, fulfilling, and always an adventure. Let this book be your guide!

DEDICATION

To my nephew, Jesse.

AUTHOR'S ACKNOWLEDGMENTS

I must first and foremost thank my charming and intelligent fiancé, Sarah, for her indefatigable patience, advice, and bi-lingual proofreading skills. This book would have never come to fruition without her input and listening capabilities. Sarah has been a constant source of support and advice. Together with her, I have been able to improve and expand this project.

I am fortunate to have a number of generous colleagues who agreed to be victimized by my sophomoric interviewing technique, among them: Ellen Rissinger, Angela Fout, David Blackburn, Damon Nestor Ploumis, Nadine Weissmann, Delia Tedeschi, Robert Tannenbaum, and Helene von Orlowsky. To those who were kind enough to read through my various drafts and put their good names behind my work: Garnett Bruce, Kirsten Gunlogson, Corey McKern, Monica Yunus, Erin Williams, Larry Cotter, Aaron Judisch, Patrick Carfizzi, and Kate Aldrich—I am immensely grateful for your feedback. Ravil Atlas was a frequent source of helpful advice and brainstorming, and he encouraged me to think big. Ravil was often there with creative ideas that helped take this project in new directions. I thank my father who has been a constant supply of *pro bono* legal advice, certainly saving me from an onslaught of libel litigation. He was also the venture capitalist who helped get this initial project off the ground. I must also thank Matt Treviño for his help posting the original guide to the Web and for giving me the Web domain. I still owe him a big beer four years later. Thank you to my future brother-in-law, Dr. Christopher Schäfer, who prepared the medication table; and thank you to Julie Baron, who informed me of the importance of having a Shengen Visa.

1 EINS
How Good Are Your Goods?

So, you've been thinking about coming to Europe—more specifically, Germany, Austria and Switzerland—for an audition tour. You certainly have plenty of questions about the entire process: *Where do I begin? What do I do in preparation for an audition tour? Whom do I write? Is there even any work left over there? What kind of competition am I up against? How much does this cost? How long should I stay? What is life like in the Festsystem? Do I even want to live over there?* There are a thousand questions to ask and answer, so you need to get organized. It's best to start at the beginning.

Is a Fest contract right for you?

This book presents you with plenty of vital information for auditioning and working here. However, merely having this information is not going to get you a job. You need to honestly assess if you are ready for this new career direction.

Accepting a *Fest* contract means that you are essentially a member of a large theater family, performing a number of roles in repertoire over the course of a season (generally 10 1/2 months). You are a full-time employee of the theater and are (for a finite time, at least) no longer your own boss. It is up to you to decide if this is a wise move for you and one you wish to make. Keep in mind that a *Fest* contract will keep you occupied in Europe, and it will be a challenge to maintain personal relationships and professional contacts in your home country while you are in an ensemble.

Before you embark on this adventure, ask yourself a number of important questions and answer them honestly. You should candidly assess if you are able and willing to take on the vocal, mental, and physical challenges of a *Fest* engagement. Are you working now in your home country? Yes? Good. No? Why not? What kind of feedback are you getting from opera professionals? Do they give positive feedback and encourage you to come over to Europe and further your career, or do they say your technique is not together and your skills (e.g., languages, stage skills, etc.) need more work?

First thing is first. Your technique absolutely must be together for your *Fest* engagement to be a success. Is your technique in good shape and will it be in even better shape at the end of a busy season? If you are a *Dramatischer Koloratursopran*, can you juggle Norma, Fiordiligi, Violetta, and Miss Wordsworth in the same season, singing performances in repertoire? If you are a *Lyrischer Tenor*, can you sing Ernesto on Tuesday, Belmonte on Thursday, and Almaviva on Sunday, all while in final dress rehearsals for Alfredo in the mornings? The morning dress rehearsals are all with orchestra, so the conductor will probably want you to sing out. Of course, not every week is so severe, but I cannot remember how many times I have faced similarly challenging schedules. You will frequently rehearse and perform on the same day, and the opera you rehearse in the morning will often be a different opera than what you perform in the evening.

While opinions about opera and aesthetics are certainly different here in Europe than in North America, a tenor without high notes, a mezzo with a wobble, and a baritone who sings a half tone flat, all sound the same whether they are in New York, Sydney, or Mainz. If these problems are keeping you from getting work at home, the same is going to happen here, I promise you. Or even worse, you may actually get work and exacerbate your technical problems. Bad idea. Spend your money first on resolving these issues. If you have some serious technical problems, getting a *Fest* engagement is just going to put you in a world of hurt when you run out of gas in the middle of a production during the middle of the season. Being in an ensemble can take its toll on you if you are not prepared for the work. On the contrary, you should not wait until everything is perfect (although there really is no "perfect") before you come.

Once you begin performing an opera as a member of the ensemble, the next production will often begin rehearsals. By the end of the season you may be juggling four, six, or ten shows, including rehearsals for the opening opera of the next season. If you think you can sing from forty to over one hundred performances in the same season (I'm not joking) and still be in good shape at the end of the season, this may be for you. Moreover, you will have few, if any, chances to get back to your teacher in New York, London, or Sydney, during the season.

The work is hard and can be immensely rewarding. Being in an ensemble can be an artistically fulfilling and enjoyable lifestyle. Life is good! If you are ready for the challenge, this is an ideal way to build your repertoire, improve your craft, and give your career a solid foundation on which to build. Imagine the experience of performing Gilda seventeen times over the course of a season. Such an experience is invaluable and you certainly are not going to find that opportunity so easily in America or England. Believe me, after you perform a role fifteen or twenty times, your stagecraft improves in ways you could never imagine, and (if your technique is together) the role really gets into your voice, so to speak.

So if you are in doubt about whether this is the right step for you, hop to it and get some professional advice. Consult people who know first-hand the business of *singing professionally in international theaters for a living*, preferably with experience working in German-speaking theaters.

Can you really live over here? Do you really want to live here?

You should really ask and answer this question truthfully. Germany, Austria, and Switzerland are completely different cultures from America, Britain, and Australia. Although German is spoken in all three countries, you will find the cultural differences significant. I find the pace of life over here refreshing, and in contrast to life in America, people take more time to enjoy the present and are not riddled with guilt by taking a couple hours in the afternoon to relax and take a walk. Most rehearsals take place in the mornings and evenings, leaving the afternoons free for life outside the theater. Don't misunderstand me; we also work hard here, but the culture here places importance on relaxation and the pleasure of everyday simplicities. It's a good life.

Although there are some reminders of home (i.e., MTV in German, McDonalds, the occasional Starbucks, etc.), the cultural differences far outweigh the similarities. The Germanic mentality is much different from the American or British mentality, and the Austrian mentality is something else altogether. Then there are the Swiss: friendly, organized, punctual, productive, and the list goes on. They are an international, multi-lingual culture, and speak their own brand of German: Swiss-German (*Schwyzerdütsch*). It is almost impossible to understand (even after months of working there), but they almost immediately switch to *Hochdeutsch* or English when they hear that you are not Swiss. The only time this did not happen was when I opened my Swiss bank account. The sweet teller explained everything to me in the city's *Schwyzerdütsch* dialect, and I still do not understand what kind of bank account I actually have.

Are you all right with being away from your family and friends for an extended period of time? Is your spouse or significant other supportive? If you have children, is this a move that the entire family is willing to make? When you have a death in your extended family, can you live with yourself because you had to sing a performance of *La Bohème* instead of making it back to America for the funeral? Can you live with not shopping on Sundays?

Although stores in Germany used to all close at 8 PM Monday thru Saturday, this is changing. The German government has just deregulated shopping hour restrictions and passed a law allowing each individual state to set their own shopping hours. This means that some stores may now stay open until 10 PM, and some until Midnight. The stores still often close early on Saturdays, and a sizable part of the country shuts down on Sundays. If you want to buy shoes on Sunday, forget it.

Austria is more extreme; on weekdays, stores here stay open until either 6 PM or 7 PM, many close early on Saturdays (i.e., 2 PM) or are closed altogether, and virtually nothing is open on Sundays. I must say, though, that while I initially had trouble adjusting to the relatively limited shopping hours here, I now enjoy that things close down in the evenings and on Sundays. (When in dire need of a jar of mayonnaise or other essential items, I can always go to a gas station; they stay open late into the evening.)

What the Fach?!

There are many wonderful aspects to raising children in Germany, Austria, and Switzerland, but it is different in so many ways from life in Indiana. If your spouse or partner does not speak German, the first few months can be difficult. But don't freak out; you are not moving to the Moon. With a bit of effort and a positive attitude, it is possible to learn German and assimilate into European society.

German society is somewhat rigid and formal compared to America, the degrees of which depend on where you are in Germany. Just as in America, some cities have incredibly friendly inhabitants and others not so much (I am not giving examples). What we Americans sometimes consider good social graces, the Germans often consider superficial (*oberflächlich*). The phrases "How are you," and "It's pleasure to meet you," for example, are just not thrown around like they are in Omaha. If you ask how someone is, be prepared to chat about it for a minute or two because they assume that you are genuinely interested. And vice versa; if someone asks you how you are, they are genuinely interested.

Customer service in stores and restaurants is, diplomatically stated, dreadful. With some exceptions it is common to be treated as if I should consider myself lucky I am gracing a store or restaurant with my business. It is also quite common to be nudged, pushed, and bumped into on the street and to receive no "excuse me" (*Entschuldigen Sie*). Each city and state is different, and the degrees of decorum and rudeness vary, you'll see.

Shopping here can be an adventure. When you are out shopping, you may notice that Germans love to cut in line. They will do almost anything to squirm their way in front of you. It is actually quite humorous (when it is not infuriating), especially when you call them out on it and they innocently respond that they did not even see you there (as they pushed you out of the way)!

Once you get to know German people, they can be quite warm. They do not, however, traditionally open right up to newly met acquaintances as Americans might do. Germans value friendship greatly, something you will appreciate when you are invited to a new friend's home for your first coffee and cake (*Kaffee und Kuchen*), a tradition of afternoon coffee and dessert. But be warned that they are very direct. If you ask a question, you will get an honest, often unedited, response.

I find Austria much different than Germany, in that people take pains here to engage in the simple social graces reminiscent of my Midwestern American upbringing. Life appears also to be a bit more relaxed here. I find the pace of life in Austria to be a bit slower than life in Germany; there is an everyday optimism evident with people, and the customer service is generally better than Germany. One of the many great things about Austria is the abundance of coffee houses. They are everywhere, the service ranges from just ok to fantastic, and you are expected to not only enjoy your café, but also stay for a while and soak in the atmosphere. The wait staff will not put the pressure on you to pay and turn over the table to the next customer.

There is cigarette smoke absolutely everywhere in Austria, something with which I constantly struggle. People smoke everywhere in Austria including in the theaters. In fact, I was on stage a few seasons ago singing my big duet with the soprano and I smelled smoke! That's amazing, no? The duet came right after intermission and the audience had just been blazing it up in the foyer. While they have passed token anti-smoking laws in the past couple years, it is window dressing at best. Austria's stong pro-tobacco lobby seems to step solidly in the way of any progress.

Germany has changed their smoking laws greatly in the past three years, and the benefits are easy to see. Smoking is now banned in public places, including bars and restaurants (www.howtogermany.com/pages/nosmoking.html). You will unfortunately get used to the smoke to some degree. The good news is that the anti-smoking movement continues to pick up momentum.

None of my cultural observations are meant maliciously, and if you have been here you may likely have conflicting views. Let me make it very clear: I absolutely love it here and I am comparing apples and oranges, so to speak. I do not mean to challenge or question you by suggesting you ask yourself all these questions. Rather, it is best to face any fears or concerns head-on to see if you are ready for this career and life change. When you come to Europe, resist the urge to constantly compare the culture here to that of your home country. Jump in and try to assimilate; let yourself be open to new experiences. Simply being here can be a thrilling and life-changing experience.

How old are you? Are you hot? How much do you weigh?

My colleagues in America often ask me what role physical appearance and age play in the hiring of singers in Germany and Austria. These factors play a role of varying degrees depending on the tastes of the theater, and they are often a part of the hiring equation. Some theaters want an ensemble of singers fresh out of school that look like Abercrombie & Fitch™ models, while other General Directors (*Intendanten*) hire singers based just on singing and/or acting. They want you to look like the roles you might sing.

Age. It is simply a matter of taste whether the *Intendant/–in* likes younger or older singers. Younger singers in *Fest* engagements (very generally speaking) sound not only fresher than their older colleagues—they have not been singing eight productions and one hundred performances in repertoire, per season for twenty-five years—but they are also cheaper to hire. What young singers often cannot do effectively is sing some of the heavier, more dramatic repertoire. A twenty-five year old baritone cannot sing everything from soup to nuts unless he wants to make his first season here his last. Our more mature and experienced colleagues are essential to rounding out an ensemble. They often lead by example and are a great source for wisdom about how to survive and grow in the *Fest* system. I have colleagues from ages twenty-three to sixty-seven, and the sixty-seven year old is one of the best singers I have heard in a long time. While some theaters and agents have asked my age, I only know of it once working against me (I am thirty-*something*!) though I assume it has on other occasions, as well. Who knows and who cares; I cannot change how old I am. Somehow, age seems to matter much more to Americans than it does to the Europeans. In fact, getting your first *Fest* engagement at thirty, while not the norm, is certainly not unheard of. Being thirty-five years old should not palpably discourage you from coming here and looking for work. And in the end, who cares how old you are if you have a great voice.

Physical appearance. The truth is that being beautiful is an asset, or so people tell me. For the rest of us in the vast middle, with a little makeup we look beautiful from the fourth row, or as I once heard a colleague say, "Opera beautiful." I can think off-hand of one German theater where each member of the ensemble is drop dead gorgeous. They are also mostly under twenty-five, singing roles for which they are nowhere near ready, burning their voices out, and many will be finished in three years.

Weight. I understand that the issue of weight is sensitive, but you deserve candor. I cannot issue statements of infallibility regarding weight and hiring in German-speaking theaters. Rather, I can merely share my observations from experience. Although I do not pretend to read the minds of *Intendanten* or Agents, one look at the singers on the stages here proves that either weight is influential with hiring decisions or there are fewer overweight (i.e., obese and morbidly obese) singers auditioning for work in theaters here. Working singers here are often physically fit and height-weight proportionate. The stages in Germany and Austria are much smaller than America (many houses here are under one thousand seats), and your extra weight will not be so easy to conceal. With that said, weight plays less of an issue when there are difficult voice types (*Fächer*) and roles to fill, such as the heroic and Wagner repertoire. If you sing a hell of an Otello, nobody is going to care if you are one hundred eighty lbs or three hundred twenty lbs; it is a tough role to cast. If you sing Susanna in *Le nozze di Figaro* and weigh two hundred ten lbs, you are going to have considerable difficulties being cast; there are a lot of Susannas running around looking for work and *Intendanten* can therefore afford to be picky.

If you are considering an audition tour and are overweight, now is the time to begin losing some of that weight and getting into better shape. I can confidently say that since I have worked in Europe, the vast majority of my performing colleagues have been height-weight proportionate. Some have big bottoms, some have hips, some have love handles, some have bellies, some are built like cover models, many are average, and *none* are hindered on stage by extra weight. You will be expected to move easily on stage, and while ten lbs of junk in your trunk is not going to keep you from getting the gig, sixty lbs very well might.

Here is an example where being overweight is not an obstacle: I saw a production recently of a Wagner opera in a well-known, international house with a large seating capacity and big stage. The leading soprano was clearly overweight and while she is certainly not well known, she is working around in very good houses. She was overweight, completely believable in her role, moved very well on stage, and had a voice directly from Heaven for a difficult-to-fill role. However, every other soloist was height-weight proportionate.

You may believe the weight conscious mindset by European theaters and audiences is discriminatory, and it very well may be. Although it may sound rude and you may not want to hear it, if you want to work here you simply need to accept and understand this mentality. Only you can decide if you need to make lifestyle changes to increase your ability of being hired.

Am I at an advantage or disadvantage because I am a native English speaker?

My opinion of fellow English-speaking colleagues is bound to be somewhat biased, so I have asked numerous colleagues for their opinions of American, Canadian, British, Australian, and New Zealander singers working here. Below is a compilation of not only my observations, but also those of a number of colleagues.

Americans and singers from other English-speaking countries have a great reputation in Germany and Austria. We are known to be extremely well prepared, we learn quickly, we are proficient at singing a number of languages, we come from good schools of singing where we received high-quality training in everything from acting to sight singing, and we are considered good colleagues. (You will be surprised with your first *Fest* engagement by how many of your wonderful European colleagues have never sung a word of French.) While we expect every professional singer to have the above skills before being engaged, this will not be the case with every singer in your particular theater (diplomatically put, I hope).

Europeans enjoy seeing and hearing uniqueness in performances. I have heard from a number of Europeans that we (Americans, in particular) are too "perfectly" prepared, so much so that our performance package sometimes borders on the generic. Many times I have seen theaters hire the more exciting performer with an inferior technique over the more technically proficient, yet generic singer. But of course, most theaters would prefer to have not only the exciting performance, but also the great technique in the same package.

2 ZWEI

It's All in the Preparation

As a well-regarded American acting instructor and director says, "preparation is the key to success." This holds particularly true to your audition tour; the better you prepare for a European audition trip, the more enjoyable and successful it is bound to be. Before you come to Europe you should do your research, and it begins with your *Deutsch*.

Alles auf Deutsch, Ami.

Kannst Du Deutsch sprechen? Wenn Du diese zwei Sätze nicht lesen kannst, musst Du etwas mehr Deutsch lernen. Wenn Du kein Problem damit hast, wirst Du bestimmt keine Probleme mit deinen Vorsingen haben.

Learning the German language is a challenge, but by doing so you earn the respect of your fellow colleagues and open yourself up to a completely different culture. It is in your best interests to become fluent in German, and learning German will maximize the return on your audition tour investment. Yes, many people speak English here and when you first arrive (during your first season, at least) they will be patient as you try to grasp the language. But if you accept a *Fest* engagement, your colleagues will expect you to learn the language well. You will certainly have to speak German dialogue in productions, especially in operetta and musical theater.

I have worked in *Fest* ensembles with a few colleagues from various non German-speaking nations who did not bother to learn German and mangled the most basic of German phrases. These were cases of complacency and laziness, not a struggle with German in an effort to grasp the language. These singers lost the respect of their colleagues and the theater. So continue your study once you land the job; people notice. With a bit of effort you will pleasantly surprise your colleagues. Your effort will also help overcome the prejudice here against native English speakers who do not bother to learn German, a prejudice that is unfortunately alive and well.

How about learning Some German before you come?

Your chances for success increase significantly when you are able to speak German. When you do not speak German, it just another excuse for a theater not to hire you or an agent not to represent you. So take German courses before you come, brush up with your old college textbook, find a tutor, take a class at the local community college, play Scrabble™ in German, or find a good self-teaching course on iTunes University. Whatever you do, study your German.

There are a number of self-study German courses with books and CDs, including the reputable Rosetta Stone Language Study Series (www.rosettastone.com). Should you have the funds to take a private course in America before your audition trip, the Goethe Institut (www.goethe.de) in New York City (and various other cities) along with Berlitz (www.berlitz.com), should give you a good start. I have colleagues who learned a great deal of German in a very short time at The Middlebury College German Program for Singers (www.middlebury.edu) in Vermont.

With that said, it is not imperative to speak fluent German when you get off the plane for your audition tour. If you have an understanding of the grammar, you can order food, exchange social pleasantries and small talk, and get through an audition with your dignity intact, this is a good beginning.

If you have no German experience, you speak no German, you cannot take a course before coming, and you still insist on coming for an audition tour, you should *really* take a German course before you come. But if you *still* insist on coming, at least learn important words and phrases: "hello" (*Guten Tag*), "goodbye" (*Auf Wiedersehen*), "thank you" (*danke schön*), "please" (*bitte*), "stage door entrance" (*Bühneneingang*), and the difference between an "exit" (*Ausgang*) and "emergency exit" (*Notausgang*). I learned the difference between the last two in the Duisburg Opera House—a very embarrassing learning experience.

I found the Berlitz German Phrasebook (www.amazon.com), a good German dictionary, and my old college German textbook great companions to get me through my first months here. They should be your friends, too.

How about learning some German in Germany before your audition tour?

If you would like to prepare for your audition tour with a German language course in Europe, try (again) the Goethe Institut (www.goethe.de) or Berlitz (www.berlitz.com), two of the most respected language schools. Do your research before you make your decision, though; there are countless language schools offering to teach you German and not all of them are equal. Ask for first hand recommendations from people who have already been to language schools, or get back in touch with your old college German professor for a recommendation. To profit most from your experience, search for a program with low teacher-student ratios and the option of taking private lessons. You will also get the most out of your experience if you live with a German-speaking family during your course and you do not hang out with fellow English speakers. Duh.

The work climate

Perhaps you have heard some colleagues tell you that finding work in Germany as a singer is not as easy as it was in the past. This is unfortunately true, and while I considered most of these claims as exaggerated just a few years ago, some seem to be more accurate in 2010. Before I arrived in Europe in 2004, many American colleagues warned me that "there is no work over there anymore," that the German Theaters "are in peril," and other apocalyptic observations. The truth is that since the reunification of Germany and the fall of the Iron Curtain, the extra strain of aiding the economic growth of the former East Germany (to whom workers in Germany pay a tax), and the perennially struggling German economy, it is a greater challenge to find work than it was just five, ten or twenty years ago. There is considerable competition here, there are more theaters with serious financial problems than there were in the 1980's, and the current economic meltdown has only deepened the financial woes. Singers come from all over the world in hopes of starting or advancing their careers here. At one of my recent auditions, for example, there was another American, a Swede, an Austrian, a couple Germans, an Italian, and a Bulgarian.

Austria is a different theme on the same story; there is competition from singers of many nations, but there is also strong financial support for the theaters. Austria places a high priority on investing in their culture, and this includes generous financial support of the theaters. Once you hear the reverence with which Austrians speak when they mention the Wiener Staatsoper or Salzburger Festspiele, you will understand what I mean. It is not uncommon for opera singers here to be not only cultural icons, but also subjects in the daily papers and gossip columns.

Switzerland is also a wise place to look for employment. The wages are higher than Germany and Austria, and the taxes are lower. However, Switzerland is not part of the EU, and the cost of living is significantly higher than either Austria or Germany. There are also relatively few theaters in Switzerland (and Austria), while there are still close to one hundred full-time theaters in Germany with *Fest* ensembles, all in need of a certain number of guest singers presenting full seasons of opera (along with plays, ballet, modern dance, children's theater, and orchestral concerts).

The sky is not falling at a fast pace. However, while there is work to be had, budgets and positions are continually being cut. At the time of publication in 2010, for example, the opera house in Essen has just been told that they must immediately enforce a 30% budget reduction, Flensburg is closing their opera, Würzburg is in serious financial peril, and Wuppertal keeps threatening to shut the doors to their *Schauspielhaus* (drama theater). The budget cuts in Essen are at least being met with protests in the streets. The numbers in the chart on the next page, taken from the 2006 through 2010 *Deutsches Bühnen Jahrbücher* (the Bible of the German-speaking opera world), show the number of full-time employees in the German theater system (not including Austria and Switzerland) and the trends over the past five years:

NUMBER OF FULL-TIME SOLOISTS, CHORISTERS, COACHES, AND DIRECTORS IN GERMAN THEATERS ~ www.buehnengenossenschaft.de					
ACCORDING TO DEUTSCHES BÜHNEN JAHRBUCH					
(NOTE: NUMBERS DO NOT INCLUDE ARTISTS IN AUSTRIA AND SWITZERLAND)					
YEAR	**2006**	2007	**2008**	2009	**2010**
SINGERS (SOLOISTS)	**2,987**	2,963	**2,947**	2,941	**2,916**
SINGERS (CHORUS)	**2,983**	2,966	**2,951**	2,941	**2,912**
CONDUCTORS/ COACHES/ CHORUS MASTERS/ PIANISTS	**740**	740	**744**	744	**748**
STAGE DIRECTORS	**703**	691	**681**	683	**681**
ASSISTANT STAGE DIRECTORS	**414**	395	**390**	381	**387**
PROMPTERS	**334**	312	**298**	290	**283**
ORCHESTRAL MUSICIANS	**6,502**	6,478	**6,471**	6,428	**6,398**

Let's talk Fach. Ohhhhh yeaaah.

The German system of classifying singers, called the *Fachsystem*, divides operatic voices into specific classifications depending on voice color, weight, range, and beauty. I call it "unable to think outside the box," and I am not a complete fan of the *Fachsystem*. But whatever you may think or do, you must make sure you give agents and theaters the impression that you know your voice type (*Fach*). Consider it a necessary love–hate relationship if you wish to succeed here. While your *Fach* limits the repertoire you can perform, it can also protect you from having to sing repertoire you do not want to sing, or are actually unable to sing. The *Fachsystem* can be advantageous for both theaters and singers. Imagine if you had no *Fach* classification: a theater could theoretically make you sing Despina, Brünhilde, Salome, Violetta, Rosina, and Blonde—all in the same season and all in repertoire. It would surely be one hell of a first and last season for you. While I do not enjoy being classified as one particular "type" of singer, I play by their rules and have added great roles to my repertoire in well-regarded theaters.

Before you contact theaters and come to Europe, figure out which *Fach* is yours. In what *Fach* is the bulk of your repertoire? More importantly, are you able to sell yourself to agents and theaters in this repertoire, and can you maintain stamina and grow while singing this repertoire over many seasons? Do you think someone will pay €60 to watch you perform roles in your *Fach*? You can save yourself potential needless struggle and anguish if you honestly answer these questions. With that said, I do not know of many people who sing repertoire listed only in their *Fach*. I have sung roles in four different *Fächer* (plural of *Fach*) and it has not hurt me one bit. But the bulk of my repertoire certainly belongs in one—or perhaps two—*Fächer*.

The definitive guide to *Fachsystem* is the *Handbuch der Oper* (www.amazon.de), written by Dr. Rudolf Kloiber, Wulf Konold, and Robert Maschka (Bärenreiter/Dtv, 2006). This book—popularly known as "The Kloiber"—lists much of the operatic repertoire, synopsis, roles with their *Fach* classification, and an explanation of the *Fachsystem*. The Kloiber is a wise and necessary addition to your library. Go buy it today. The lines between *Fächer* are sometimes a little blurry, and I take Kloiber's *Fach* classification as a strongly advised guideline with certain exceptions.

Europeans have different views about which types of voices should sing particular roles. For example, they often cast different voices in the roles of Pamina and Tamino than they might in America. It may be that you present yourself to agents in one particular *Fach,* and they have different ideas of how to sell you.

This happened with me. I came to Germany auditioning in a *Fach* where I sang the leading romantic roles. I was already having success in America singing this repertoire and was getting plenty of work in Germany singing the same roles, including my first two seasons here. However, many agents and colleagues whom I trusted told me that if I switched my *Fach*, I would have much more work. I considered the move a shrewd marketing decision to capitalize on the weight and color of my voice combined with the fact that I am in good shape and can move on stage. Since I was comfortable with making such a change, and had already been contemplating it for a while, I made the switch with an optimistic outlook and did not look back. Within three weeks of switching *Fächer* and re-auditioning for agents (and also after three months of preparing new repertoire), I had a *Fest* engagement. I entered into a *Fach* where the demand was high, the supply was low, and I had certain clear advantages over the competition. Most people with my voice-type want to be the romantic lead, it seems. I asked myself, why do I want to be the romantic lead whining about my broken heart when I could play the stuttering next door neighbor who likes to dress up like a clown and snort cocaine—then somebody hands me a paycheck for that? Are you kidding?

As you prepare your audition arias, still abide by the rule of singing what you sing best. Do not offer an aria just because it is in your *Fach* and people say you should sing it "because it is in your *Fach*." If you sing the aria wonderfully and can sell it, then offer it. If you do not sing it wonderfully, do not offer it. Remember that although you are theoretically required to sing every role in your *Fach*, there are sometimes a few roles in there you are not yet willing or able to tackle, or that do not show you off well. If, though, there are a great number of roles in "your" *Fach* that you cannot sing, or you cannot sing some of the most frequently done roles, you should perhaps re-examine if you are really marketing yourself correctly.

Here is a personal example of how you can do yourself a disservice by offering repertoire in your *Fach* when it does not show you off fantastically: I used to audition with a particular Rossini aria, and I knew deep down that the role was not for me. Before I came to Germany, I was told that I must offer this aria for auditions because the role is a staple of my then-*Fach*, and everyone in America told me I should sing this role because I "looked" the role. So I prepared the bane of my then-existence, this (absolutely gorgeous, stunning, so not for me) Rossini aria, and sang it at my first three auditions in Germany. Because that aria did not show me off at my best, I was told "no thanks" by one agent and two theaters. As soon as I took that aria off my audition repertoire list, the feedback suddenly changed for the better. And being free of this Rossini aria was so liberating!

It is not imperative for you to choose repertoire from each period of classical music history, including arias in French, German, Italian, and English. Only do this if you sing each selection extraordinarily well and can sell yourself in each role. If you present a survey of operatic history for your audition and you do not do it exceedingly well, it may very well appear to agents and theaters as if you have no idea what kind of repertoire you should be singing. While you should show versatility to help your chances of landing

Fest engagement, you do not need to offer Idamante, Gaea, Dalila, Eboli, Baba the Turk, Meg Page, and Rosina to get a job. Be calculating about the versatility you show in your audition arias. What do you do the best? Find out what it is and offer it.

With that said, you really need to sing Mozart. I cannot say that you absolutely must offer Mozart, but all theaters do it and if you are in an ensemble, the chances are great-to-certain that you will sing Mozart. Europe is, after all, the land of Mozart. If you do not offer Mozart, most agents and theaters will still ask for it, and if you answer that you do not sing Mozart, this will certainly raise eyebrows with many.

If you are in doubt about how you might fit into the *Fachsystem*, cover your bases and get some advice from people actually working in the theaters here. Work with coaches on the staff of opera houses here before you audition for agents. There are also coaches in your home country who have extensive experience working in German-speaking theaters. Sing for them and listen to their advice.

Operetta

The German-speaking world is the land of operetta, and you've never seen an audience drool over a piece like they do when they sit through *Gräfin Mariza* or *Der Vogelhändler*. They love this repertoire. If you are cast in an operetta, you will not only have a lot of German dialogue to speak and numbers in which to dance, but you will also almost certainly have numerous performances (thirty or forty performances of a production in a season is common); operetta sells very well. What you also may or may not already know is that operetta is a huge challenge to perform well. It is its own genre; not opera or American Musical Theater.

Although the thought of lengthy monologues *auf Deutsch* may seem intimidating to you, with a lot of effort you can do it. I did my first operetta in Belgium with an international cast and a German director who wanted to pull her hair out when she heard me bungle my dialogue. Now, many years and operette later, I no longer make such a mess of my operetta dialogue.

It is wise to prepare an operetta aria or two for your audition tour. If you are engaged for a *Fest* contract, you very well may find yourself performing this repertoire. Do your research first, though; operetta roles are classified by *Fächer*, as well, and you will want to bring an aria from an appropriate role. What am I getting at, you may wonder? If you are a tenor, *Dein ist mein ganzes Herz* is not the only tenor operetta aria ever composed in the history of the world. Bring *Dein ist mein ganzes Herz* only if you know for certain that the role of Sou-Chong is right for you and that you can also sell *Immer nur lächeln* (many of the *Lyrische Tenöre* operetta roles are written with a low tessitura and heavy orchestration). Some agents here find it both hilarious and painful that so many English-speaking tenors from virtually every tenor *Fach* bring this aria for auditions. The same goes for sopranos and *Viljalied*.

If you are a *Spieltenor* or a lighter soprano, you will often be cast in the supporting roles (often as the second, comedic couple) where you will have plenty of dialogue and dancing. You will also need to speak very good German on stage to be cast in these roles. For the lyric tenors and bigger-voiced sopranos, there's plenty of dancing and dialogue for you, too. Explore the repertoire and do your research before you decide on an audition aria.

There is a great amount of operetta repertoire out there. If you are not in the German-speaking world, finding a good selection of operetta repertoire may not be particularly easy. Look on Operabase (www.operabase.com) to see which operette are performed often, though just a few of the most popular pieces are *Wiener Blut, Gräfin Mariza, Der Vogelhändler, Der Graf von Luxemburg, Die lustige Witwe, Der Bettelstudent, Die Csárdásfürstin, Eine Nacht in Venedig, Orpheus in der Unterwelt, Der Zigeunerbaron* and *Im weissen Rössl*. There are many, many other operette besides just *Die Fledermaus* in the repertoire. *Guide to Operatic Roles & Arias* by Richard Boldrey is a good resource showing what operetta roles fit into particular *Fächer*. Schott (www.schott-music.com) also publishes a fairly comprehensive five-volume set of operetta arias called either *The New Operetta* or *Das neue Operettenbuch*, though it is poorly organized.

Theater sizes

Theaters in Germany and Austria are classified as either A, B, C, or D houses. This letter designation is decided by the size of the theater's orchestral budget:

Orchestra with a budget from under 56 members: D house

Orchestra with a budget from 56 to 65 members: C house

Orchestra with a budget from 66 to 98 members: B house

Orchestra with a budget for at least 99 players: A house

There are all kinds of different theaters here: *Stadttheater* (City Theaters), *Staatstheater* (State Theaters), *Landestheater* (Regional Theaters), and *Nationaltheater* (do I need to really translate that for you?), among others. Historically, the State and National theaters have been the larger, more reputable companies, while the City and Regional theaters have operated on a less-international level. Do not take this as a rule, however. The internationally respected Oper Köln is a city theater (*Stadttheater*), and Grazer Oper is actually a regional theater (*Landestheater*), with a solid international reputation.

Not all "A" theaters are equal, and this goes for each theater classification. For example, though Hamburg and Kassel are both "A" theaters, there is no question that Hamburg operates on a much higher international level. Once you are here and working you will begin to get a feel for reputations different theaters have. If you look on theater Web sites to see who is performing there and which press review the productions, you will begin to see how different theaters compare to each other.

The quality and international reputation of a theater is generally higher with "A" and some "B" houses, though this is occasionally not the case. Do not simply equate the size classification to the quality of the house. I once worked in a "C" house whose quality was much better than my next engagement at a "B" House. You can find some excellent singers in provincial "C" houses and some talent-free singers in "A" houses. To get an idea of quality, attend performances in all different sizes of theaters, especially theaters where you plan to audition. You will then see where you might best fit in.

When should I come? How long do I gotta stay?

Unlike just ten or fifteen years ago when there was an annual fall audition season, there is no longer just one audition season. Anyone who tells you otherwise has either never worked here or has not been working here lately.

The odds for success in finding a *Fest* contract increase the longer you stay and audition. Between getting around Austria, Germany, and Switzerland to sing for agents (there are many), the agents sending you to auditions, and you landing the right *Fest* contract, you should plan on an absolute minimum of six to eight weeks. Eight to twelve weeks is optimal. However, if you can stay for even longer than twelve weeks, there is an ever-greater chance of reward. With very few exceptions, the agents and theaters will not bother to call you once you are back in America. You are not going to be engaged unless you are able to take the call and go to the audition, and it sometimes simply comes down to timing and good fortune.

In Germany, the theaters have until October 15th to let singers know if they are fired or re-hired for the following season. The singer has until October 31st to let the theater know if they intend to stay or go. Then, starting November 1st, everyone theoretically knows where the vacancies are for the following season, and the audition fun begins. In reality, it takes a while for information to trickle down to agents and for the auditions to get started. Even then, some theaters are disorganized and do not hold auditions for several months.

Because of a number of issues, some of which have to do with the struggling economy in Germany (unemployment is hovering around 8.2% nationally and in some of the German states, as high as 25%; in Austria it is at 5%, all according to 2010 figures), theaters are waiting longer and longer to hire singers for following seasons because they often do not know what their budget will be. I was hired for my first *Fest* job two months before the season began, but this was only because the administration was terribly disorganized and going through turnover. And just today I was called by my agent for a *Fest* job next season in a large theater. This is, in fact, the theater where my future bride works, and although they have known about this vacancy since the end of last season (nine months ago), they are just now hearing auditions. I won't be auditioning.

Generally speaking, you will have more *Fest* contract auditions for the following season starting in the late fall thru the spring. The later in the spring/summer one auditions, the fewer positions there will be for the next season. In the bigger, international theaters, in theaters where the administration is well organized, and in theaters where the administration may change at the end of the next season, you may sometimes audition for *Fest* and guest contracts two or three seasons away.

3 DREI

Me Write Agents and Theaters Real Good With Real Neat Publicity Materials in German

Whom do I write, you ask? Write both agents and theaters. And how might I find the names? The Bible of the German-speaking theaters is the *Deutsches Bühnen Jahrbuch* (www.buehnengenossenschaft.de), also known as the DBJ. Although you can live without a DBJ, don't. Go buy the book and save yourself a lot of time and hassle; life is so much easier with one. The DBJ is published in November or December for the following calendar year (i.e., the 2010 DBJ came out in December, 2009). The DBJ lists everything: theater personnel, addresses, sizes of theaters, singers, and agents, and even kitschy ads that singers and actors take out for themselves. You may order this book online and they will ship it to you with a bill. Pay either with a bank transfer (*Überweisung*) or Euro Check. So, when it comes time to pay for the book and you have no German bank account, you should transfer the money to their account or send them a Euro check. Please see p. 209 for their bank information. If you choose not to buy the DBJ, you may find listings of all theaters at Operabase (www.operabase.com)—a fantastic resource for everything having to do with opera.

Writing agents

You will find agents listed at the back of the DBJ and in the Resources Section. As well, a quick Google search (remember, www.Google.de, .at, or .ch) will often yield fruitful results. When you write agents and theaters let them know how long you will be over and for what kind of work you are searching (i.e., guesting and/or festing).

I will resist the urge to make specific recommendations and warnings regarding agents. They come in all shapes and sizes: good, bad, fantastic, honest, dishonest, scheming, caring, motherly, fatherly, enabling, competent, incompetent, connected, completely out to lunch, and a few asses to round out the bunch. They also operate much, much differently than artist representatives in the U.S. or United Kingdom. German-speaking agents are almost always non-exclusive, and it is nowhere near the Olympic accomplishment that it is in America or Great Britain to begin a working relationship with them. It is relatively easy to get agent auditions (depending on your *Fach*, experience, and level of talent), and they will tell you right then and there if they want to work with you. If you hear nothing, it is safe to assume they were not interested.

How do you know which agents are good, bad, lazy, nice, jerks, etc.? Ask colleagues, friends, colleagues of friends, friends of colleagues. There are some agents for whom many people should sing, a few for whom just a few should sing, and some for whom nobody should sing. In between, there are about ninety agents who are always going into and going out of business. With the right combination of agents in your corner, you are in business. But acquaint yourself with each agent and their roster (again available at Operabase or on agents' individual Web sites) before you send your materials. If you are fresh out of school and are looking for a *Fest* contract in a regional German house, you might look silly sending your materials to Dr. Germinal Hilbert (www.hilbert.de). Take the time to inform yourself.

Beware, however, that although you may legally work with as many agents as you wish, if you have too many working for you and they keep calling you about the same engagements, you will inevitably damage the singer-agent working relationship. These are working relationships you want to nurture.

The ZAV (Zentrale Auslands- und Fachvermittlung: www.zav.arbeitsagentur.de), formerly the ZBF, is the German government agency and you should sing for them. They have offices in Hamburg, Köln, München, Leipzig, and Berlin, and as one colleague says, singing for the ZAV is "a must." Consider them the biggest singer's temp agency in the world, and they do not charge you a commission when you get a job through them. The ZAV is not a regular agent and will essentially be looking at what possibilities for you they have sitting on their desk that particular day. Do not count on them to be thinking of your future as a singer. As soon as you sing for one branch, you are in the centralized computer system, and they should call should something appropriate come up. They actually sometimes do call even if they do not know you. However, it is not a bad idea to sing for as many as you can and call them occasionally, like any other agent. They will give you their honest opinion (often well-informed, occasionally merely entertaining), and they often have connections that—since they charge no commission in contrast to private agents—other agents do not.

Send your materials (there is no need to send them a CD) and they will often get back to you with an E-mail invitation (see p. 235). Make sure that when you go you take a repertoire list of roles you are able to sing right now; ZAV is also the one-stop connection for jumping-in (*Einspringen*). Most importantly, when you sing for the ZAV (especially in the fall or winter) you will wait to sing. You will wait like you have never waited before. Bring snacks, bring a good book, and be prepared to sing at 4:30 PM if your audition was scheduled for 1 PM. Walk around, stay warm, and speak with your colleagues/competition; you will see some of them again and again. Consider yourself warned.

Writing theaters

Writing theaters can often be fruitful, and if you do write, send a CD. I received a number of auditions, for both *Fest* and guest contract, by writing the theaters directly. When you write theaters, you should write the head of the KBB (*Künstlerisches Betriebsbüro*—say that three times fast), called the *Betriebsdirektor/-in*. Some theaters jump at the chance to work directly with singers; if they engage you they are not saddled with paying an agent fee (theaters pay half of the agent's commission in the *Festsystem*) and can often negotiate a lower fee by speaking directly with the singer, depending on how shrewd you are. Read more about *Einspringen* in chapter Zehn.

The KBB is the German equivalent of the American or British "artistic administration," and when you are working in the theater they are either your best friend or worst enemy. Make friends with everyone in that office, be good to them, and do not be a pain in their butts. They often work hard to make your life easier.

Publicity materials: cover letter, résumé, and biography

Publicity materials for agents and theaters are much different than in America. You do not need a fancy folder or even a separate photo to send along, but it should still look elegant and professional. After consulting with people in the KBB in different theaters (the people who actually read singers' publicity materials) and looking through piles of pitiful publicity materials sent by aesthetically challenged agents and singers, I pared my materials down to three pages:

- Page 1: Very brief cover letter—see p. 231
- Page 2: Short biography (*Biografie*), 100–150 words, with a small .jpg thumbnail of your headshot. The font size of the biography is at least 12, if not 13.
- Page 3: Résumé (*Lebenslauf*) listing operatic roles, with what company, when, where, and—if they are well known in Europe—directors and conductors. If the directors and conductors are not known in Europe it is a waste of space. Exclude the concert/recital work from résumés for theaters; they have little interest in your concert/oratorio experiences. However, it might be good to list your concert experience on résumés for agents. View a sample résumé on p. 230.

As I stated above, a small, yet clear, .jpg thumbnail of your headshot on each page will suffice for a separate photograph in your envelope.

Everything fits nicely into a large envelope (do not fold your materials into a business envelope), you save the hassle and cost of reproducing 4x6 photos (the standard size in Europe), and you will save postage when sending your packets from overseas. Do not worry about trying to find A4 paper (the common paper size in Europe and just a little different from U.S. Letter paper) if you are sending your materials from America; you can easily make formatting modifications when you get to Europe.

Important note: German biographies are worded differently than English, in that they are generally drier and without the self-congratulatory "I am the second coming of Maria Callas" language. I can tell you from embarrassing personal experience, do not simply translate your English biography to German. This will give them a lot to laugh about (they do not understand why we write that, "I am the best and most versatile singer of my generation and my voice is creamy and rich," or something along those lines). Pay someone to professionally translate it and convert the format to that of a typical German biography. And keep it short and easily-readable; when you send your materials to agents and houses, they will spend just a few seconds deciding whether or not to invite you to audition.

CDs

Some agents will hear virtually any singer who walks through the door while others prefer pre-screening with a CD. It is a good idea, however, to send a demo CD and bring some extra copies with you. Only send it, though, if you think your CD shows you off well and your German is *wunderbar*. Moreover, if you have no working experience in Europe or you are in a high-supply *Fach* (e.g., *Lyrischer Sopran*), the chances are much greater that agents will want to first hear a CD.

With all that said, I did not send CDs along with my package for two reasons: I already had a bit of professional experience in the U.S. that I believed would help get me auditions, and I was in a high demand/lower-supply *Fach*. Simple math (and knowledgeable colleagues) told me I would have favorable chances of getting auditions.

Web sites, E-mail, and fax

If your Web site looks professional and includes a German biography, it is an asset to your paper materials. Agents are happy to be able to refer theaters to your Web site.

As for making initial contact with E-mail and/or referring agents and theaters to your Web site, only do it if you are referred by another singer on their roster or have already spoken with the agent or theater. Many agents still prefer to deal with paper, so use caution in making initial contact via E-mail. I am of the strong opinion, as well, that it is much harder for an agent to lose your paper materials on the desk than it is for them to lose an E-Mail. E-mail and/or phone, however, are certainly the communication of choice once your working relationship begins.

I have rarely needed a fax number, though I do have one through www.myfax.com. You may send and receive faxes via E-mail with this service, and it costs around $10 USD per month. Also, when you fax via E-mail, not only is it easy, but the agent or theater also receives a hard copy of your materials. A hard copy of your resume is much harder for someone to lose when it is sitting on their desk instead of their inbox.

When to send your materials

You should send your materials to agents and theaters soon enough so that they have ample time to review them and invite you to auditions. My experience has been that they waste no time reviewing materials. I consider it advisable to mail packets anywhere from two to five weeks before your arrival. Keep in mind that nothing happens in August; it is vacation month. If you plan on coming on September 1st, mail your materials at the end of June and then they will have plenty of time to review everything.

4 VIER

I'm Gonna Need a Sugar Daddy

You are going to need a chunk of money for a successful audition tour. Unfortunately, the glory days of the strong U.S. Dollar are long gone thanks to "creative" domestic and foreign policies by the American government leading to a vast financial meltdown, as well as other factors that I will never understand with only my meager musical education. In fact, it is safe to say that many of us are experiencing economic hardships not seen in generations. Although the Euro remains relatively strong, it has recently taken a hit due to the insolvency of Greece (yes, the entire government! It seems someone was cooking the books over there...) and hard economic circumstances of countries such as Portugal, Italy, Ireland, and Spain (fellow EU countries lovingly refer to this group as "PIIGS"). Even the British Pound is weak as their economy reels from the fallout of the World Recession. What does this mean for the you, if you are coming from the U.S. or Canada? Your dollar will stretch a bit more here, particularly in comparison to just last year. The current exchange rates as of March 2010 are represented in the following table:

EXCHANGE RATES AS OF MARCH 29, 2010:		
(Visit www.xe.com/ucc/convert.cgi for real-time exchange rates)		
1 USD ~ US Dollar	=	.74 Euros
1 GBP ~ United Kingdom Pound	=	1.11 Euros
1 CAD ~ Canadian Dollar	=	.73 Euros
1 AUD ~ Australian Dollar	=	.68 Euros
1 NZD ~ New Zealand Dollar	=	.53 Euros
1 VND ~ Vietnam Dong	=	.0000524384 Euros

You need to budget for plane, train, health insurance, food, apartment sublet, hotels, agent audition fees (theater auditions are free), vocal coaching, and incidental expenses. I will let you figure out the transportation cost since you will purchase tickets in your home country and prices vary greatly. But first, you need to actually get into the country...

Passports and visas

If you are not a European Union (i.e., EU) citizen and do not already know that you need a Passport to enter the EU, you have just failed the intelligence test (You might want to keep that day job).

If you are a citizen of America, Canada, Australia, or New Zealand, you are allowed to visit Germany and Austria for up to ninety consecutive days without an entry visa. If you are South African, you will need an entry visa to enter Germany and Austria: for a German visa application visit www.what-the-fach.com/pdfs/German-Visa-Application.pdf, and for an Austrian visa application see the Austrian Embassy's South African Web site (www.aussenministerium.at).

If you are a non-EU citizen and plan to stay in Germany for longer than ninety days, it is wise to apply for something called a Schengen Visa (see the hyperlink in the paragraph above). The terms of the agreement allow non-EU passport holders to spend ninety out of every one hundred eighty days in any and all Schengen countries (Belgium, France, Germany, Greece, Italy, Luxembourg, Netherlands, Portugal, Spain, Denmark, Finland, Iceland, Norway, Sweden, Austria, Czech Republic, Estonia, Hungary, Latvia,

Lithuania, Malta, Poland, Slovakia, and Slovenia). This means that the old idea of spending ninety days in Germany, leaving for a few days to a non-EU country and returning is no longer viable. If you wish to stay in Germany longer than ninety days within one hundred eighty without having obtained a visa through an engagement, you will need to apply for the Shengen Visa.

The first thing you need to do is go to the *Einwohnermeldeamt* (registration office) and complete your *Anmeldung* (registration). This is your registration with the authorities to tell them where you are living. (Technically, you are supposed to do this within seven days of your arrival in Germany, and every time you move.) You will then make an appointment at the *Ausländeramt/Ausländerbehörde* to apply for the visa (see the visa application on the previous page). In addition to the Schengen Visa application form, you will need all of the documentation listed in Chapter Eight.

Here is a tip: Before you come to Europe, make two color copies of all bankcards and passports. Scan all documents, as well, and send the file to your E-mail account. Take one photocopy with you to Europe and leave another copy at home with someone who could fax it to you in an emergency. Should you actually have an emergency and lose everything, this simple act will save you much pain with your bank and your Embassy here (view listing of all Embassies on pp. 206-207). This act of prevention has saved me twice in just the past two years.

You are legally obliged in Germany and Austria to carry proof of identification with you at all times, and the police can ask you for it whenever they wish. This means carry your passport with you especially when you travel away from your home base for auditions; your drivers license from Iowa does not count here. If you do not have your passport with you and are asked for identification, you may be in for some problems. And they do ask. In fact, I was recently asked for my passport as I was sitting in an international train between Nürnberg and Frankfurt. I was the only person they chose out of a train compartment packed with one hundred people.

Finding a home base

If you have any type of support system over here (friends, family, etc.), find a home base near them unless they are in the boondocks of the former Eastern Germany—difficult to reach by train. An audition tour is stressful and you will be thankful for any emotional support you can find while being here. Simply having the possibility of going out with a familiar face (and speaking a little English) after an audition can be a welcome relief.

Finding a centrally located home base is crucial. München and Frankfurt are extremely expensive, while Berlin is relatively less expensive. Frankfurt is arguably the most central spot in Germany for train travel, and Berlin is a little bit out of the way, though accessible by numerous fast trains and discount airline connections. A good number of agents are located in München and Berlin, and you will inevitably spend time in both cities. In between are a hundred other viable possibilities: Düsseldorf, Mannheim, Stuttgart, Hamburg, Hannover, Bonn, Nürnberg, and Köln. As you may gather, there is no perfect home base and choosing a city is a matter of priorities and taste. But remember: stay somewhere with frequent, fast train connections that will minimize your travel time as much as possible. That cheap sublet in Heilbronn or Pforzheim is just a bad, bad idea; you will spend much of your audition tour on a slow train getting to a faster train to get to the fast train to get to your audition. Take some time to look at a map, get on the Deutsche Bahn Web site (www.bahn.de) to see how long train trips to various cities take, and consider where you think you might feel the most at home for a couple months.

Keep in mind that you may often be traveling and may not be "home" very much. You may be home two days per week and you may be home five days per week; you never know what auditions are going to come your way. You also do not have to set up base in the biggest cities in Germany or Austria to have an effective audition tour, and you do not have to rent a luxury apartment. I began in Düsseldorf thanks to the generosity of an old friend and colleague who sublet me her flat and relocated for a month. It was an excellent, central location and one that had countless fast train connections. I have also had numerous friends who based their audition trips in Berlin and München, and they were generally happy with their decisions. The atmosphere, though, differs in these two cities (i.e., LA and NYC); Berlin has a reputation for being a hip, young city with lots going on while München is known as a more culturally-conservative (some say Yuppie-ville) city. I love both Berlin and München and have no reason to recommend one over the other.

If you are coming for any length of time longer than two or three weeks, find an apartment. Do not even think of staying in hotels. Not only is it ridiculously expensive to live in a hotel, you will never have the luxury and necessity of having a home base with a kitchen. Are you still considering just staying in hotels? Don't. Expect apartments to start at €350–400 per month and rise depending on the city and your taste.

Remember that you are not moving here with grandma's china. Rather, you are setting up shop in a sublet for a limited amount of time while you spend (we hope) a majority of time on the road. You need to make sure your accommodations are situated before you come over; not only do you not need the stress of having to look for a place once you land, but you also need to write down your German address on the materials you send to agents and theaters.

Finding an apartment

If you know anyone in Germany or Austria, get in touch and ask them to get the word out that you are looking for a sublet. Put a posting up on NFCS (www.nfcs.net), Craigslist (www.craigslist.com) München or Frankfurt. There are a few Web sites out there and more than plenty possibilities for short-term, affordable subletting: Immobilienscout (www.immobilienscout.de), MWZ (www.mwz.de), Homecompany (www.homecompany.de), Mrlodge (www.mrlodge.de), ToyTownGermany (www.toytowngermany.com), Mitwohnzentrale (www.mitwohnzentrale.de) and Zwischenmiete (www.zwischenmiete.de).

If you are looking for something very economical, look for an apartment with roommates (*Wohngemeinschaft* or *WG*), often with University students. Try Googling "WG" or "Wohngemeinschaft" together with the name of the city where you want to be based, or "Zwischenmiete" (sublet) and the name of the city for more possibilities. These combinations often yield fruitful results.

Hotels. No, I didn't say hostels.

When I audition I usually stay in hotels costing between €60–100 Euros per night. Depending on various circumstances (i.e., conventions in town, holidays, Carnival, Pope is visiting, European Soccer Championships, etc.), hotel prices could sometimes be a little higher and sometimes even lower. There are hotels cheaper than €60 per night but my experience has been that the "maid" wakes me up at 6:30 AM as she tries to get a head start on "cleaning." This happens after being kept awake half the night by the drunk Eastern European truck driver staying in the room next door. And your mattress has no box spring. (I absolutely tanked that audition, by the way.) Do you get the picture? You get what you pay for. Do yourself and your audition a favor: invest a few extra Euros in a comfortable hotel room. You will be happy you did it. I have always used Hotel Reservation Service (www.hrs.de), though I am sure there are other good sites, as well. HRS has affordable rates in mostly good hotels, and all with private bathrooms and showers.

When you travel to a theater for auditions and need a hotel, you may also call ahead to the KBB. Theaters receive special rates with hotels and you should certainly ask them to either help you reserve a room or put you in touch with a hotel. These hotels are often right by the theater and are quite nice.

Pay attention to the checkout time before you reserve your hotel. Remember that if you must check out at 11 AM and have to wait until 3 PM for your audition, you will have a lot of time on your hands with your luggage. Hotels are generally not too flexible with stretching the checkout time (although with nicer hotels you can often play the "I'm running late and I need an extra thirty minutes" game). Drop your luggage off in a locker at the train station or go by the theater and ask to leave your suitcase with the stage door security guard (*Pförtner/–in*). They are used to this and usually do not mind at all.

Note: With the comfort and convenience of train travel, you can often travel on the day of an audition. I generally travel on the day if my total travel is under three hours. And if you spend just a little more on a comfortable 1st class Rail Pass, you may make the price difference up by not always having to spend €60 on a hotel. You then get to spend the night in your own flat. But do this only if you are already used to traveling here and are sure it will not negatively affect your audition. You have come so far and it would be a shame just to blow an audition because you wanted to save paying for a €60 hotel room.

Audition fees

Agents generally charge €10–20 for an audition fee which includes the pianist and use of the space. ZAV does not charge an audition fee. I know a few agents who charge more but I find it too much to pay and strongly suspect they stay in business just by charging singers outrageous audition fees. If someone wants to charge you €30 for an audition, strongly consider if you want to make that investment. Make sure you have the exact amount in cash ready to give the agent or pianist before you sing your audition. At my very first audition ever in Germany I had only a €50 bill and the pianist (also an American) did not have change. When I told him I had to go get change he did not believe me and was very rude, even when I returned to pay him. Somehow I have not forgotten his name.

Coaches

Here is some good news. Coaching is often cheaper than elsewhere, particularly in comparison to New York City. If you want to coach, it often costs €25–35 to coach with someone on the staff of an opera house, and the prices can go up to €70 per hour. This all depends on the geographical location and résumé/theater of the coach (*Korrepetitor/–in*). It is always a good idea to try and coach with people on the music staff of theaters; they can give you some valuable insight and your name also starts to circulate around at least a little.

Food

Here is even more good news. Going to the grocery store in Germany is often cheaper than America, depending on where you are. Those of you coming from New York will fall over when you see the prices; they are drastically cheaper here. However, Austrian and Swiss grocery stores are considerably more expensive. According to a 2008 article in the *Süddeutsche*

Zeitung, food prices in Austria are 17-22% higher than Germany.

When you go grocery shopping here, though, pay attention; it is a different sport entirely. As you have already read, folks love to cut in line here. They do it agressively. *Especially* grandma. If you want a shopping cart, you will need to deposit a coin (€.50, €1, or €2) into the cart that you will get back when you return it. When you check out, you will either need to purchase a grocery bag (*die Tüte* for Germany and *das Sackerl* for Austria) or bring your own. And finally, as the checker rings your purchases up, get them into a bag or your cart as fast as (un)humanly possible. They will not wait for you to bag your groceries before they begin with the next customer's purchase, and this can lead to uncomfortable moments. I still sometimes get dirty looks from cashiers when I am not fast enough.

As for eating in cafés and restaurants, it is also somewhat cheaper in Germany, and you tip—at the absolute most—10% (often just rounding up to the next Euro). When the service is bad many people do not tip. Unlike America, the wait staff here is often salaried with full benefits; they are not living off of tips and this frequently translates into bad service.You will have to ask for the check when you are ready to go (*bezahlen*). Otherwise, you will be sitting there for a while.

Expect to pay €1.50–3.00 for a sandwich at a bakery and €7–8 for a simple sit-down lunch. A good café, cappuccino, or latté costs in the neighborhood of €1.50–3.00. Of course, prices vary according to which city you visit. If you are traveling and must eat on the go, budget €15–40 per day depending on your style and appetite. If you have a kitchen you can easily eat well for under €10 per day.

There is a magic word in Germany and Austria: *Döner*. Just writing the word makes me salivate. Though it comes in many variations, this Turkish delicacy is a flat bread filled with lamb or chicken, lettuce, tomatoes, and a yogurt/garlic sauce, with an added option of a spicy sauce. They are cheap and if you have a strong constitution and flexible dietary restrictions, you can eat for about €3 per meal. I did it for my first month in Germany and I somehow even lost a couple pounds. Don't ask me how. For an exciting variation, try the *Yufka Döner* (sometimes known as a *Dürum*)—an alternative where they wrap the meat in a very thin, freshly made tortilla they roll and toast right in front of you—it is culinary art.

Cash machines, banking, and travelers checks

There are cash machines everywhere in Europe, so check with your local bank to see if your debit/credit card is set up for international use. I found this the best and most convenient way to get cash from my American account. Talk to your bank before you come and let them know where you are going. Otherwise, because of security measures, they may shut your card down when they suddenly start seeing cash machine withdrawals from Karlsruhe. Do not forget to bring an international toll-free, collect number with you for your bank back home. Even if you do call and make proper arrangements with your bank before your trip, some idiot may still shut off your account at some point. This happened to me. For extra security I suggest taking a few hundred Euros in travelers checks.

If you want to open a German/Austrian/Swiss bank account, hold your horses. You will have to wait until you have a contract in hand.

Health/Travel insurance

Don't leave home without it. It is illegal *not* to have health insurance in Germany, and if you get a job and have to apply for a residence permit (*Aufenthaltserlaubnis* or *Aufenthaltsbewilligung*) and work permit (*Arbeitserlaubnis*), you must first show proof of having health insurance. Before my first trip, I purchased travel insurance thru STA Travel (www.statravel.com) and that also carried me thru the process of getting my first residence and work permits. If you drop dead on stage in Bremen during the middle of your audition, the insurance below will even ship your body home. Now, that's even cheaper than cargo.

Below are the prices for travel insurance with STA Travel as of May 2010:

TRAVEL/HEALTH INSURANCE RATES THRU STA TRAVEL (www.statravel.com)	
Rates in USD as of May 2010	
Length of Stay	**Price**
Up to 8 days	48
9-15 days	70
16-22 days	100

23-31 days	125
32-45 days	165
46-60 days	195
Up to 3 months	240
Up to 4 months	290
Up to 5 months	340
Up to 6 months	390
Up to 7 months	430
Up to 8 months	480
Up to 9 months	530
Up to 10 months	580
Up to 11 months	630
Up to 12 months	680
Up to 13 months	730

What to pack

Packing for your audition trip should be rather simple and painless. Follow these rules: pack only what you can comfortably carry or roll, pack wrinkle-resistant and non-dry cleaning clothing, and bring a carry-on suitcase with wheels (you will walk a great deal with your luggage). You will pay out the nose in Germany for dry cleaning, and your beautiful linen blouse that you decided to bring along will certainly be wrinkled after your four-hour train trip to Dresden. Keep in mind that you can get away with just one or two audition outfits. Most importantly: pack light. For information about audition attire, see p. 70.

5 FÜNF

Planes, Trains, and Automobiles (and Buses and Bicycles and S-Bahns)

Getting to Europe

When buying a plane ticket to Europe, look all over the Internet. This is common sense, right? There are not only discount ticket Web sites such as Orbitz (www.orbitz.com), Expedia (www.expedia.com), Travelocity (www.travelocity.com), but also meta search sites such as Kayak (www.kayak.com) and Mobissimo (www.mobissimo.com) that search hundreds of sites (including the above-mentioned discount sites) for the lowest fares. Of course, there are also web sites for the actual airlines.

    I have often found great deals through Airline Consolidator (www.airlineconsolidator.com) in Chattanooga, Tennessee. This friendly travel agency specializes in consolidator fares (buying seats in bulk and then selling them at deep discounts). I have used Airline Consolidator numerous times when they had unbeatable prices on one-way and round-trip tickets. There are, of course, other consolidators out there but I have never used them.

If you decide to use a discount site and can find the same fare directly from the airline, I strongly advise you to go ahead and purchase your ticket directly from the airline; in case of travel problems at the airport or other unforeseen difficulties, the airlines are more willing to help you if they see you purchased the ticket directly from them. And the airlines are also more flexible with changes in travel (you might get a gig or decide to extend your audition tour). Airlines are just not known for their stellar customer service—sad but true. View a complete listing of travel web sites on pp. 210-214.

When you choose a European arrival city, remember that trains connect you to other cities very quickly and conveniently, even directly from airports. If you base yourself in Düsseldorf, for example, it is quite easy to either arrive in Amsterdam (two hours by train), Frankfurt (one hour by super fast train), or even Köln (right around the corner). Find a cheap ticket and then take the train.

Before you choose an American-based airline...

Airlines vary widely in their Trans-Atlantic service, and I suggest you shop around for the best fare combined with the best airline. Though everyone has different opinions on which airlines are good and which are bad, one thing is for certain; the service offered by American-based airlines (i.e., Continental, American, Delta, United, USAirways, Northwest, etc.) on Trans-Atlantic flights is meager in comparison to that of European and Asian airlines, to put it diplomatically. At their absolute best, American-based airlines provide glorified domestic service on international routes. I have flown back and forth to America on nine different airlines and the European/Asian airlines always outperform the Americans. On such a long flight before and after a stressful audition tour you will want the added comfort of full meals, perhaps a free drink, and sometimes a little more legroom. If the cost of booking a ticket on a European- or Asian-based airline is not prohibitive to your budget, I suggest you take the plunge.

Singapore Airlines (www.singaporeair.com) often comes up as the best option. Though I have not flown them, many friends regularly do (they offer reasonably priced flights to America), and I am told the service is fantastic. The next best option is choosing a European airline, the best among them—according to my experiences—are British Airways (www.britishairways.com), KLM (www.klm.com), and Lufthansa (www.lufthansa.com).

I speak from experience when I say that the American-based Airlines belong in one group entitled "mediocrity" or "if you really must do it and are in a fix." American, United, Continental (especially sub-par) and USAir lead this category. I have had continued good luck in the past few years with Delta, however, leading me to almost believe that their continued good service is no anomoly.

Do some research and sign on with frequent flyer programs before you fly. After two to three Trans-Atlantic flights you often have enough mileage accrued for a free U.S. domestic ticket. Many airlines are connected through partner mileage programs (Star Alliance/www.staralliance.com, being among the biggest), thus giving you the choice of flying different airlines while accumulating points under one account. Do not make a single flight without racking up some mileage.

Important Note: When I purchase tickets to America originating in Europe, I use Orbitz or Kayak, as well, and take advantage of the USD–Euro exchange rate to get cheaper tickets. Many of the online travel sites and airline sites in America now let you book tickets originating in Europe, thereby letting you sometimes take advantage of the Euro–USD exchange. Two other good options for buying tickets originating in Europe are Billiger Fliegen (www.billiger-fliegen.de) and Opodo (www.opodo.de).

Getting around Europe by train

The fastest and often most affordable way to get around Germany, Austria, and Switzerland—and much of Western Europe for that matter—is the train system. For an audition tour you should almost certainly buy a rail pass before you arrive. The only question is, what type of pass?

There are German Rail Passes (good only for German trains, as well as free rides to Salzburg and Basel, both right over the border of Germany), Eurail 3, 4, and 5 Country Select Passes, and then the unlimited Eurailpass covering almost every train in Western and Central Europe. You essentially have a salad bar of options when it comes to what kind of pass you wish to buy. Regardless, buying a rail pass before you come is a smart decision.

Buying full-priced tickets is ridiculously expensive and a rail pass gives you the luxury of cheap, spontaneous travel—perfect for auditions. To drive my point home, here is an example: A full-priced, roundtrip ICE train (that's the fast train, ideal for longer trips in Germany) ticket from Berlin to Stuttgart costs €262, up from €236 in 2007($353 USD; £236; $387 AUD).

Most of your auditions will take place in Germany, followed by Austria and Switzerland. Though your options are numerous, a 3 Country Select Rail Pass (Germany, Austria, Switzerland), a German Rail Pass, or a German/Austria Rail Pass, are all practical options. With a German Pass you must pay extra for your travel in Austria and Switzerland, and with a German/Austria Rail Pass, you must pay extra for travel in Switzerland.

I have a good friend who came over recently for an audition tour, and he decided to purchase an unlimited Eurailpass good for an entire month. We spoke about his decision to buy this pass instead of a limited German or 3 Country pass, and he reiterated how happy he was to have paid the extra money; he never had to worry about rationing his train travel days, and if he had some down time between auditions it cost him nothing extra to hop on a train (1st class, of course) and go to Leipzig or München for the day. If you can afford it, the unlimited Eurailpass will give you the most travel freedom and flexibility for both auditions and recreational travel, and it will also save you the stress of having to ration your use of a limited rail pass.

There are, as you clearly see, numerous possibilities for rail passes, and it is wise to invest some time looking on the Eurail web site (www.eurail.com). STA Travel (www.statravel.com) also does a wonderful job of clearly explaining your rail options.

These passes can be used by anyone except residents of Europe, The Russian Federation, and Turkey (a resident is defined by Eurail as someone who has been living in a country longer than 6 months). The Eurailpasses are available for purchase in Europe, as well, but the prices are 20% higher than in America. The German Rail Pass is available for purchase at limited German train stations, but in Euros and without the discount.

If you are twenty-five years old or younger, you will save heaps of money because you are eligible for the "youth passes." The following are price tables for different options (prices good as of May, 2010, and all in USD). The prices are for adults (people twenty-six years and older):

Planes, Trains, and Automobiles...

GERMAN RAIL PASS (www.eurailtickets.com)

Days of Travel	Adult 1st Class	Adult 2nd Class
4 Days Within 1 Month	361	258
5 Days Within 1 Month	394	297
6 Days Within 1 Month	441	327
7 Days Within 1 Month	489	359
8 Days Within 1 Month	533	389
9 Days Within 1 Month	586	424
10 Days Within 1 Month	633	453

EURAIL AUSTRIA/GERMANY ADULT PASSES (www.eurailtickets.com)

Days of Travel	Adult 1st Class	Adult 2nd Class
5 Days Within 2 Months	407	347
6 Days Within 2 Months	448	381
8 Days Within 2 Months	533	453
10 Days Within 2 Months	620	527

EURAIL 3 COUNTRY SELECT PASS (www.eurailtickets.com) ~ (Germany, Austria, and Switzerland) *For adults, this pass is only available in 1st Class*

Days of Travel	Adult 1st Class
5 Days Within 2 Months	459
6 Days Within 2 Months	507
8 Days Within 2 Months	602
10 Days Within 2 Months	697

EURAIL UNLIMITED PASS (www.eurailtickets.com) ~ (Unlimited travel in 18 European countries) *For adults, this pass is only available in 1st Class*

Days of Travel	Adult 1st Class
15 Days	726
21 Days	941
1 Month	1,169
2 Months	1,650
3 Months	2,035
10 Days Within 2 Months	856
15 Days Within 2 Months	1,126

The price difference between a 1st class pass and a 2nd class pass is relatively small, but the difference in quality is substantial, particularly with the added "luxury" of 1st class travel and the stress it relieves before auditions. While certainly not essential, a 1st class pass will insure you extra comfort, much smaller crowds, fewer screaming children, and larger seats. In 1st class, you may often have a six-passenger cabin to yourself (perfect for stretching and warming up before an audition). The extra cost pays for itself in tangible and intangible ways. If you can part with the extra sum of money, do it.

There are discount cards for the Deutsche Bahn (German Rail System; www.bahn.de) called Bahncard 25 (25% discount off a full price ticket and €57 per year) and Bahncard 50 (50% discount off a full price ticket and €230 per year). Contray to some information floating around, you may purchase these cards without a German bank account. Go to the Deutsche Bahn Web site for all train schedules and information. You may also purchase heavily discounted tickets on the Deutsche Bahn Web site if you buy ahead of time.

You may also purchase a discount train card from the ÖBB (Austrian Rail System; www.oebb.at) called a VORTEILScard. The card entitles you to a 45% discount on your Austrian train travel (50% if you buy tickets online or at the automated machine), as well as a 25% discount for travel in foreign countries. As well, you do not need a domestic bank account. However, you will need an Austrian address. Although you immediately receive a temporary card, the permanent card takes about a month to arrive. Welcome to Austria. They have their own Austrian pace for things here.

As for Switzerland, they have a discount card called the Halbtax (www.sbb.ch), costing CHF 150 per year and entitling you to a 50% discount. With both the Austrian and German discount cards you still receive a discount (albeit smaller) in Switzerland. But if you will travel a lot in Switzerland, it may be a good idea to purchase a Halbtax since the trains are expensive.

Speaking from (yet again) unfortunate personal experience, if you are traveling 2nd class always reserve a seat on the super-fast trains (ICE/Intercity Express) and the fast trains (IC/EC or Intercity/Eurocity). A reservation saves you pre-audition stress and often insures that you have a seat when you otherwise would not (like one morning when half of Germany was with me on the train to Stuttgart for a football/soccer match).

Reservations are relatively inexpensive (€4.50 for domestic 2nd class travel and €5.50 for domestic first class travel) and you may purchase them directly from the automated machines in the train station (*Bahnhof*) or online. There is an English option with the automated machines. You will want a seat either by the window (*am Fenster*) or on the aisle (*am Gang*). German trains are now all smoke-free! Check the connections (*die Verbindungen*), as well, to see that you leave yourself a second option should your train be late and you miss your connection; trains do not run perfectly on time like they did back in the good old days before privatization (like this morning when my train was an hour late and I missed my connection). In all train stations, departures (*Abfahrt*) are printed on yellow posters and arrivals (*Ankunft*) are printed on white paper. All times are posted on the 24-hour clock system instead and not the American AM/PM system.

Once again, be aware of when the holidays are because the trains will be packed, and you will have no seat when you ride from Berlin to Düsseldorf. If you are traveling on Friday or Sunday, don't even think of getting on that train without a reservation. View a full listing of holidays on pp. 228-229.

Public city transportation (Bus/U-Bahn/S-Bahn)

The local mass transit system in the German-speaking world (and most of Western Europe, for that matter) is unbelievably efficient. You usually need to buy a ticket before you get on board (*einsteigen*), and very few buses and S-Bahns actually have ticket machines onboard. Though authorities do not check every customer for tickets, there are undercover ticket checkers on the lookout. You can try your luck and ride without a ticket, but if you get caught the fine is around €40 along with an embarrassing ten minutes in front of other passengers as the undercover ticket checker fills out the paperwork. In some cities they make you pay on the spot, and if you cannot pay they take you to the police. Playing the dumb American will probably not get you very far, either; they know that game. Yes, I have been a passenger without a ticket (*Schwarzfahrer*) a couple times but only in emergencies. Although I have never been caught, just doing it scares me.

Should you need to find a public transportation site, Google the city's name and "public transportation," or see p. 214 for a list of public transportation sites. Your Eurailpass does not cover local transportation (e.g., buses, S-Bahn, and U-Bahn), but if you buy a roundtrip ticket with Deutsche Bahn, your local transportation is sometimes covered, and it will say on your ticket.

Ride sharing

If you want to save a little money, you can always hitch a ride in a car through the *Mitfahrgelegenheit* (www.mitfahrgelegenheit.de), a service connecting drivers with paying passengers. Depending on the trip, ride sharing sometimes costs significantly less than a train ticket and can even save you time. Plus, it is a good chance to brush up your German skills. But if you want relative peace and quiet without the obligation of making conversation, take the train. We just used the *Mitfahrgelegenheit* for the first time to carry passengers. It was easy, convenient, we met nice people, and we covered our fuel costs. Our passengers, all of whom were regular *Mitfahrgelegenheit* users, said that is is generally faster, easier, and cheaper than taking the train.

Air travel within Europe

For longer stretches such as Berlin–Geneva or Hamburg–Vienna, or for trips with enough advance notice, there are numerous discount airlines with good safety records. Wegolo (www.wegolo.com) is the European equivalent of Orbitz for discount airlines. German Wings (www.germanwings.de), Air Berlin (www.airberlin.com), and Ryan Air (www.ryanair.com) are just a few of your discount airline possibilities. Lufthansa (www.lufthansa.de) often has €99 Roundtrip Specials (including tax), so do not assume there are no deals to be had with them. Other European Web sites for air travel include Expedia (www.expedia.de) and Opodo (www.opodo.com), among others. Other comparison sites for discount airlines include WhichBudget (www.whichbudget.com) and Flylc (www.flylc.com).

When you fly Ryan Air (and I sincerely hope you don't), do not let it frighten you that the entire interior of the plane is bright blue and yellow, it is a free-for-all mad dash race to get a seat, you are forced to stare at the emergency ditching instructions pasted on the seatback in front of you, and that you bought your plane ticket for €.99 (no joking). In spite of everything, they somehow have a good safety record. Just remember why their prices are so cheap: their airports are often difficult to reach, and they charge for absolutely everything including all checked baggage. They have also been threatening for the past year to begin charging to use in-flight lavatories, so bring your own Stadium Pal™ (www.stadiumpal.com). Ryan Air flies to Frankfurt-Hahn Airport, not Frankfurt am Main International Airport. There is a huge difference between the two, mainly that Frankfurt-Hahn is almost in Luxembourg and it takes two hours to reach from Frankfurt am Main. There, you've been warned.

Auto rental

If you are rich, you can rent a car (approximately €250 per week) and pay for gas (€1.42 per liter, *not* per gallon). Then please call me and drive me to my next audition. But before we get there drop me off at the train station so I do not get stuck in the traffic jam (*Stau*) on the Autobahn and miss my audition. This will happen to you. Get the picture? If not, you have once again failed the intelligence test.

However, remember some basic rules if you decide to drive here: The rule for right-of-way at intersections is right before left when neither street has the marked right-of-way; when driving on the Autobahn stay out of the left lane unless passing; when passing make sure there are no BMWs coming up behind you at 220 km/h; and never ever ever pass on the right side. This is deadly in Germany. Also, Germans are very orderly drivers with the occasional bout of tailgaiting. Flipping a fellow German driver "the bird" (while sometimes entertaining, often cathartic, and always illegal!) awakens some pretty scary pent up German anger (also entertaining—yet disturbing—to see). Austrians are unpredictable behind the wheel, and the Swiss are manaically and needlessly agressive, giving the Italians a good run for their money. While I'm at it, the Danes and Dutch drive 90 km/h in the left lane on the *Autobahn*, and is seems as though every single person who drives a BMW in Germany is an agressive and rude male driver. There, I'm done.

For more information on obtaining an EU drivers license once you have settled here, see p. 95.

Buy a used bike

No, I am not joking. A bicycle is an optimal way to get around town here. Europe is very biker-friendly and you will find paved bike trails (*Fahrradwege*) and bike lanes seemingly everywhere not only in metropolitan areas, but also throughout the continent. One of my favorite sights is seeing old ladies peddling around town on their bicycles—quite a common sight.

Look in the newspaper (*Zeitung*) or one of the many weekly newspapers under classified ads (*Anzeige*) and bicycles (*Fahrräder*) to see what you can find. It is typical to find a perfectly decent bicycle for €40–50 (cheaper than three months of city bus tickets, no?). When I first arrived, I found a fantastic (and fantastically ugly) 21-speed city bike for €40, and it ran beautifully until it died many years later.

6 SECHS

Your Trip Over and Arrival to the Mother Continent

Pre-Audition Tour Checklist:

- Get a passport and/or visa.
- Study your German.
- Write agents and/or theaters from 2 to 5 weeks before your departure.
- Prepare your budget.
- Purchase: plane ticket, Eurailpass/es, travel/health insurance, travelers checks, plug converter (http://travelstore.ricksteves.com) for appliances.
- Arrange to rent an apartment in Germany or Austria. Use the address on the publicity materials you send agents and theaters.
- Photocopy your essential documents (passport, etc.) twice, leaving one copy with a person at home and taking one copy with you.

- E-mail yourself scanned copies of your essential documents, as well as your publicity materials.

- Call your bank to let them know you will be using your debit/credit card in Europe, and get a toll-free international number to reach them in case of an emergency.

On the trip over to Europe, sleep. It is that simple. Turn off your little individual movie theater on the seat in front of you and sleep. Drink water. In fact, start drinking extra water a couple days before your flight. Save the double scotch for the trip back. If you do not sleep you will be screwing yourself (for lack of a more appropriate term) for your first many days here.

When you first get here do not forget to validate your Eurailpass in the train station before you get on the train. However, if your first trip on the train to your home base apartment is not so long, you might want to think twice about spending an entire day's worth of a Eurailpass on a thirty minute train ride you could just as well buy full-priced for €15.

I have always found that a short nap of an hour or less to be useful, and then I go out in the sunlight all day to get acclimated. This sounds much easier than it actually is. Every time I arrive back from America, I am the walking dead and every ounce of me wants to find the nearest bed and crash for two days. Fight this impulse. Instead, go have a café and walk around. Welcome to Europe! You're going to have a great adventure.

Handy/Mobile phone

What in the world is a Handy?! It's the first thing you need when you get here and what the rest of the world calls a mobile phone. It will take about three weeks before you can actually say the word "Handy" without snickering (who is the idiot who came up with that name?). Buying a Handy and setting up service is quite easy to do and you do not need to worry about it until you arrive. Make it part of your to-do list for your first day in Europe. It will give you a reason to get up and about in the city. You may go to a number of different shops (where they often speak English, so don't worry) and get a prepaid SIM card (take your passport with you and know your local address). You can avoid any kind of service contracts, as well, when you stick to the prepaid option. I suggest either Blau.de (www.blau.de), Aldi (www.aldi.de),

Netto (www.netto.de), O2 (www.o2online.de), or E-Plus (www.eplus.de) in Germany. I strongly advise against T-Mobile, after having been through numerous negative customer service experiences with them. They are also terribly expensive. If you see the third-party Handy store "The Phone House," run in the other direction. I had nothing but agony and frustration with them. That story will be my next book.

In Austria, Orange (www.orange.at) is a very good option (prices for handy use in Austria are also much lower than in Germany). Another even cheaper option is Yesss (www.yesss.at). Go to any Hofer grocery store (www.hofer.at) and pick up the entire yellow letter-sized starter envelope in the checkout line. The packages are inexpensive but come only with a SIM card. In Austria, unlike Germany, you must first be officially registered (*angemeldet*) with the local authorities before you can get a prepaid Handy. This is easy to do and you do not have to have a residence permit before registering.

Once you have a prepaid card you can plug it into your unlocked cell phone you brought from your home country (if it is a dual- or tri-band GSM phone). An unlocked cell phone is a phone with which you can use many different SIM Cards (the brains of the phone). If you do not have an unlocked cell phone, many of these companies sell entire starter packages (including phone) that cost €40–80, or you can try to have your phone company unlock your phone before you make your trip over. You can also try and find a shop in Europe that can unlock your mobile phone, thereby saving you a little money. Most small Handy stores will do this for a nominal fee.

A note about Handys in Europe: You do not pay for incoming calls unless you are in another country besides the country where your service is based. All you have to do to load up your credit is to buy a card either from the individual stores, a newspaper or cigarette store (*Tabak/Kiosk*), the internet, or automated machines. It's all fairly easy. In Austria, Germany and Switzerland you may load up at the cash machines (*Geldautomaten*) and even sometimes at the automated ticket machines in train stations. If you are in a country other than the country where your service is based and your credit runs out, the phone companies provide a free number to call and reload. When you are outside the country where your service is based, make sure you have already uploaded plenty of credit on your Handy. Otherwise it will not even accept incoming calls (I could have once saved a two day train odyssey from Ancona, Italy, to Bremen, Germany, had I known this).

Once you have your new number you have a perfect excuse to make contact via E-mail with every agent and theater you wrote. Write to tell them you are here, how long (once again) you plan to stay in Europe, and that you have a Handy number. I remember getting more than a few additional auditions from my "Hi, I am here and have a Handy" E-mails. See p. 233 for examples.

Üben/Practicing

It is not easy to find practice space in Germany, but with a little perseverance it is certainly possible. With some exceptions (and with a relatively sound-proof flat), it is not a good idea to disturb your neighbors by practicing at home; you will, after all, have to endure their dirty looks for a couple months. However, if you do practice at home, make sure you are at least quiet for a couple hours in the afternoon during the quiet time (*Ruhezeit*; http://de.wikipedia.org/wiki/Mittagsruhe) and that you do not practice in the evening. That's just being a good neighbor.

Many cities have conservatories of music (*Hochschulen für Musik*) and you can sometimes sneak in and find practice rooms (*Proberäume* or *Überäume*). Private music schools and music stores sometimes have practice space for rent, and city libraries sometimes also have practice rooms.

If all this fails, you can go to churches and ask to practice. I have done this and they were happy to oblige, sometimes in exchange for a solo on Sunday morning or a small donation. Go to the secretary of the church, explain your situation, and ask as nicely as possible.

But I will not mince words: finding practice space is generally a challenge.

Internet and your laptop

If you have a laptop and you do not mind carrying it around, I suggest you bring it along. (Just don't be an idiot like me and drop it on the train platform in Braunschweig.) There are now so many places to connect via wireless internet, and you will really appreciate having that added convenience of instant access while getting your Internet fix instead of always having to enter a dirty, smoky Internet café by the train station every time you want to read E-mail. As well, more and more cafés have free WIFI for customers. Visit Jiwire (www.jiwire.com) for a decent listing of wireless connections, or just open your computer and see who didn't bother to add a password to their WLAN. More and more cities are also creating free wireless hot spots in public areas. Make sure to buy a plug adapter for Western Europe (230-50hz) such as those from Rick Steve's store (http://travelstore.ricksteves.com).

It is not the end of the world if you do not bring your computer. There are smoky, dirty Internet cafes everywhere. Just bring all files you need (i.e. publicity materials, scanned copies of your vital documents, etc.) on a USB stick, and make sure you E-mail a backup copy to your own E-mail account before you leave home.

Internet telephoning

Internet telephoning is the best thing since the invention of sliced bread. I use Skype (www.skype.com) and love it, though there are certainly other Internet telephoning/ IM programs. With Skype you can not only have a regular U.S. telephone number where people in the States can reach you for free, but you can also set it up to have your American cell phone forward to this number, thereby saving lots of money by not having to answer it in Europe. Skype is a wonderful convenience, a money saver, and it keeps you in touch with home. In addition, most Internet cafés have web cams, thereby making it possible to speak and see your friends back home, even if you did not bring your laptop with you. Downloading, installing, and using Skype is a very quick and easy process: just go to the Web site (www.skype.com) and choose to download. Follow the simple instructions and then open the application on your computer. You will need to create a user name and password, and you will also need either a built-in microphone or a headset. Then you're in business.

So, you're krank/sick.

You wake up one morning and you're sick. It's time to find some drugs or see a doctor. You need to go to the Pharmacy (*Apotheke*) to get medication and not to a drugstore or supermarket. *Apotheken* are full-service, and I have always found them staffed with courteous and knowledgeable pharmacists. There is always an *Apotheke* that is open. So if you are in dire straits at 3 AM or on Sunday afternoon, go to any *Apotheke* and look on the front door. It should say on the door where the nearest pharmacy with late/weekend/emergency hours (*Notdienst*) is located. If you do not find the information there, try the information desk at the entrance to any hospital. *Apotheken* take turns providing this service and when you find the *Apotheke* that is open, ring the doorbell and they will open a tiny window to help you.

If your illness has anything to do with your voice, you will want to see an ENT; an Ear, Nose, and Throat Doctor (*HNO* or *Fachärzte für Hals–, Nasen–, und Ohrenkrankheiten*). You may either call an *HNO* for an appointment (be sure to tell them you are an opera singer and it is urgent) or visit the ENT Emergency Doctor (*HNO-Ambulanz*) at the hospital (*Krankenhaus*). If you decide to go to the hospital, be aware that the HNO-Ambulanz is not always open for business. If you are in Berlin, I suggest you call Dr. Gerrit Wohlt (tel +49 (30) 31 50 76 55; www.stimmarzt.de), a *HNO* who treats many opera singers.

If you are sick with any other malady, you may want to see a General Practitioner (*Facharzt/–ärztin für Allgemeinmedizin*). These doctors have regular office hours (*Sprechstunden*) just like your college professor. You need an appointment, so it is a good idea to call ahead and see if they are able to see you.

If you need to visit an OB/GYN, you will want to find a *Facharzt/–ärztin für Frauenheilkunde und Geburtshilfe* or *Facharzt/–ärztin für Gynäkologie*. They often have a heavy load of patients so if it is extremely urgent, spit out the magic words, "extremely urgent" (*sehr dringend*). If you have no luck with that, go to the hospital. If you need to see a dentist, look for a *Zahnarzt/–ärztin*.

If you are sick and need emergency care, go to the emergency room (*Notaufnahme*) at the hospital. The hospitals also have emergency rooms for specialties (e.g., internal medicine, cardiology, proctology, plastic surgery, tropical diseases, etc.). And finally, here is a tip in case you call the doctor, tell them it is urgent, and they tell you the first available appointment is in three months: just show up at the doctor (during their *Sprechstunden*) and tell them it is an emergency; they are then obliged to see you, although some may still try to kick you out the door.

Let me tell you how much I love the health care system here. As I originally wrote this chapter I was suffering through my annual sinus infection (*Nebenhöhlenentzündung*). Fortunately, I noticed it coming on at 9 PM, so I walked to the hospital to have them take a look. Within thirty minutes I had been seen by an ENT in the ENT emergency room, she had scoped my throat to look at my vocal chords and had taken X-rays of my head to look at the infection. The doctor prescribed me antibiotics and other fun drugs, which I immediately filled at the Pharmacy (*Apotheke*). By 10 PM I was already on antibiotics. Not bad, eh?

For a list of medications and their German equivalents, please see pp. 221-227.

7 SIEBEN

Agents and Theaters: They Love You, They Hate You, They Love You...

What to expect at agent auditions

Expect to have no place to warm-up (*einsingen*). In fact, you will almost never have a place to warm-up (aside from a couple ZAVs, zav.arbeitsagentur.de) and a couple other agents who hold auditions in music conservatories. I have warmed-up on the street in ten degree Fahrenheit weather (incidentally, for the agent that helped me get my last *Fest* engagement), in dozens of bathrooms, city parks, and empty train compartments. It does not hurt to call the agent and ask if they can recommend a place where you may warm-up. See pp. 215–216 listing practice spaces for rent in certain cities, although this listing unfortunately remains sparse. Expect the process of singing for agents to take several weeks. They are not waiting with baited breath for your imminent arrival to Europe. It will take a bit of time for you not only to coordinate your schedules, but also to actually do the auditions. Be patient and be ready for the process to take a while.

Warming up for theaters is a different topic, one to be covered shortly. But here is another tip until then: If you are traveling by train to an audition, the small six-passenger compartments are convenient, private places to do some light warming up and stretching. With some luck you may sometimes find them empty.

A note on what to wear and what not to wear

Think business casual. Although the Germans and Austrians are sometimes much more "casual" (i.e., not looking very professional) with audition attire, it still makes a difference in your presentation. Make sure you feel comfortable in your outfit, and make the investment to look good for your auditions. Do not look like that singer at one of my auditions who was wearing a faded black t-shirt (not tucked in, of course), a different shade of black pants, and cheap brown shoes—an unfortunate combination. When you consider which audition outfits to bring, do not forget that dry cleaning here is less common and more expensive than in America. Bring audition outfits that pack easily and are wrinkle-resistant.

Men, wear slacks and a blazer with either a sweater or shirt, or just slacks and a shirt. Although you can get away with jeans and shirt, it still looks as if you are at a monster truck rally instead of a professional opera audition. Do not wear jeans. Somehow, though, I have seen male singers hired on the spot—on two separate occasions—wearing dirty jeans, sweatshirts, and work boots. This is your career so dress like it. What you do not need, however, is to wear a suit with a tie. It is not the norm and the agents and theaters will not expect it of you.

Ladies, an elegant, understated dress or pantsuit will suffice. I often see women wearing a simple blouse and skirt. Leave the ball gowns at home unless your audition is on Halloween. As for jewelry, opt on the side of understated elegance instead of debutante ball. See the interview with Robert Tannenbaum (beginning on p. 135) for more information.

For the boys *and* the girls: buy some nice shoes and make sure they are polished. They look at shoes here, too.

Repertoire to bring

Aside from the ZAV (zav.arbeitsagentur.de), which requires 5-6 arias, singers are expected to offer 3-5 arias. It should go without saying that you should bring something in German and your repertoire should lean heavily on the "standard" side. In fact, if you do not offer anything in German, you might want to think twice before coming over for an audition tour. Mozart is often requested and, if offered, almost always heard. Use caution by offering repertoire that is not terribly difficult for the pianist. You never know if you will have John Wustman or an accompanist who apparently lost his digits in a woodworking accident. Because I am American (and stubborn), I have always brought something in English. They almost never want to hear it.

Most German agents are not looking ahead three years to what you might sing or what you think you will grow into. They want to hear arias from roles you can sing right now and for which they can sell you. Avoid the temptation to help them see what you might become; they are generally not interested, have little time, and they often take away the impression that you are not quite certain what repertoire you should be singing. There is no harm in having the "I might be able to sing Don Carlos in four years" repertoire with you, and if they want to hear it you'll be ready. But don't count on it, and I would suggest you do not offer it unless they start asking you.

If you have doubts about your specific repertoire, see (as I have already written) "The Kloiber" (www.amazon.de). "The Kloiber" is my favorite resource to use and, once again, it needs to be part of your library.

Do not expect to always choose your first piece or any piece, for that matter. Each agent has his or her different style. They know what they want to hear and they do not have time to waste. If you have a staple aria of your *Fach* on your audition repertoire list they will sometimes ask to hear it first. If you can sing it well they might be interested in hearing more, and if you can't they have just saved themselves the agony (and four minutes) of hearing a second aria. Your flexibility is noticed, and sometimes even appreciated. But if you know what you want to sing and the agent or theter does not have a special wish for the first aria, go ahead and offer it. Just do not say, "I don't care," when they ask you.

Forms, etc.

You will be asked to fill out forms for agent auditions, not unlike theater auditions. Know your size in cm and kg (see chart below). One agent, Karl-Erich Haase in München, always asks for names of other agents with whom you work or for whom you have auditioned. I often hear that people decide to be crafty and say "none," thinking it will help their chances. Just be honest. I sat there and told the secretary a list of 10–12 agents with whom I already worked, and it had absolutely no negative effect. Your other option is to lie, and when they catch you in that lie you will have lost one of the more valuable agents for finding *Fest* engagements in Germany.

All agents here understand that you work with them non-exclusively, and you must work with other agents. Speak as much German as possible in the audition. Even if you stumble a bit, it will be beneficial to show them you are trying.

METRIC CONVERSION TABLE (www.worldwidemetric.com/metcal.htm)		
1 inch	=	2.54 centimeters (cm)
1 lb	=	.453 kilograms (kg)
1 cm	=	.393 inches
1 kg	=	2.204 lb.

The ZAV Informationsformular (www.what-the-fach.com/pdfs/ZAV-form.pdf) is what you will fill out when you arrive for your ZAV audition. Many agents and theaters have variations of this and while not all forms are the same, the form above gives you an idea of what to expect. Acquaint yourself with the terminology (see the Phrasebook and Dictionary beginning on p. 188, for further assistance).

Make sure you get a written confirmation of the audition (*eine Bestätigung*) from the agent, regardless if they love you or hate you. This is common practice and you will need it for tax purposes if you stay in Germany and wish to deduct the cost. Don't forget.

The agent wants to work with you!

My experience has been (without exception) that if an agent is interested in working with you, they will tell you on the spot. If they do not say anything to you or just thank you for your time, you can safely assume that there will be no working relationship. Don't take it personally; just move on. With that said, I am sure that someone, somewhere, has experienced something different.

Agents are looking at you differently than theaters look at you; agents want to sell you as a product and the good agents realize there are just as many different tastes out there for singers as there are *Intendanten*. Agents often are in tune with what sells and what does not sell, but do not blindly assume they know everything. This is a sense you will acquire and cultivate as you begin to work with them. Most importantly, are they sending you to appropriate auditions, and are the sizes of the theaters and the repertoire right for you? Some agents intelligently and strategically present their singers, while others throw everybody at theaters—including the kitchen sink—hoping that somebody will come home with the gig.

When will they send me to theater auditions?

Sometimes agents have auditions to which they send you right away, sometimes it takes a few days, and sometimes you will not hear a word for months.

Here are four examples of agents A, B, C, and D, to give you an idea: 1. Agent A, for whom I auditioned when I first arrived in Germany, said she wanted to work with me, and I did not hear another word from her. No phone call—nothing. Five months later she called me out of the blue for an audition that led to a guest engagement and my first *Fest* engagement. She was hard working and honest, and we happily worked together until she left the business. 2. I auditioned a few seasons ago for powerful agent B who said he definitely wanted to work with me. Just a few days later he called me about two auditions. I was hired at my second audition for my last *Fest* engagement just three weeks after my original audition for this agent. Unfortunately, after three seasons in this engagement and thousands of Euros paid to him in commission, Agent B never bothered to see me in performance. His apathy infuriated me, and I chose to end that working relationship. He somehow has one of the better reputations in Germany. 3. I sang four years ago for powerful agent C who was very complimentary and said he definitely wanted to work with me. I never heard a word from powerful agent C about a single audition, although he was very friendly when I called him to tell him I was still alive. I eventually quit calling figuring out that he was simply giving me what my dad calls "lip service." 4. Finally, we come to Agent D. While at an audition two years ago for one of the biggest theaters in Germany, I struck up a conversation with an auditioning soprano who was quite friendly and also very good. The talk inevitably turned to agents and she mentioned hers, saying he was an old friend and his agency was "klein und fein." I sent Agent D my materials the next day, he called me two days later, I sang for him that next weekend, and we spoke for two hours. After six seasons over here, I had finally found an artist manager who knew what he was doing, was sincerely interested in me and my career, and had the tools and connections to help. After a short period of time, I decided to let working relationships with other agents slowly fade away, and I continue to be impressed with Agent D. He will have a long and fruitful career in the opera world.

So, you see there are many different possibilities and you never know when the agents will call you. Unfortunately, some agents tell you during your audition that they want to work with you and then you never hear anything from them, ever. There is one, in particular, who does this with many singers, but he or she shall remain nameless. It is just an unpleasant part of the business and you should just move on.

Follow-up and nurturing the singer-agent relationship

Agents are people, too. The good ones work like hell as do many of the bad ones. Many agents are actually very nice people, too. Keep in mind that if an agent wants to work with you, you must make an effort to nurture the working relationship. Make contact with your agents monthly (a rough estimate), sometimes to just pass on a piece of news, sometimes to invite them to a performance, and other times to inquire about auditions. Just because they do not call you does not mean there is nothing for you. On the contrary, they often hear so many singers that your name might not automatically come to mind when they have an audition. These agents are not exclusive and often deal with over one hundred singers.

Be judicious, however, about calling your agents too often. They cannot give you the daily, personalized attention that we expect from our American and British artist representatives. By simply and subtly keeping your name in the agents' minds without making them feel that you need your hand held, you substantially increase your odds of receiving auditions from them.

Mind your manners, too. A simple and sincere verbal "thank you" to an agent for sending you to an audition goes a long way—most agents would construe a thank you card for each audition as overkill. And when you get the job, at least a thank you note if not a nice bottle of wine, are appreciated gestures.

My experience tells me that agents are much more interested in you getting a job and earning a commission than actually developing your career (in the American/British artist representative tradition). Unfortunately, some may not have your best interests in mind. Some agents care about you, some do not, and they all want to make a living. You have to be the judge if they are sending you to appropriate auditions. While you should listen to what they have to say, do not assume that everything coming from their mouths is a statement of infallibility. If the agent has no understanding of what is good for you or little respect that you have a strong sense of what you should and should not do, move on. There are other agents out there.

You also receive a finite number of chances once agents start sending you on auditions. If you get good feedback from theaters but do not get the job, they may be receptive to sending you out again. Sometimes they give you one chance, sometimes two, and sometimes four. But if you bomb and tank and choke, expect that agent relationship to be either severely damaged or finished. Even when you get the gig, some agents will then consider you "employed" and ignore you, as one of mine did for a *Fest* engagement. Go figure...

So the agent does not want to work with you

Forget it, move on, and do not take it personally. There are plenty of agents out there. Do not let it get you down if one or two say "no thanks." However, if most of them are saying "no thanks," then there may be something wrong. Contact the agents and ask for specific feedback (if they did not give it to you in the audition), and pay attention carefully to the similar comments you hear from them. They do, after all, often know what sells and what does not and that is all they are trying to do with you. It could be your repertoire, technique, German, or even (don't hate me) your physical appearance.

Theater auditions

Now is when the fun begins. Here are a few things that hold true to virtually every theater audition: they are free of charge (except for your travel/housing costs), you will have a place to warm-up, and they will provide a pianist (of widely and sometimes shockingly varying capabilities). You will have a short rehearsal (*eine Probe*) with the pianist and you should always arrive at least an hour to ninety minutes early, if not even earlier. Many times I have arrived an hour early, and because there were so many singers auditioning I did not receive a chance to rehearse with the pianist. As you cue up with your fellow auditionees to rehearse, make sure you get your two minutes; it very well can make the difference. Although you may not feel you need the rehearsal, your accompanist will need it just so you do not throw him or her any curve balls. Do not assume anything. Some pianists are not familiar with the entire standard repertoire, some can play absolutely everything, and some play as if they were wearing mittens after that wood working accident.

A typical theater audition

Let me walk you through a typical theater audition that begins at 2 PM. You arrive at 12:45 PM, go thru the stage door entrance (*Bühneneingang* or *Hauptpforte*), and check in with the doorman/receptionist (*Pförtner/–in*). He or she then gives you complicated directions through an often-antiquated theater to find the KBB and check-in (sometimes they just give you a form there at the *Pförtner/–in* and you save the entire trip to the KBB.) If you do not lose your way (which happens 30% of the time), you will then check-in with the KBB. You give them an updated copy of your materials (*Unterlagen*) and—with your own pen you brought with you—fill out an audition form they provide. The forms are generally the same: vital information (again, know your height and weight in cm and kg), roles performed and where, and audition arias (*Vorsingarien*). This is also a good time to ask for a written confirmation of your audition (*eine Bestätigung*), once again for your German tax deductions should you stay here. Then the KBB takes you to a practice room (*das Repetitionszimmer*) to warm-up. They will also tell you where the pianist is, where the auditions are, and if they will pick you up and take you to the audition room or stage. At least, they should tell you. If they don't, ask them.

Now comes more fun. Seven times out of ten you will sing your audition on the stage. Many auditions take place in the afternoon because that is often the only time the stage is free from morning rehearsals and evening performances. You are often called at the same time as all other singers, and the group auditioning will be anywhere from just you to (believe it or not) eighteen tenors—that audition was hell. Then, you wait. Depending on the theater there is either a pre-set order or first come first serve. If you are on a tight time schedule let the theater know as soon as possible, preferably before the day of the audition; they are usually very understanding.

It is at this point when I notice a difference with native English-speaking singers; the way we are taught to carry ourselves onto the stage in auditions sets us apart and frankly, it looks good. Perhaps this is also our superficiality (*Oberflächligkeit*) at work. Walk out confidently and say "Guten Tag." (Your audition really begins the second you step foot in the theater and check in at the *Pförtner/–in*.) In fact, I had a conversation about this exact topic with a colleague. He snuck into the auditions one day, sat in the fourth balcony, and was shocked at what he saw. One singer after another walked on stage with their heads down, hands in pockets, no charisma, no attempt to greet the audition panel, and even scratching themselves. It should go without saying that these are no-no's. You are not applying for a data entry position at the phone company. This behavior can easily cost you the job.

The audition panel sometimes engages you in small conversation to see how your German is and to determine what kind of colleague you might be. If you flounder with the language, do it with grace. They often ask you to walk upstage before you sing, and when you stop they may ask you to keep walking (*noch weiter...*).

You may often choose your first aria but some theaters make the first choice—no reason to freak out, just remain flexible. Theater folks are incredibly busy and they do not waste time in auditions. You know they do not hate you if they ask for a second piece, and you may even get a job from just two arias (I know of plenty of colleagues who have, and I have, as well). You know they find you interesting if they hear a third piece. You know there may be a chance that they are in deep lust/love with you if you sing four arias. And if they ask you to stay and talk with them, you may very well be on the edge of being offered a job. Although I do know of a colleague who was hired for her first *Fest* engagement after singing just the "Seguidilla" from Carmen, this is the exception and not the rule. When a theater hears just one aria, do not worry about staying up late for a phone call. Once an *Intendant* heard just one aria from me and actually said, "Thanks, we'll call you." I began to laugh right there which was probably considered rude. But that only happened once, and he never called.

  The audition panel wants to see you use the stage and use it well. If your aria calls for some movement and action, do not be afraid to use the set of that evening's performance of *Tosca* in front of which you may be singing. I consider it a gift having a set on stage, and I use it when appropriate. But that does not mean run around the stage like a jackass regardless of the aria. If you are singing *Un'aura amorosa*, there is no need to jump on the scenery like a monkey just to show them you can move.

8 ACHT

You're Hired (You Like Me, You Really Like Me!)

Take a minute to go get a glass of wine and then take a deep breath. If you have not worked or lived here yet, everything you are about to read may seem (and probably is) fairly complicated and confusing. Frankly, the first time going thru the process of German, Austrian, or Swiss bureaucracy is the hardest. But the following steps are meant to relieve you of much of the stress and uncertainty that go along with this process. Just relax, do not freak out, and read this chapter slowly.

What do you do now?

1. Negotiate the contract (*Verhandeln*).
2. Go find an apartment (*Wohnung suchen*).
3. Register with the city (*Anmelden*).
4. Apply for residence and work permits (*Aufenthaltserlaubnis/Aufenthaltsbewilligung* and *Arbeitserlaubnis*).
5. Get an Income Tax Classification Card (*Lohnsteuerkarte*). Don't forget. Seriously.

6. Get a bank account (*Bankkonto*).
7. Choose your health insurance (*Krankenkasse/Krankenversicherung*).
8. Get a driver's license (*Der Führerschein*). Don't forget. Seriously.
9. Go party. You have job *and* health insurance!

1. *Negotiate the contract/Verhandeln*

Trust but verify. — Ronald Reagan

(This means: **GET **EVERYTHING** IN WRITING.**)

A very refreshing thing about German-speaking theaters is that they sometimes hire people on the spot. It has happened with me a number of times, and I have seen it many more times with fellow singers—each time, either for colleagues or myself, it is a thrill. But do not let this thrill cloud your judgement.

If an agent sent you to the theater and the theater wants to hire on the spot, do not accept and do not negotiate yourself. This is the agent's job and they will be upset if you take their bargaining power out from under them by accepting the position. Do not do the agent's job for them. A good theater will know this. Of course, it is alright to speak with the theater right then and there to discuss repertoire, but give them no answers and refer them to your agent. Let the agent earn his or her commission.

If you came to the theater by yourself, it's up to you to negotiate. Have fun. I am not going into detail about negotiating with theaters—this is another book entirely. Just remember that the people with whom you are negotiating do this hundreds of times per year and are well practiced at squeezing the most out of you for the least amount of Euros. And believe me, they are quite often seriously interested in getting you for as cheap as they can, particularly in this economic climate.

If the theater has made you an offer on the spot, they will sometimes try to get an agreement right then and there. If you are like me, when you are hired on the spot your blood is pumping and you might not be operating in prime-negotiating-skill mode. If the theater really wants you, they can wait a day so you can come down off your high, get out of their office, and get a grip on reality before you sign a contract with terms you might be able to better negotiate two days later. It is within your rights to tell them you are interested and that you need a couple days to contact people and do some thinking. I learned my lesson the hard way about accepting a contract on the spot; I did it once and talked myself into an agreement for 60% of what I could have received, all because I was just happy to be hired on the spot. Of course, if the audition is for a job that starts next week (quite common), you might not have the luxury of putting them off by a day or two. But still try and take your time. It is not your fault that the theater is hiring at the last second.

And whatever you do, never *ever* start work without a signed contract. Never. It is big-time illegal (*Schwarzarbeit*). In fact, do not even travel to the city without a signed contract. An E-mail is not a signed contract, a promise to have a contract waiting for you is not a signed contract, and a friendly phone conversation with the *Intendant/—in* is **definitely** not a signed contract. Your signed contract protects the theater and you, and no matter what the theater may say, you need it in your hand before you step on that rehearsal stage. One of the theaters where I used to work often plays the game of waiting to give their singers contracts until they are already in rehearsals. Then, when the singer finally gets the contract, the terms are different than initially agreed upon. This is certainly the exception to the rule but a good lesson for why you must always have a signed contract before you begin. No exceptions. You are your own CEO—time to act like it.

THE CONTRACT

Germany

Negotiating your first *Fest* contract can be a daunting experience and you should tread with cautious optimism. There is a standard contract in Germany called *Arbeitsvertrag Normalvertrag (NV) Bühne Solomitglied*, commonly known as the *NV-Solo Vertrag* or *Normalvertrag Bühne Solomitglieder*. You may buy a copy of it from the German Stage Workers Union, *Genossenschaft Deutscher Bühnen-Angehöriger* (www.buehnengenossenschaft.de)—also, the same company from whom to buy a copy of the *Deutsches Bühnen Jahrbuch* (www.buehnengenossenschaft.de/dtbuehnenbuch.htm). The contract is a standard form with plenty of negotiable variables:

Fach classification and specific roles

Your *Fach* is written into Section 1 of the contract, and there are numerous different possibilities.

The sentence defining your *Fach* may be described as follows: "Frau Schmidt wird als Solomitglied mit der Tätigkeitsbezeichnung Dramatischer Mezzosopran und Partien nach Individualität eingestellt" (Ms. Schmidt will be employed as a soloist with the occupation term dramatic mezzo soprano, and roles according to individuality). The second part of the statement, *Partien nach Individualität*, means that the theater could, in theory, get you to sing parts outside of your *Fach* and this is *carte blanche* for the theater.

Occasionally, the theaters will simply list your *Fach* but they retain much more wiggle room when they insert a qualifying clause such as "Partien nach Individualitäten." If they just list your *Fach*, you are legally obliged to sing everything in your *Fach*, but you do not have to sing roles outside of your *Fach*.

Be very wary if the theater just wants to list your voice type (i.e., *Sopran, Bariton*, etc.); then they can get you to sing everything. You want your *Fach* listed, even if it is followed by a qualifying phrase.

One of the best possibilities is having the following listed: *Lyrischer Sopran, Partien nach Absprache* (Lyric soprano, roles contingent upon agreement). This means that the theater must consult and ask you before they assign you roles. (A good theater will do this with or without this clause.) While a few theaters may interpret this as simply needing to inform you of your upcoming roles in writing, most theaters take this to mean that they are obliged to consult you and ask your permission before they assign you roles. As you might imagine, it is not easy to have this put into your contract; the theater really has to want you.

Duration of contract, salary, and per performance/broadcast fees

Sections 3 and 4 contain many of the negotiable points of the contract, and they are becoming rarer. They include specific duration of the contract, monthly salary for each of the seasons, and per performance fee (*Spielgeld*) for exceeding a pre-agreed number of roles and/or performances per month and/or season. Additionally, there are options for negotiating a fee for more than one performance per day, performances for radio or television, and performances recorded for radio.

Agent commission

Section 5 identifies your agent and the percentage of their commission. Here is some good news: the theater pays half of their commission. The half that you pay will generally come directly out of your monthly salary, but be sure they are actually taking it out. During my first *Fest* contract, the head of payroll (who also happened to be a certifiable *Fachidiotin*) forgot to deduct my agent commission until near the end of the season. Then she decided to take it all out in one month (which I begged her to spread out over three months). All I could do was tell her that she was incompetent, a fact she had probably already heard many times. Her answer was, *I did not read the contract. But you should have seen it on your pay stub, so it is your fault.* Passing the buck can be the olympic sport of *Beamter/Beamtin* (civil servants) here.

Other variables include: *Gage* (salary), *Abendbegrenzung* (a limit to the number of performances you can sing in the season), extra compensation for TV/radio broadcasts, and paid vacation while you are away guesting. The two most important variables are pay and *Fach* classification. If you have a suspicion you might have to sing a high number of performances (e.g., one hundred performances), an *Abendbegrenzung* might be something in your interests, although—again—it be be more difficult to receive in this economic climate.

Pay

This is a long subject but, in short, do not expect to break the bank. If you have just won "Operalia!," you will probably have a good financial offer on the table. If you are just starting out and have limited European experience, expect something along these lines: *Anfängerverträge* (beginner's contracts) pay € 1,600. If the contracts are classified as "Anfängervertrag," the theaters must offer you a two-year contract (unless the Intendant is leaving at the end of your first season). So, you do not have much main stage experience and these jokers are calling you a "beginner?"

Relax—that is how people who have very little or no professional experience in Europe are sometimes classified. In an informal survey of friends in different sized theaters, monthly salaries range from €1,600 to €3,600 per month. One thing is clear, though: salaries are either stagnating or going down.

If you have some professional experience, the pay begins to rise and you should be careful about accepting an *Anfängervertrag*. The pay naturally varies from theater to theater, is somewhat better in Austria than in Germany, and depends particularly on the financial state of the particular city/state that pays the theater's budget (all theaters belong to the government) and the size of the theater. There are some wealthy cities, some bankrupt cities, and many in between. Your pay also depends (of course) upon your experience and how badly the theater wants or needs you. Keep in mind that you are not taking a *Fest* engagement to get rich. You really can live a decent, fulfilling life on €1,000–2,000 per month after taxes, and you may even have other concert and opera engagements to supplement your Fest income. The cost of living is often significantly below that of New York, Chicago, or London, depending on the city where you will live.

One good thing to keep in mind is that with a German *Fest* Contract, you often receive a 13th month pay as a bonus. Although this has traditionally been without exception, some theaters are discontinuing this practice because of budgetary restraints, and many more—I suspect—will follow. In Austria, you receive a 13th and a 14th month as a bonus. Depending on the theater, there are other small perks like extra pay for free days that you work, extra pay for overtime, among others. In Austria, there are two more weeks of vacation than with theaters in Germany, and you also receive a discount on the taxes you pay if you rehearse over a certain number of hours per month in the evening.

Plane tickets

I have had success with negotiating plane tickets from the U.S. into my contracts. While this may not always happen, it is worth trying to work into the agreement. If the theater is contracting you in February and your contract starts in September, let them know they need to get you over here. Some theaters will do this and others will look at you like you are on crack.

Do not expect to get everything you want when negotiating your contract. Be reasonable and be happy if you have negotiated a contract where you feel like your needs are met. Make sure to have everything—*everything*—in writing (remember, *trust but verify*), and have your contract professionally translated before you sign it. Exception: theaters may or may not agree to write your specific roles into the contract. There you must unfortunately remain flexible. But at least discuss your possible roles with the theater before you sign your contract.

Austria

Negotiations and contracts are not much different in Austria, although there is no *NV-Solo Vertrag* here. The contract looks different from that of its counterpart in Germany, but many of the negotiating points remain the same; particularly pay, paid vacation days, and listing of the *Fach*.

2. Find an apartment/Wohnung suchen

Now the fun is taken to a new level. Getting an apartment here can be an adventure. Whatever you do, make your new theater the first stop in your search. Theaters are like small cities employing hundreds of people, and you should certainly ask the KBB or artistic liaison office for tips. They may suggest putting up a flyer in the house, a very smart idea. If you have particularly good fortune, the theater actually owns apartments to rent, or they have working relationships with landlords. I was lucky to be able to rent a flat from my last theater and avoid a mess of paperwork, plus a ridiculous deposit.

If none of the above steps work, either look in the local paper in the real estate (*Immobilien*) section under rentals (*Wohnung zu vermieten*), or put an ad in the local newspaper. Unlike some other countries such as America, putting an ad in the newspaper to find an apartment is a very successful strategy here; many landlords (*Vermieter/–in*) look in the apartments wanted section (*Wohnung gesucht*) so they can select prospective tenants. It does not hurt to mention in your ad that you are a singer at the theater; some landlords like renting to artists from the theater, and I know of landlords who appreciate the occasional free tickets to a premiere. Search the online sites for the local papers, as well.

Just like other countries, there is a specific language of abbreviations in advertisements for apartments. They are listed in the Phrasebook and Dictionary, courtesy of the wonderful *Handbuch für Deutschland* (www.what-the-fach.com/pdfs/Germany-Handbook.pdf), a comprehensive guide published in English by the German government.

Be prepared to pay a large rental deposit (*Kaution*) in Germany, sometimes as much as two months. You will pay up to six months of rental deposit in Austria! And you get to supply your own kitchen in both countries; the sink, the fridge, the oven, the counters, absolutely everything.

3. Registration/Anmelden

Und jetzt comes more bureaucracy, which is really not so horrendous once you figure it out. After you get your apartment, you need to register with the local officials immediately—it's the law. I am convinced that if the German government could find a way to legally staple a UPC barcode to everybody's' foreheads, they would. They love to keep track of their people.

Go to the registration office (*Einwohnermeldeamt*) to register, often in either the city hall (*Rathaus*) or city office (*Bürgeramt*), and ask to register (*anmelden*). You will need confirmation of your address in the form of either a rental agreement (*Mietvertrag*) or a rental confirmation letter (*Mietbestätigung*). It doesn't work to give them the address of the theater because that is not your residence (although it may sometimes feel like it). Is the bureaucracy giving you a headache yet? Filling out the registration form (*Anmeldungsformular*) is free, painless, quick (by German/Austrian standards), and necessary to show the Foreigner's Office (*Ausländeramt* or *Ausländerbehörde*) when you reach the next step of applying for a residence- and work permit (*Aufenthaltserlaubnis, Aufenthaltsbewilligung,* or *Arbeitserlaubnis*). View a list of apartment rental Web sites on p. 214.

4. Residence permit and work permit/Aufenthaltserlaubnis/ Aufenthaltsbewilligung and Arbeitserlaubnis

Once you have your contract, you have an apartment, and are registered (*angemeldet*) with the local authorities, you need to apply for a limited residence permit (*Aufenthaltserlaubnis*). Check first with your theater; some theaters save you the trouble by taking care of applications for one or both.

If you need to apply yourself and have plenty of time—at least three months—before your contract begins, you might want to apply through your local consulate or embassy. However, applying this way takes a long time and you forego the advantage of any special relationship the theater most likely has with the local foreigner's office (*Ausländerbehörde* or *Ausländeramt*).

This is the point where things get confusing and frustrating, and you may start saying, *what the hell am I doing here?* Depending on the city, the mood of the lady behind the desk, the vernal equinox, and other unknown factors, you will either need to get your residence permit first or your work permit first. If you show up to apply for your residence permit, they may tell you that they need to see your work permit first. And if you show up to get your work permit, they may tell you they need your residence permit first. Ah, German bureaucracy... Whatever you do, do NOT get upset at these people. Just like your new best friends in the KBB, you want to do everything short of bribery to make these people love you. Never ever make them mad and never be difficult. Do not talk back and do not argue; you will lose. These people wield unknown power over your precarious life in Europe. They can make your life hell. Smile, say "danke schön," and go back to square one. Call your other new best friends at the theater if you're ever in doubt. They have engaged you, you have a signed contract, and it is in their best interests to make sure you get all the paperwork in order.

Depending on the city (and, I suspect, also, the number of foreign residents there), the foreigner's offices have varying degrees of strictness to their policies. When I first came to Germany I would receive visas in my passport good only until the last day of my next contract. Now, after a few years, plenty of forced small talk, and my charming German/Danish fiancé by my side, the process is now more of a social visit. The lady did not even bother to review my last application; rather, she just printed out another visa for my collection.

Here is what you need:

In Germany

When you go to the foreigner's office (*Ausländeramt* or *Ausländerbehörde*) in Germany, bring:

- Two completed copies of the residence and work application (www.what-the-fach.com/pdfs/Germany-Residence-Permit-Application.pdf) and *signed* declaration (www.what-the-fach.com/pdfs/Germany-Residence-Permit-Declaration.pdf)

• Two passport photos

• Your passport (duh?)

• Your *signed* contract from the theater

• Your *Anmeldungsbestätigung* (registration confirmation) if you are applying in Germany

• €50–100 cash (Some do not take credit/debit cards.)

• Police Certificate of Good Conduct (*Polizeiliches Führungszeugnis*) available from your local precinct; and a photocopy

After five years of continuous residence in Germany, you are eligible for a lifetime work permit and visa (*Niederlassungserlaubnis*). You are then no longer restricted to a particular geographical area, your permit does not expire, and you will no longer have to seek permission to look for other forms of employment. In other words, you will almost be German!

In Austria

Things get a bit more complicated in Austria. They have their own way and pace of bureaucracy here. Just hop on board, be obedient, and follow all the rules. When you are engaged by an Austrian theater, speak with the theater immediately about the process. Just explain to them that you have no idea what is going on, and if you are fortunate they may hold your hand through this process. You may also ask your agent for help and cross your fingers that they will lend you a helping hand. They may help you with your residence and work permit application process. In some cases such as with my theater, they are contractually obliged to help you. You will need numerous documents and it does get a bit confusing. The theater will provide you with some of them and others you will have to hunt down yourself. It is important to note that you must have some of the documents below officially translated into German (*beglaubigte Übersetzung*) by a notary public. Get ready. Here they are thanks to the Austrian Government's Web site:

- Valid and signed passport (passport must be valid for at least three months beyond date of return and must have a blank page to affix the residence permit). Include copies of *every* page in your passport.

- Copies of previous passports

- Application Form (www.what-the-fach.com/Austrian-Residence-Permit-Application.pdf), completed and signed, available only in German. For an explanation of the application in English, visit www.what-the-fach.com/pdfs/Explanation-of-Austrian-Residence-Permit-Application.pdf.

- One recent picture (passport format, color, front view)

- Original or notarized copy of Birth Certificate officially translated into German (*beglaubigte Übersetzung der Geburtsurkunde*)

- Original Certificate of Good Conduct/Criminal Record (*Polizeiliches Führungszeugnis*), available at local police station and not older than three months. Again, officially translated into German

- Proof of health/travel/accident insurance (original letter from insurance company confirming coverage in Austria) Speak with your theater about providing you with proof of your insurance coverage.

- Your *signed* contract

- Proof of lodging in Austria (e.g. rental contract). If you do not yet have a rental contract, speak with your theater and ask them to help provide proof of residence for you.

- Statement of Financial Liability. *Again, speak with your theater.*

- Proof of your education (copy of degree or transcript), again, officially translated into German

- One set of photocopies of all documents

Whew, I think I need a cigarette. And you thought it could not get more difficult. It is hell to get a visa in Austria—they do a very good job of controlling their immigration.

The Austrian Embassy will only accept complete applications and only in person. Let me give you an example of how frustrating and time consuming this process can be, just so you are forewarned and can keep that smile on your face. When I received my present contract in Austria, I already had a valid work/residence permit for Germany. However, this made no difference to the Austrians who have their own style of bureaucracy. I am not an EU (European Union) citizen so I had to start at square one with the Austrians. My new theater was (thank God) obliged to help me with the process and even pay my processing fees. They sent me the forms two months before my contract began and I got started.

Austria wanted lots of interesting things (see above) included with my application, and I took them all to the Honorary Consulate in Frankfurt. It was the beginning of a really long, bad, frustrating wild goose chase where everybody was extremely polite. Once at the Frankfurt Honorary Consulate, they told me I had to send everything to the Austrian General Consulate in München. There's a difference between the two, apparently. Ok, fine, no problem. I sent my application to München and heard back from them just four weeks before my contract was to begin. "Vaht ahh you siiinking just sending your siiings in?" asked the very nice gentleman on the telephone. I had to come and apply in person. Huh? Ok.

So, I got a one day release from another engagement to take a six hour train to München (and back) just to hand in the form in person. Once at the Austrian General Consulate in München, the very friendly gentleman (same friendly voice from the phone conversation) took my application form, marked an "x" in the box that said "applied in person," and told me they would send it in a diplomatic pouch to the office in my new city in two weeks. "Vaht ahh you doingg vaiting so long to apply for a wisa und vhy did you not just take your application to [your new city] in Austria?," he asked. Because you told me to bring it here, you *ass*, I thought, but did not say.

The application arrived in my new city for processing at the local foreigner's office one week before my contract was to begin. The people at the theater were freaking out, not to mention that they were a little irritated with me. But it wasn't my fault so what could I do? The theater informed me that my contract was null and void if I had no work permit by the first day of my contract. Two days before my contract started, the Intendant called to say, "Don't worry; I've made some calls and everything is taken care of."

The purpose of telling my saga is that even when you do everything by the rules it, can all still go terribly wrong. Be prepared. Be prepared to get the run-around and to get false, conflicting information. It shall all soon be in the past, and you will soon be admiring a shiny new visa in your passport.

As for Switzerland, speak with your theater for help. As you already know, they are not part of the EU but they do give EU citizens priority with some processes.

5. Income tax classification card/Lohnsteuerkarte

In Germany you must get an income tax classification card (*Lohnsteuerkarte*) before you begin work. The *Lohnsteuerkarte* shows your employer in which tax bracket you belong and determines how much tax you will pay. Where do I go, you may wonder? Either ask the person when you register (*anmelden*) at the residency registration office (*Einwohnermeldeamt*), or ask in the theater if all else fails. It is different in different cities. Welcome to Germany.

In which tax bracket (*Steuerklasse*) do you belong?

- *Steuerklasse 1*: Those single or separated, but not falling into either category 2 or 3
- *Steuerklasse 2*: Single and separated, with a child, entitling them to a child's allowance
- *Steuerklasse 3*: Married or widowed employees who are within the first year of a spouse's death
- *Steuerklasse 4*: Married employees both receiving income
- *Steuerklasse 5*: Married persons who would normally fall into category 4, but whose spouse is in tax class 3
- *Steuerklasse 6*: Employees who receive income from other employment on one or more different tax cards OR people married to someone with a significantly higher income

If you do not specify in which Steuerklasse you belong, they will automatically put you in *Steuerklasse* 6 (the highest tax bracket), and you will be in for a rude awakening when your first check comes with all kinds of extra taxes taken out. Don't forget to do this. I forgot and it cost me hundreds of Euros. Stupid.

In Austria, you do not need to get a *Lohnsteuerkarte*; they have a different and much more streamlined system than in Germany.

6. You have to put all that money somewhere. Get a bank account and learn how to transfer money back home for free./ Bankkonto

This is the easy part, but it can still be hard. There are a few good options for Germany. If you want the free bank, try the bank operated by the Post Office (no, I am not joking), Postbank (www.postbank.de). However, when you are back in your home country, you will be charged to use your cash card. But the service is generally acceptable and my favorite Postbank customer (my fiancé) is very satisfied. To receive a "free" account from them, though, you will need to set up direct deposit.

If you want to be able to use your cash card for free in many different countries and with other participating banks in Germany, I strongly suggest my German bank, Deutsche Bank (www.deutsche-bank.de). Fees start at €4 per month for an account, you have free use of cash machines in many parts of the world (including all of Bank of America's cash machines), and I have always found the service very good. I have never had a bad experience with Deutsche Bank. A third option is to try a local bank that charges nothing for an account. There is also Citibank but I do not recommend them just because they actually refused to give me a bank account when I first arrived in Germany, even with my work contract in hand!

Where else not to go? I have a close friend who was a banker for Dresdener Bank, another institution in Germany. As she always said, "Whatever you do, do not use Dresdener Bank. They suck." Dresdener Bank was purchased by Commerz Bank. My friend now says, "Whatever you do, do not use Commerz Bank. They suck." Add Sparkasse to the "no" list. There are just too many bad stories to tell about bad customer service and not enough ink available.

In Austria, I use BAWAG (www.bawag.at), and have had positive experiences. Although their former CEO was recently hauled back to Austria after being suspected of Embezzlement and fleeing to the Caribbean, I receive good service for just €3.95 per month (that is good for Austria). One fantastic perk with the cash machines in Austria is that they do not charge fees; it is against the law. And this goes for the entire EU—I can use my Austrian cash card all over Europe for free.

Just because some banks here are under the same names as those back in America (i.e., Citibank, Deutsche Bank, Bank of America, et al.), does not mean that they are actually the same bank. For whatever reasons, some of these banks are not connected with the banks of the same name in America. So, if you have a Citibank account in New York, for example, do not expect the Citibank in Frankfurt to help you. They are a different company. When you go to open your account, you should take the following documents with you:

- Passport
- Residence and Work Permits
- Your signed contract
- Registration form
- Signed apartment lease (if you have one)

A note about Banks in Europe: it is common to give out your bank information to people. People pay most bills (your *Deutsches Bühnen Jahrbuch* bill, for example) by bank transfer (*Überweisung*). It is actually very convenient, free EU-wide, and I wonder why America has not caught on yet. You may fill out a form in the bank, do it on their automated banking machines in bank lobbies, or do it thru online banking.

Once you are here and earning money, you will inevitably want to transfer some of it home. If you transfer directly through your European bank, you will pay a hefty transfer fee, a fee you will also pay when you receive the money into your home country account. I have found a service, XETrade (www.xetrade.com), that offers fantastic currency conversion rates and that eliminates all the fees. Although it takes a few days to set up (you must fax then information and actually speak with them because of strict money laundering laws), it is well worth your time. You may transfer the money for free as an *Überweisung* (transfer) to their Bank of America account in Frankfurt and have it transferred into your home country account as an EFT/direct deposit, which is free (an option for the U.S. and Canada only, though they plan to expand this option to additional countries). Then you pay no bank fees on either end and you receive a great exchange rate. Yes, it is a little confusing at first but if you plan to work over here it will save you copious amounts of ridiculous bank fees.

7. Choose your health insurance/*Krankenkasse* and *Krankenversicherung*

Before you begin work at a theater in Germany, you need to let them know which health insurance provider (*Krankenversicherung*) you would like. There are quite a few providers from whom to choose and they work hard to get and retain you as a customer. They provide excellent customer service unlike so many other parts of German society.

There are two types of insurance in Germany: state subsidized, (*gesetzlich*) and private (*privat*). If you are a Fest member of an ensemble you will be eligible for the less-expensive *Gesetzliche Krankenkasse*, and do not need to worry about private health insurance. The prices do not vary wildly and services are generally similar. I had wonderful experiences with the Techniker Krankenkasse (www.tk-online.de) and my girlfriend swears by Barmer (www.barmer.de). In fact, since the first printing of this book, I have switched to Barmer and am thrilled with them. These providers are certainly not the only wise choices, but I mention them because I have experience with them. The providers generally, if not always, cover you throughout the European Union, though you should confirm this with them. As well, when you travel back home outside of the EU, check with them about adding extra worldwide coverage to your policy. I did this thru Barmer Krankenkasse, and it cost me just €6 per year for each trip up to forty-two days. For all trips over forty-two days, you will pay €1.50/day. To compare all your choices in Germany visit Krankenkassentarife (www.krankenkassentarife.de).

If you work for a theater in Austria, the state health insurance provider will cover you. You pay less in Austria for insurance and that includes prescription drugs. I had to buy some prescription medication recently for a drug that would have cost plenty of money in America. It cost me €2.90! I about had a heart attack, and thankfully that would have also been covered under my health insurance. Having health insurance is unquestionably a cause for celebration, especially if you come from America. You are now fully covered and it is not breaking your bank account!

8. *Get your driver's license/Der Führerschein*

And take my word for this, please. If you are from an EU land, skip ahead. If not, read this carefully. After first moving to Germany (read: when you get a residence permit), you have six months to transfer your foreign license to a German license. At this point you may think that you will never drive in Germany or you are only staying for a season. But it is better to do it at the outset and prepare for that potential rainy day when you actually may need it. If you wait past six months, you will be forced to take the German written and practical exams (that may be taken in English, if you wish). But you cannot just take the exams; you have to sign up for driving school and pay potentially thousands of Euros for the lessons. In each other the eighteen German States the rules are different and the German government has a specific agreement with each and every U.S. State. Why? I have no idea. This means that people from some States may just simply exchange their U.S. driver's licenses for a German equivalent, and other people from other States must take all tests. Educate yourself and get a German driver's license, if you are able. The complete information is here: http://www.howtogermany.com/pages/driving.html.

9 NEUN

Taxes and Kindergeld
(Money For The Kids)

If you are reading this chapter before you actually have an engagement, everything may quickly get confusing (just like the previous chapter). There are numerous taxes you will pay here, and it is not an easy system to understand. Simply put, if you are working in Germany, you should expect to take home around 50% of your gross income (if you are single with no children). If you are working in Austria, expect to take home around 65% of your gross income. If your curiosity is eating you up, pop your Xanax and read on.

Taxes in Germany

The Germans tax for sport (they are world champions, second only to Scandinavian countries), and trying to read your monthly pay statement from the theater is like trying to read Braille in Chinese. But I am going to do my best to make it as simple as possible for you.

I took home approximately 50% of my gross income when I was in a

German ensemble (I was single and without children—*Steuerklasse* 1). Yes, it hurts seeing so much money taken out, but that is the price of being here. Suck it up and be a big boy/girl. Don't forget that your total net income includes the payment of your health insurance.

The following will be taken out of your paycheck and is calculated for a person without children (If you have children, you will pay less tax):

<u>Lohnsteuer (Income Tax):</u> According to the 2010 German tax law, depending on your income level and *Steuerklasse*, you will pay 0–42.5% *Lohnsteuer*. If you are single and have an income of less than €7,664, or if you are married and have a joint income under €15,328, you will pay no *Lohnsteuer*. However, many of you may fall into this next group: If you are single and earning up to €52,151 or are married with a joint income up to €104,302, you will be taxed at a progressive rate starting at 15% and rising to 42.5%. If you are single and earn over €52,151 or married with a joint income over €104,302, you will be taxed at 42.5%.

<u>Krankenversicherung or KV (Health Insurance):</u> Starting in 2009, all health insurance costs 15.5% of your gross income (*Bruttogehalt*) in Germany. However, the theater will split the cost of this with you: you will pay 7.6% and the theater will pay 7.9%. If you are married—with or without children—you will *all* be covered under this insurance, inclusive in this price you pay to insure yourself. Your children may be insured under your coverage until the age of twenty-five if they are still studying. For comprehensive comparison-shopping, visit Krankenkassentarife (www.krankenkassentarife.de).

<u>Pflegeversicherung or PV (Nursing Home Insurance):</u> The cost varies from 1.35% to 1.70% of your gross income. You split the cost of this with the theater, and the curent rate you will pay—as of 2010—is .975% of your gross income.

<u>Rentenversicherung or RV (Social Security/Retirement Fund):</u> 19.9% of your gross income, but you pay only half of this because your theater pitches in the other half. So, you will pay 9.95% of your gross income for *Rentenversicherung*.

Taxes and Kindergeld (Money for the Kids)

Solidaritätzuschlag or SolZ: A tax of 5.5% from your income tax (*aus der Lohnsteuer*). The *SolZ* was initiated after the reunification of East and West Germany to help rebuild and subsidize the East's game of catch-up with capitalism. Note that it is 5.5% of your *Lohnsteuer* and <u>not</u> your gross income. All in all, it is a relatively small amount to fund a black hole of bad policy.

Arbeitslosenversicherung (Unemployment Insurance): You will pay 1.4% of your gross income.

Kirchensteuer (Church tax): A tax of 8–9% from your income tax (again, *not* gross income) that goes to either the Protestant Church (*Evangelische Kirche*) or Catholic Church (*Katholische Kirche*). If you are Jewish, you may opt to pay a Culture Tax (*Kultursteuer*). When you register in your new city of residence, you must either choose a religious affiliation on the registration form and pay this tax, or write "*konfessionslos*" and be exempt from this tax. If you do not write anything, you may end up paying both, as I did my first few months here. It is your choice if you would like to pay this tax—so untypical for the Germans...

Bayrische Versorgungskammer (www.versorgungskammer.de): This is the retirement fund for German theater workers and, frankly, a good deal. Once you start working in Germany you become a member of the *BVK*, and then with every engagement you pay 4.5% of your gross income into your private retirement fund. The theater matches your contributions with an extra 4.5%. You will receive a big, intimidating packet from the *BVK* when you first begin working. Save it. Click on the above hyperlink to see information in English and acquaint yourself with all your options.

Agenturgebühren (Agent Commission): The standard agent commission in Germany is 6% for a two-year *Fest* contract and 10% for a one-year *Fest* contract. The theater then pays half of this commission for you and the other half is almost always taken directly out of your paycheck.

Working a Teilmonat (partial month): The following is an absolutely disgusting practice, and fortunately you should only worry yourself with these details if you have a contract—either *Fest* or guest—when you are employed for partial months. Common sense, decency and moral conviction dictate that if you worked a partial month and therefore received a partial salary, you would be taxed for the actual income you earned. But, no. Not here. The theater (and government—it is the law, after all) estimates what you *would* have earned for the entire month and then taxes you for that estimated amount. Criminal, in my opinion.

Here is an example: if you sign a contract for €2,000 per month and begin the contract on the fifteenth of the month, you would have a gross income of about €1,000 for the first month. However, to the greedy eyes of the theater and government, they see that you would hypothetically earn €2,000 in that first month, and therefore they tax you for €2,000 of income. Grotesque, but true. If you have a contract starting on the fifteenth of a month and ending on the fifteenth of a month, you will be taxed *twice* (for both half-months) for double the income you actually earned.

Taxes in Germany when you are a guest

When you work as a guest in Germany, your taxes change significantly. This is very confusing and I suggest you speak with the business office (*Verwaltungsbüro*) of your theater after you read this to clarify any confusion you may have. As well, consult an accountant whenever you have questions.

On important general tax note: ff you earn less than €800 in a given month and you are in Steuerlasse 1, 2, 3, or 4, you will pay no tax at all.

Ausländersteuer (Foreigner's Tax): If you do not have a permanent residence in Germany, you will pay a "foreigner's tax" (*Ausländersteuer*) of 25% for the income you make here. This is in lieu of the regular income tax (*Lohnsteuer*) you would normally pay. If you are not an EU citizen, you are ineligible to get this tax back should you file a tax return in Germany. If you are an EU citizen, you may be able to recoup this tax in you home country under double taxation laws. The German government charges this flat "foreigner's tax" because they are essentially unable to estimate your income and tax rate. The German government considers you to be a resident in Germany and not a candidate for the "foreigner's tax" when you have a tax card (*Lohnsteuerkarte*; see p. 91), a work permit (*Aufenthaltserlaubnis/ Arbeitserlaubnis),* and when you are registered (*angemeldet*) at the local city hall (*Rathaus* or *Einwohnermeldeamt*). Confused yet? Speak with your accountant in your home country to see if you may recoup these taxes at home.

<u>Taxes for guest performances:</u> When you come to a theater as a guest without being engaged as a *Fest* singer in another German theater and are a part of the production (i.e., not an *Einspringer/-in* for just one performance), you will pay in most cases either *Lohnsteuer* or the *Ausländersteuer*, PV, RV, SldZ, BVK and health insurance.

If you do have a *Fest* engagement in any other EU theater and you work as a guest in another theater, you will only pay *Lohnsteuer* . If your *Fest* theater is outside of Germany, you will need the form "E-101" from your *Fest* theater saying that you are employed there. You will then be exempt from paying the double insurance on PV, RV, AV. You still have to pay BVK, though. But remember that the BVK is an investment similar to an American 401k, and not a tax.

<u>Einspringen taxes:</u> If you are *kurzfirstigbeschäftigt* (short-term employed) and are engaged with a theater for under seven days, you will receive your entire fee with nothing deducted. Since 1.1.2010, if you work under 7 days for an engagement, you do not have to pay into BVK. The theater will inform the local *Finanzamt* of your fee, so you will have to declare this is income.

<u>Lodging:</u> If you negotiate any kind of lodging for a guest engagement—even if it is "free" to you—you will pay the tax (*mehrwerter Vorteil*). The crafty Germans consider it income to you that you were given accomodations for "free." Let me give you an example: if you are engaged for a performance and earn a fee of €2,000 and your apartment cost the theater €500, you will be taxed for a total income of €2,500. Deplorable, I believe, but not surprising.

There is an exception to this practice, however. If you already have a residence (*Wohnsitz*) in Germany, they will not tax you for your accomodations because they consider it a double residence/upkeeping of two households (*doppelte Haushaltsführung*) within Germany.

Taxes in Austria

The good news about working in an Austrian theater is that you pay less taxes than in Germany. You will pay the following taxes:

<u>Lohnsteuer</u> (Income Tax): If your income is under €10,000 per year, you pay 0% income tax. When your income is from €10,000 to €25,000 per year, you pay income tax on a sliding scale up to 23%. From €25,000 to €51,000, the sliding scale increases to 33.5%. If you make over €51,000 per year, you pay 33.5% income tax. There are numerous deductions one can take, and for a comprehensive (and easy-to-read) explanation of the streamlined Austria tax system, visit www.what-the-fach.com/pdfs/Austrian-Tax-Booklet-2007.pdf. We have tried to find a newer version of this document for 2010, but to no avail.

<u>Sozialversicherung/SV</u> (Social Services Tax): This is where the Austrians got it right. Instead of all those individual taxes the Germans take out, you pay 18% of your gross income for an all-inclusive package of health insurance, retirement, nursing home insurance, and unemployment insurance. The theater then contributes an extra 21%.

<u>Agenturgebühren</u> (Agent Commission): The standard agent commission for *Fest* contracts in Austria is 6%, of which the theater pays half. (For guesting, the agent commission is generally 10% and for concert work it is 12%.) In other words, if you make €2,000 per month for a *Fest* engagement, your agent will earn a monthly commission of €120 but you will only pay half of that. The theater deducts this commission directly from your check and the tax is already included in the commission.

Doing your taxes/Steuererklärung

I am not an accountant and will not pass along tax advice aside from this: do your taxes (*Steuererklärung*) when you are here. Ask around in your theater to see if anyone can recommend an accountant (*Steuerberater/-in*) who is familiar with doing taxes for musicians. Just like America, you can take all kinds of deductions (*Absetzungen*), which will increase the amount of your tax refund. Just do not forget to save your receipts; you will need to actually show them to the local finance office (*Finanzamt*) where you bring your tax return to be eligible for the deductions. Yes, doing taxes here is complicated, out of my realm of expertise, and it drives me absolutely crazy. Hence, I always have my accountant do it.

I also strongly suggest you contact your accountant in your home country to answer questions of double taxation law and other complicated issues for which my music degrees did not prepare me.

Kindergeld

The governments of Germany and Austria actually *pay* you money, called *Kindergeld*, to have and raise children. Germany—in particular—is having a tough time maintaining their population, and by most estimates the German population is estimated to drop from eighty-six million people to sixty-nine million people within the next twenty years. In both Germany and Austria you should apply through your theater or the employment office (*Arbeitsamt*). This is how it works: the government pays you a certain amount every month for every child you have. This money is paid to you until the children either complete their education or they reach their twenty-seventh birthday, whichever comes first. For more information about *Kindergeld* in Germany (complete with diagrams a three-year-old could understand), read the Merkblatt Kindergeld (www.what-the-fach.com/pdfs/Germany-Kindergeld-Booklet.pdf).

In Austria, the mother begins receiving payments for a protection period (*Karenz*) beginning eight weeks before the birth of a baby and lasting through the baby's first eight weeks. For complicated births such as caesarian sections and premature birth, this assistance lasts even longer.

The monthly payments for *Kindergeld* in Austria are considerably higher than those in Germany, and you should check with your theater about the application process. Just like Germany, payments of *Kindergeld* in Austria are made to the parents until the children either complete their education or they reach their twenty-seventh birthday, whichever comes first.

10 ZEHN

Pot Luck Dinner

There are a number of other loose ends worthy of addressing and they all go together untidily in this chapter.

Festing and guesting

If you want to make some money and grow your career, you should hit the pavement and find guest work (*Gastengagements*). As a guest, you also have the potential to earn in one evening what you earn during an entire month in a *Fest* ensemble.

However, it may be naïve to think you can come on over and earn a good living by accepting only guest work. If you have a very good artist representative and impressive professional credits on your résumé, then yes, it may be more realistic to accept only guest work. Those in a rarer *Fach* (e.g., Verdi/Wagner Soprano, Heldentenor, Countertenor, Male Soprano, Bass, etc.) also have a greater chance of making a good living doing only guest work. However, if you are a *Lyrischer Koloratursopran* fresh out of school or young artist program with no experience and no management, you might have greater luck riding a unicorn to the pot of gold at the end of the rainbow than starting out by making a good living taking only guest work in Germany.

I am sure there are exceptions somewhere to this rule.

Due to the fact that North American-, British-, and Australian-based singers survive almost solely on freelance work, we generally have a much greater tolerance than our German-speaking colleagues for the ups and downs of this lifestyle. Frankly, this confounds many of my German and Austrian colleagues who often consider a stable *Fest* engagement a pinnacle of their careers. There is absolutely nothing wrong with that; I know many colleagues who are able to have wonderful and stable lives by sticking to just one theater. I prefer, though, not to put all my eggs in one basket, so to speak.

Society in Germany and Austria places great importance job stability, and this is exactly what a *Fest* engagement offers. *Fest* contracts are generally either one or two seasons, the salary is enough on which to live and even put a little money away, and you have a stable home base. A *Fest* engagement is useful for a number of reasons: you gain incredible experience, get your feet wet in Europe, and learn the language. Believe it or not, when you fest you may also have some time to accept guest engagements.

For those of you wishing to do only guest work, it is wise to keep in mind that it is not easy with the economic climate in Germany and Austria (only since there are fewer theaters in Austria).

A combination of guest and *Fest* work is possible and often the best option for a few seasons until people begin to know your name and you build your reputation. If you have just a little free time in your *Fest* contract, you can notify your agents that you are available to guest, and this work sometimes comes just a few months—sometimes weeks—before rehearsals begin.

Künstlersozialkasse / KSK

If you decided to be a freelance artist in Germany, you have the possibility of being insured by the Künstlersozialkasse (www.kuenstlersozialkasse.de) for health insurance and social security. See the pdf form (www.what-the-fach.com/pdfs/ksk.pdf) for information in English. It is a little time comsuming, but in the end it is well worth it. You will have to submit an application with copious supporting materials proving that you make at least €3,900 per year as a freelance artist. They very well may initially require you to submit more proof, and I beleive they do this to discourage non-eligible people from applying. I have been a member on two separate occasions, and on both occasions it took a couple months and additional documents from me to gain approval. You may also not apply retroactively. If approved, you first date of coverage will be the day they receive your application.

Once you are approved, you will keep the insurance company you already have (i.e. Barmer, TKK, etc.), and you will pay the Künstlersozialkasse directly. They will then pay your insurance and Social Security directly. The amount you pay is determined by the amount you earn. It is a good deal and almost too good to be true. But it's true.

Jumping in/Einspringen

With so many full-time theaters and thousands, if not tens of thousands of performances per season, singers inevitably get sick and cancel. Then an *Einspringer/–in* (last-minute replacement) comes to the rescue. Not only is it nerve wracking and financially rewarding, but it is also is much fun. There is no reason why you cannot begin to set yourself up to jump in once you get off the plane. This work does not come along on a regular basis so do not count on making it a significant part of your income. In fact, do not count on getting any *Einspringer* work at all. It comes when you least expect it.

If you would like to let agents know you are ready and able to jump in, you should prepare a repertoire list of roles you have performed professionally and that you have ready to go at a moments notice. Let them know, especially ZAV (zav.arbeitsagentur.de), that you have these certain roles ready to go now (*Rollen parat*). It does not hurt, as well, to directly contact theaters that are performing this repertoire just to let them know you can jump in. Then if you get lucky your phone will ring. Make sure that you actually can perform these roles at 7:30 PM if called at noon on the same day. This is, after all, how I got my start in Germany.

What can you expect to be paid as an *Einspringer/–in*? It depends on the role, how common it is, how big the theater is, how much advance notice you have, what experience you have jumping in, and—perhaps the most important factor—the desperation level of the theater. The financial range can be from €400 per performance (Giannetta in *L'elisir d'Amore* with 5 days notice) to €2,000+ per performance (*Tannhäuser, Otello*, etc.) in larger theaters. I was once able to negotiate a significantly higher fee than usual with an *Einspringen* simply because nobody else knew the role, the scheduled singer had not bothered to learn it, and the theater waited until the last second to contact me.

Keep all this in mind if and when you receive an *Einspringen* offer; you do not want to price yourself out of a nice opportunity that could lead to even more opportunities. Ask yourself the question: do I need the money more than the gig, or the gig more than the money? That should help determine how much you want to push your luck while negotiating (if you even have room to negotiate).

When you take an *Einspringen,* make sure you discuss—and have in writing—how and when you shall be paid. Each theater has different payroll systems. Sometimes you are paid cash on the spot, other times they transfer the money to your bank account right away, often you are incorporated into the theaters bi-weekly/monthly payroll, and yet other times they conveniently "forget," and you have to keep calling to get paid. Many theaters like to hang on to their money for as long as possible. Be firm, yet professional, when discussing payment.

Tipping with festing, guesting, and einspringen

You are not required to tip (or give small gifts to) your dresser and makeup artists for festing, guesting, or *einspringen*. This essentially means that nobody is holding a gun to your head saying you absolutely must tip. However, not only is it a kind gesture to show your appreciation for others who made you look good on stage, but also a greatly appreciated, chivalrous gesture that people will remember.

What do I tip in my *Fest* engagements? If I tipped everyone €5–10 per performance with a *Fest* engagement I would go broke. Nobody is expecting it. It is kind and good form, though, to remember the backstage personnel (i.e., your makeup artist, dresser, stage manager, assistant director, prompter, etc.) with a small gift for every opening night. In addition, at the end of the season I give my dresser and makeup artist either cash or gift certificates to show my appreciation. The amount I give depends on how good they were to me during the season.

There are some colleagues in the theater who do not tip and believe that because the dressers and makeup artists earn a decent living, "Why should I tip them?" I think that attitude is selfish and ignorant; these people are always there to make us look good and their work should not go unrecognized. Furthermore, these small, tangible gestures repay themselves many times over in intangible ways.

In my last *Fest* theater, for example, I had an absolutely wonderful, highly professional dresser. This man was always (and I mean, always) there to make me look good, and he was a kind person. He went above and beyond his job description and I gladly gave him a generous tip or gift certificate of €100–150 at the end of the season. Sadly, he passed away and his presence is sorely missed.

What do I tip with guest engagements? I tip my dresser (*Ankleider/–in*) and makeup artist (*Maskenbildner/–in*) around €5–10 per show for guest engagements—a bit more or a bit less depending on the friendliness and competence of their assistance. At the very least, I give a bottle of wine or a box of chocolates, but only if they are unfriendly and unintentionally make me up to look like Liza Minnelli strung out on crystal meth.

What do I tip with an *Einspringen*? When I show up to jump into a production at another theater, everyone knows that I will be taking home a decent-sized check that evening. I am having a good day, so I prefer to share the love. I take care of my assistant director (*Regieassistent/–in*). This is the person who will spend their free afternoon to help stage me into the production. They never ever want to be there (they often rehearse with me on their afternoon break), and they often get paid nothing extra to help.

You need them to help make you look good, so tip them if they were helpful. If you are stingy, get them a €5 box of chocolates. If you have a little class, get them a nice box of chocolates or a bottle of wine with a card. If you are feeling particularly generous, put a €20 bill in a card for them. This goes a long, long way, and when the assistant director speaks with the KBB the next day about your performance (and they will), it will surely not hurt to have greased the wheels a little, so to speak. Also, a nice bottle of wine or chocolates is a nice gesture for the makeup artist and your dresser. If your cast helped guide you around stage, take them out for a beer afterwards.

It is not obligatory to tip. Plenty of people will disagree with me about the size and scale of generosity necessary to show your backstage personnel. I ask, though, why not be generous?

Renegotiating your Fest contract

Once you are working as a *Fest* singer in an ensemble, there is a good chance that you may be called upon to renegotiate your contract with the theater. Depending on your circumstances (i.e. if you negotiated the initial contract yourself, or if it was done through an agent) and the particular theater, you may be asked to do this directly, or the theater may contact your agent. I have had the experience that *Intendanten* wanted to renegotiate my contracts directly with me, although the intial contracts came through agents. This made me uncomfortable and it should make you uncomfortable, as well. Let the agent earn his or her fee and take that pressure off of your back. Thank the *Intendant/–in*, tell him or her how flattered you are, and let him or her know that your agent will be in touch with the theater.

Although some theaters may believe that since you are a fixed employee there and you see each other every day in the theater, it would be fine to just deal directly with each other. I say, though, that you will most likely benifit in the end from the distance you keep by not discussing money and contract particulars directly with the boss.

And whenever you do meet with the *Intendant/–in* to discuss anything at all (i.e. repertoire, vacation releases, future programming, etc.), take this wise advice that was given to me: always write the boss a short E-mail after the meeting thanking him or her for meeting with you, and (very clearly yet diplomatically) confirm the details of the meeting. Then you will avoid the potential altercation with a "forgetful" boss who "forgot" that he offered you one role and not the other. *Intendant/–in* are extremely busy. Some forget and others "forget." Don't let them. Get it in writing.

Teaching English during your audition tour

You have decided to come for an audition tour and would like to financially subsidize your trip by teaching English while you are here. I have not done this and know very little about teaching English and what kind of qualifications it entails.

However, I can speak about the following: if you are coming for an audition tour, you will undoubtedly have enough stress just with auditioning, staying in vocal shape, adjusting to a new culture, and trying to order your lunch in German. Why put an extra burden on yourself? What happens if you start teaching English and you receive a call from an agent that conflicts with your English class in three days? You may be forced to make a difficult decision. If you need to earn the money to pay for the auditions, I strongly suggest you have the money in hand before you arrive in Europe. You have already invested so much into your audition tour—why spread your time and resources thin by teaching English at the same time?

I do know of some people who actually moved here and decided that teaching English was the most sensible way of supporting themselves while they started to get their operatic careers off the ground. If this is you and it floats your boat, go for it.

Opera studios and young artist programs

There are a number of opera studios in Europe: Düsseldorf, Hamburg, München, Frankfurt, Nürnberg, Zürich, Paris, La Scala, Strasbourg, and Netherlands Opera, to name a few. While North American and British singers often gain our first professional experience in young artist programs/opera studios, the trend is not so prevalent in Germany, Austria, and Switzerland. On the contrary, many beginning singers here start with a beginner's *Fest* contract (*Anfängervertrag*) in various theaters, which substitutes for opera studio experience.

Though opera studios here are not the standard path to a career, this does not mean that they serve no purpose at all. Many studios are part of larger theaters with significant exposure to critics, singers with international careers, and powerful agents. Some companies also regularly hire alumni of these studios for *Fest* positions. Experiences in these programs vary—some theaters use their young artists for smaller roles and covering on the main stage, some have the young artists do their own productions and outreach shows, and other programs pay their artists to sit around picking their noses. But what all these programs do offer is an opportunity to be part of a theater, experience how the system works, and give you a foot in the door to a career.

Ensembles here are filled with alumni of European opera studio programs, which indicates that studios are a viable stepping-stone into careers. I have worked with alumni from a number of the programs above, as well as a couple of colleagues who are fresh out of school and were never in opera studios.

Chorus work

If you want to sing in the chorus of a theater or radio orchestra and have the positive mentality to enjoy doing it, the opportunities are plentiful. I have many friends who chose this career route and most are happy. Life in the chorus is more stable than that of a soloist. Choristers often have better job perks than *Fest* soloists (e.g., sometimes a higher salary than a soloist depending on the theater, more days off, etc.), and less individual stress placed upon their shoulders. Many choruses are filled with former soloists (and some excellent singers) who decided they preferred the job stability to the punishing stress of being a soloist. One of the most glorious voices I have ever heard, for example, comes from a woman in a chorus. She has an excellent technique and if she had the desire, she could be a soloist in large, international theaters. However, she does not want that lifestyle or stress.

Chorus members, depending on the theater, are often assigned comprimario roles and are paid a small per-performance fee. But if you have any desire to work as a soloist in Germany or Austria, you want to be a soloist in that theater, or are frustrated with your career and are bitter, do not join a chorus. I know people who fit these criteria and being in the chorus does their emotional well-being no good. Chorus singers here are considered exactly that, no matter how good. I didn't make the rules. Joining the chorus is not the way to work your way into an ensemble as a soloist, although it is somehow very occasionally done. When you take a chorus job in German-speaking countries—no matter how good you are—you are essentially telling people that you are not interested in pursuing the career of a soloist.

There are occasionally people in the chorus who naïvely believe someone will pluck them out of the choir and give them Gilda in next season's *Rigoletto*. These poor folks are often the ones trying to steal each scene by standing down stage center in every production and overacting. Everyone in the theater notices, and I do not mean with applause and flowers.

For every stage hog (*Rampensau*), though, there are an exponentially greater number of talented and happy choristers. Many of my friends in choruses really enjoy the work and live fulfilling lives, both personally and artistically. If this interests you, you should do these three things: 1. Contact ZAV (zav.arbeitsagentur.de) to let them specifically know you want a chorus position, 2. Write the theaters directly (either the *Chordirektor/–in* or KBB), and 3. sign up with Theaterjobs (www.theaterjobs.de)—they have an entire jobs section with listings for available chorus positions (as well as for other employment, including low-level guest work). If you would like to see a standard contract for a chorus singer (*Normalvertrag Bühne Chormitglieder*), head back to GBDA (www.buehnengenossenschaft.de/vertragsrechtpublikationen.htm).

11 ELF

INTERVIEWS: You Think I'm Full of Crap? Then Read What My Colleagues Have to Say.

This chapter contains interviews with a number of singers, coaches, conductors, stage directors, and administrators currently (as of 2010) working in German, Austrian, and Swiss theaters. Each has had his or her individual road to their current positions as well as varying opinions. As you may notice, a couple of them have chosen to not use their real names; the opera world is very small and these are people whose names many of you might recognize. And so, to avoid any potential uncomfortable situations while still wishing to speak freely, they have gone incognito. Enjoy...

- *Ellen Rissinger, American coach*
- *Angela Fout, American soprano*
- *Christine Graham, American soprano*
- *"Thomas Schmidt" (not his real name), European conductor*

- *Damon Nestor Ploumis, American/British/Greek bass-baritone*
- *Robert Tannenbaum, American stage director and former Oberspielleiter (Chief Opera Producer) of Badisches Staatstheater Karlsruhe*
- *Helene von Orlowsky, Swedish Künstlerische Betriebsdirektorin (Director of Artistic Administration) for Austria's Landestheater Linz*
- *Alma Wagner (not her real name), German mezzo-soprano*

INTERVIEW 1 ~ Ellen Rissinger, American Pianist, Accompanist and Coach

I have known the wonderful pianist, accompanist, and coach Ellen Rissinger (ellen@ellenrissinger.com) for several years since our time together at an American opera company. She is one of the most talented and hardworking coaches around today with a true command of numerous languages and a long-term vision for her career. Ellen's talent and perseverance helped her land her current position on the music staff of the Semperoper in Dresden. Since we first spoke in 2007, Ellen's career has continued to blossom, and she has recently begun a new Podcast, The Diction Police (www.thedictionpolice.com) available for free download at her Web Site or on iTunes. There you may get her language expertise for *free*! But first, she shares her thoughts with us.

Ellen, talk a little about yourself and what kind of experience you had in America before you came to Germany.
Ellen: Well, I earned an undergrad degree in Piano Performance from Carnegie Mellon University, worked around Pittsburgh from 1991–94, and then went for my MM in Accompanying from University of Cincinnati College-Conservatory of Music. After that, I started doing contract work for a number of American companies coaching the Young Artists in Aspen, Des Moines Metro Opera, and Florida Grand Opera. I was also Music Director of Opera Iowa and served on the Music Staff of Glimmerglass Opera, Kentucky Opera, Pittsburgh Opera, Opera Company of Philadelphia, Baltimore Opera, and Utah Festival Opera.

What prompted you to come to Germany as opposed to concentrating on building your career exclusively in America?
Ellen: I wanted to break into the top level of American Opera, so I showed Lenore Rosenberg at the Metropolitan my résumé. She told me that if I wanted to be on staff, they needed to see that I could work in a repertory house and that I could rehearse in other languages. So she suggested Europe. Germany was the easiest place to begin, because there are so many opera houses with fest positions, rather than contract work which can be difficult to break into in a new country. But I do miss the U.S. and someday I'm going back!

Describe your life since you moved to Germany. Where have you worked? How does this lifestyle differ from that in America?
Ellen: I started at the Mainfranken Theater in Würzburg for eight months, then two years as Head Coach in Pforzheim Stadttheater. I spent four years at the Deutsche Oper am Rhein in Düsseldorf, and a short contract in the Fall of 2009 with Oper Frankfurt before starting here at the Semperoper in January of 2010.

As for the difference in lifestyle, I think in some ways it's a little slower than it was for me in the States. I take more time for myself than I would have before. Everything closes down on Sundays and holidays, so in some ways you're forced to relax a little more. By the same token, everything closes down and I miss my conveniences! One thing someone had told me that I didn't believe—you will watch ANYTHING on TV that's in English, including *Flavor of Love and Rock of Love*. But aside from my TV addiction, there are upsides. Because I'm not on the road three hundred days a year, I have created a home for myself as well as a circle of friends with whom I can actually spend time. With the advent of Skype, I can call my dad every day and talk to friends back home very often. Getting home is hard, and holidays are hard away, but you create a family of friends here with whom you can share special moments, as well.

Describe your process of getting an agent and what auditions were like for the theaters.
Ellen: When I came to audition, I set up two agent auditions over the phone from the States and bought a plane ticket! Quite honestly, my first agent

audition was one of the most miserable moments of my life; all he did was yell at me (in German, even though he was *British*!), tell me that nobody wants to hire *Ausländer* ("foreigners"), I can't speak any languages (which is not true—just not German at the time!), that I don't know the repertoire well enough (at the time I had 50 operas in my rep!). And then he said, "but I think we can get you an audition in Würzburg. Talk to my colleague." She yelled at me as well—the same things—but then said, "how can we contact you for the audition in Würzburg?" So when I got to Würzburg I was TERRIFIED... and they loved me. They hired me on the spot and then we worked out all the details in English!

They were not much nicer at my second agent audition. But at that point I already had the job in Würzburg, so they couldn't tell me I was incompetent! And after that, they helped me get my next two positions. After my first two years in Düsseldorf, however, I was free to handle the contract myself, and have been working without an agent since then.

What is the standard audition repertoire for coaches? Can you also describe a typical audition?

Ellen: The standard audition repertoire for pianists is the following:

- *Carmen*: Quintet
- *Le nozze di Figaro*: Act 2 Finale
- *Otello* (Verdi): Opening scene
- *Elektra*: Magde Scene or *Salome*: Jews Quintet
- *Der Rosenkavalier*: Opening scene
- *Falstaff*: Fugue
- *La Bohème*: Complete 2nd Act

*The first three I used in the States all the time, as well.

House auditions are completely different from agency auditions. Agencies heard only one or two selections that I'd prepared, and after that had me play for singers' auditions. They don't really try to get to know you; they just want to make sure that you can play the piano. For house auditions, they heard everything I'd prepared, plus conducted me, had me coach singers, and sight-read (at the Semperoper, I sightread *Liebe der Danae* by

Strauss—there's nothing like playing Strauss in the house where so many of his operas were premiered!). Then they talk to you. Theaters are looking for someone who fits in well with the ensemble that is already in place. As opposed to the short-term contracts in the States, they hire you for two years, so personality counts!

What would you say is the general quality of pianists in German-speaking theaters? How are American pianists received by the theaters?
Ellen: The quality is extremely varied, which is due partly to the quality of education here. Administrations and singers receive Americans very well: we work hard, we're rarely sick, and we tend to be very well trained in style and diction. We also have a strong understanding of the voice. I'm spoiled here in Dresden that we have such a terrific staff of coaches who have great training in their craft, but there are many European coaches who learn to play the piano so that they can work their way up to conducting. Many of them have never played a voice lesson. In *Musik Hochschulen* [German music conservatories] they are trained to play their audition pieces and often have one semester of language training, but almost never do they learn IPA [International Phonetic Alphabet].

Talk briefly about the hierarchical structure of pianists, coaches, and conductors in theaters.
Ellen: The chief conductor is the *Generalmusikdirektor/–in* (GMD), and then there are *Kapellmeister/–in* (conductors). The next in line is the *Studienleiter/–in* (head coach) who is responsible for the daily schedule and the preparation of the singers and pianists. Sometimes coaches also get to conduct, but not very often, and usually with the small pieces. In the contract, it will stipulate either "*Solorepetitor/–in*" ("coach") or "*Solorepetitor/–in mit Dirigierverpflichtung*" ("coach with conducting responsibilities"). Coaches also perform not only in operas that require keyboard instruments (celeste, organ, piano), but also in orchestra concerts when needed as well.

You must certainly play a number of auditions for singers at the Semperoper. How do native English speakers compare to the

competition? Where do we excel and where we do we need more work?

Ellen: Technically, English-speaking singers are among the best trained as far as vocal technique, stage presence, and stagecraft. We are also very well trained in diction. That being said, we have significantly less practical experience with the languages and the cultures. In Germany you are never more than six hours in any direction from a completely different country—be it France, Austria, Switzerland, Italy, Luxembourg, or Poland. Living with another language—in another culture—is something different from learning grammar and diction; you understand not only the words, but also the *sense* of them. Here, there are so many foreigners of every nationality that you can speak almost any language you want, every day. My favorite story: I was having lunch in a Greek restaurant with an accompanying student of mine who is Japanese, an Italian work colleague, and my little American self, and we were communicating in German! I've been practicing my Spanish, French, Italian and Russian here, and even learned Modern Greek. Most of the people I know speak at least two languages, and probably half of them speak four or more. That's something we miss out on in America.

How do the administrators and our European colleagues view English-speaking singers?

Ellen: Again, Americans are seldom sick, very hard working, dedicated, and well trained. Acting styles are slightly different, which causes some directors to find singers "cold" or not as able to communicate their feelings. I think that's a function of our culture, as you write earlier in your book: when they ask how you are, it's not an "I'm fine" answer that they expect. They look you directly in the eye the entire time they speak to you, which is unusual for people in America. They also sing looking directly at each other, where we would "cheat out." These are subtle differences that you'll run into here, easily learned, and in general Americans do very well in the German Houses.

What advice do you have for pianists and singers considering the move to Germany?

Ellen: Know your technique and do your homework! Once you have a *Fest* job there is little time to work out technical issues, especially in the smaller houses. Plus, it's easy to get complacent when you have a steady paycheck and to let your own standards slide a little—don't let it happen. You have to remember why you want to do this in the first place, and keep striving to achieve that ideal. I worked my way up the regional opera houses in the States, started all over again in Germany and went from a D-house to some of the best houses in Europe in seven years by practicing and continuing to study and improve. And I'm still studying—and hopefully improving! Anything is possible, just never lose sight of your true goals.

On a personal level, I would suggest having a VERY strong family/friend base to call and cry to! Europeans have very strong opinions and have NO QUALMS telling you exactly what they think, especially unsolicited advice or criticism. Customer Service here is not friendly by any stretch of the imagination, and the first two months you'll feel like you're running from *Amt* to *Amt* (Bureaus) to get this permit or that clearance. They will speak to you in voices that vary from marginally polite to "Ve have vays of making you talk," and you will feel very much like an outsider for a while. I literally E-mailed my Dad every day for three months saying, "What the &%#$ was I thinking?!" People will walk directly into you on the street and not even notice. Seriously.

Finally, you have a special affinity with languages and—in particular—language in song. It's time for your free plug! You have a new free Podcast available on iTunes (www.itunes.com) called "The Diction Police." Here's your fifteen seconds!

Ellen: The Diction Police (www.thedictionpolice.com) is a free weekly half-hour podcast, where performers read texts from songs and arias in their native language, and we discuss the text in regard to diction. We also talk about what problems Americans have specifically with diction in their language and other useful information for voice students and young professional singers.

I had always studied languages—German in elementary school, Latin in high school, and in college French, Italian, Russian and Spanish. But my French teachers were American, as were my German and Spanish teachers. My Italian teacher was Chinese. I studied diction in both undergrad and graduate school, but in general heard Americans speaking foreign languages rather than hearing native speakers using their own language.

INTERVIEWS

When I moved to Europe in 2003 and was surrounded by all the languages I had studied, and had to use them on a daily basis, my concept of diction changed. Not that the rules were wrong per se, but rather that I started adjusting my idea of how the phonetic letters actually sounded. Learning the diction rules gave me great tools to learn quickly once I was here, but the actual sounds of the language were much different than I had previously thought.

Over the past few years I've been working a lot with young Americans and I find that they have the same sounds in their ears as I had. I've been looking for a way to offer this information to American singers, and with the advent of podcasts, have finally found a way.

The Diction Police is available for download free or through iTunes, and I encourage questions and comments. I want the information to be useful and helpful to the audience!

INTERVIEW 2 ~ Angela Fout, American soprano

I first met the captivating, gifted, and warm-hearted soprano, Angela Fout (www.angelafout.com), eleven years ago during our young artist program days in America. Since then, her performing career has taken off. She has performed with a number of North American companies, and in the past few seasons she has relocated to Switzerland where she is now a soloist with the internationally regarded Theater St. Gallen, as well as with other theaters throughout Europe. She is also happily married and the proud mama of an adorable Cairn Terrier, Knut. Angela was kind enough to share her thoughts and advice, as well as observations about living and working in Switzerland.

Describe what led you to decide to take an engagement in Switzerland.
Angela: There were a number of factors. The leading factor was that, although I was getting enough work to pay the bills and be professionally visible [in North America], I felt that it truly wasn't enough to continue improving as an artist. It takes a lot of nerve to be on the stage in a leading role, and when you have a few months off at a time, it is easy for one to lose her nerve. Singers should be singing. Also, I can sing many different things as opposed to the same four operas that continue to get recycled in the U.S.A.

Getting a *Fest* job, although at a significantly less monetary reward, allowed me to do fourteen performances of a role instead of four, and it presented me with many different opportunities and challenges that I would not have had, had I stayed in the United States. For me personally, it was the right choice.

What kind of experience did you already have before you came over?
Angela: I guess it would be considered a good regional career. I have sung leading roles with New York City Opera, Vancouver, Spoleto Festival USA, Minnesota, Palm Beach, Austin Lyric, and Wolf Trap, to name a few. It was a nice profile but there just weren't enough opportunities to keep me as busy as I would have liked.

You keep up an active career in North America, as well. What are the particular challenges with balancing between your engagements in Switzerland and North America?
Angela: It is all very new, as I have been in Switzerland for less than a year. But so far it has not been too bad. My North American engagements are scheduled perfectly with me when I am here in Switzerland. That was luck. I anticipate that maintaining the balance will be more difficult, as I will be working on productions in Europe during the New York winter audition season, leaving me with no new opportunities. That is when I must trust that my management will work its magic!

What do you find to be the biggest advantages and disadvantages of being in an ensemble?
Angela: It is mostly "advantages" if you forget about the paycheck! Every time a singer—especially a younger one—walks in on her first day of work, she has to immediately prove herself. This leaves no room for error and no space for experimentation; it becomes a bit of a musical cage. Being part of an ensemble, I am free to try new things and I am able to grow into a role. I am trusted because the administration already knows my abilities. It takes the pressure away and puts the art back into the process. My particular theater has a wonderful energy between colleagues and administration; it feels like a family environment. Therefore, the discomfort of always being with new people and all the pressures that come with it, are removed. You go to work

and you come home. When you go to work, you make music. It is a good situation.

I would also like to add that it is remarkable to have all of my clothes in my closet instead of in a suitcase for months at a time. Traveling is part of the job as a guest singer, but as a *Fest* singer you can work only in your theater or you can guest in other theaters during your free time. You have a choice.

The disadvantage (and this is not only true about being in an ensemble, but is also particularly applicable because of the long hours and many demands of your instrument) is that no one will look out for the long-term health of your instrument. You must take full responsibility for it. Have a plan. How many days a week will you sing out? How many days a month will you rest your voice? The schedule is difficult. You and you alone know how much your voice can work before the quality suffers. This is the best advice I can give any singer in general, but particularly a singer who must sing a heavy schedule.

What is life like in Switzerland?
Angela: Switzerland is like a moving postcard. It is exactly as you would expect it to be: mountains, beautiful old architecture, cows with bells, great chocolate. ... Wow, it is an extremely civilized country—very orderly, very clean. The cost of living is high but well worth it. Swiss German is a funny language; expect not to understand anything! The quality of life is high, and overall people are calm and happy.

How does rehearsing a production in Switzerland differ from rehearsing a production in the United States?
Angela: My theater does only new productions. As a member of the ensemble, I am coached on my role assignments for free. The rehearsal period for a new production is six weeks—it goes a lot slower than in The United States. We have a lot more orchestra time here, as well. The daily schedule is the biggest change and honestly the one thing about which I do not agree. Singers can be rehearsed eight hours a day and the rehearsal times are 10–2 and 6–10. It makes for a very long day and people get tired fast.

Is there anything you wish you had done differently before you came over?
Angela: The time was not there for me to do it, but I wish I would have had two months of intensive language training. I am taking classes now, but it really helps to make life easier.

What advice can you give to those thinking about coming to Europe for an audition tour?
Angela: Come over for as long as you can. Time is opportunity.

INTERVIEW 3 ~ *Christine Graham, American soprano*

I have known the gifted and one-of-a-kind American Soprano, Christine Graham (www.christine-graham.com) for fifteen years. Christine is a highly talented, intelligent, unique, blogging, singer-actor. After earning her Master's degree in Music and making it to the semifinals of The Metropolitan Opera Competition, she earned a spot in the Deutsche Oper am Rhein (Düsseldorf) Opernstudio. Formerly a member in the ensemble of a German "C" theater, Christine has had successes singing everything from Mary Magdalene in *Jesus Christ Superstat* to Zerbinetta in *Ariadne auf Naxos*. Below, she shares her candid thoughts about life and work in Germany.

Christine, describe your path to Germany. How did you make your way here, and what experience did you have before you came to Germany?
Christine: During the last year of my Master's Degree, I asked myself the question, *What the Fach am I doing with my life?* I applied for around ten YAPs [young artist programs] in the U.S., and for one YAP (an *Opernstudio*) in Germany. The Germans took me; the Ami's [Americans] did not. That was the end of the story, sort of.

The long version is, I happened to be taking German classes in the last two years of my Master's—intensive immersion type classes—so I was learning it just for fun. Then one day, one of my music professors told me that I should look into working in Germany. (I never have been a very good businesswoman and I tend to go through life lackadaisically, not knowing what I need to get where I want to be. And only on a good day do I know where the hell that is. But I've been lucky enough to have people point me in the right direction from time to time.) So I sent out seventy letters to opera studios, theaters, and agents, which all resulted in *one* single audition, which I apparently nailed. That was for an opera studio [at an international "A" house]—they hired me that very same day.

As far as experience, I was singing lead roles in University productions, working as a chorister in a large American opera company, and I had quite a few competitions under my belt, including the semi-finals of The Met Competition—but all in all I'm a pretty late bloomer.

You began in the *Opernstudio*. Describe that experience—what was it like? What did you see as the major advantages/disadvantages to being in the *Opernstudio*?

Christine: That opera studio has changed its format since I've been there. The studio members are now a lot more integrated into the big house than they were in my day. What they don't have now are individual productions, but they do scenes and sometimes perform reduced versions of shows. It was probably the worst two years of my life, and I wonder if I may ever go back there to work because they see me as "the little girl from the studio," regardless of how much progress I've made. It was just a big culture shock, getting used to the theater system, learning nine roles (albeit small roles) in five months, working almost daily, never knowing what my schedule was for the next day until 2 PM on any given day, dealing with a long-distance relationship which ultimately crumbled, and learning the hard way that flipping out does not help your reputation. Divas are "out." But I can say I now have a very thick skin as far as the grueling schedule goes. And I've reduced my flipping out to once or twice a season.

Do you recommend trying to start out here in an *Opernstudio* instead of in a *Fest* contract?

Christine: I'd say do what you can do to get your foot in the door. I never realized how much I was lacking in stagecraft, however, until working alongside the pros in the big house. In that respect, the *Opernstudio* was a really good experience. Then I did some summer festivals to get my own feet wet with playing leading roles. Then I had a *Festvertrag* in a theater that also has a drama and ballet department, so I got to see what good acting was every day. At any rate, I'm really comfortable on stage now. I'm sure back then I thought I was hot stuff, but now I know that I probably wasn't.

You were in your *Fest* position for a few seasons. What was life like for you in the ensemble? Can you describe the ups and downs?
Christine: I worked in a small theater, but it's a *Drei-spartenhaus* [a theater with three different performing arts, i.e. ballet, opera, drama]—that means I mingled almost daily with singers, musicians, actors, dancers, directors, choreographers, und und und... We were mostly on very friendly terms with one another, played soccer together, and generally had a lot of fun. I consider myself lucky to have also gotten the chance to work with these people in mixed productions (actors and singers collaborating - usually in musicals). That has been an *up*.

But what I didn't realize is, and here I'm quoting my voice teacher who is famous yet shall remain anonymous, "Repertoire flexibility can be confusing and is seldom rewarded for the special talent it is." I have now been pigeonholed into a certain *Fach* that isn't even my own. That's a *down*—fun, of course, but in the long run not accelerating my climb up the operatic ladder.

Let's play word association. Agents…? German Stage Directors…?
Christine: Agents: Be honest with them—that's all I know. But I'm a bad liar. Directors: In Germany, I have done some very, *very* rewarding work with some very smart people. You know you're working with a good director when he tries to fit the role to you, instead of trying to fit you into a role. The same goes for shoes.

People say you speak German without an accent. How the hell did this happen? What do you have to say to folks about learning the German language?
Christine: Ask me this question again after I've had a few beers! I have a knack for languages. I discovered that talent a bit too late. Who knew? I just

recognize patterns very quickly—kind of like music theory, too. I don't think learning German is different than learning any other language. You just have to realize that the language is structured differently than yours—*Have you this morning cornflakes had?* That is a totally normal sentence in German, and you have to accept that and be open to it. There's no quick way to learn. It's like learning to play an instrument—you're just going to have to practice. The intensive courses helped me with that. At certain levels of opera, though, you might not even need the language—like if you're singing Bel Canto at the *Wiener Staatsoper*. Once you start getting into Operetta, or even into the Mozart operas in German, you're going to need the language skills. Speaking, *understanding*, and sometimes even improvising, making up for your drunken foreign stage partner who messes up his lines. It all depends on your personality, though. I—for one—would not want to live here not knowing the language well. But then again, I revel in it. It's very fun for me.

INTERVIEW 4 ~ *Thomas Schmidt (not his real name), European conductor*

I first met and worked with the talented and gregarious conductor, Thomas Schmidt, many seasons ago. He has extensive experience in the German *Fest* system so I asked him to describe his career path. He also shares not only his advice to aspiring conductors wishing to work in Germany, but also his observations of English-speaking singers here.

Thomas, Talk a bit about your history: where you are from, where you went to school and where you have worked.
Thomas: I was born and raised in what used to be West Berlin. After I earned my *Abitur* [highest level of high school diploma], I began to study violin. I studied violin further [at a major university] and earned my degree, as well. While I was at the university I first began to study conducting.

While I was studying conducting, I founded an orchestra and led the orchestra for a number of years. That was a wonderful time and I give this orchestra credit for the competence I now have on the podium—every week 1-2 rehearsals, plenty of weekend rehearsal retreats every season, concerts, tours, and much more.

My first professional position as conductor was in the *Kapellmeister* position in a *Stadttheater*. After my time there, I held positions in a few different theaters and am now finishing my contract in a *Staatstheater* where I have been for a few years.

Am I correct in saying that your path to being a conductor has been a little untraditional, meaning that you did not work your way up from a *Korrepetitor* to *Kapellmeister*? What is your instrumental background? How did you come to conducting?

Thomas: Indeed it was. My path was very unusual and I know of nobody who has done it as I have. As I already said, I am a professional instrumentalist. My past with the violin has been enormously helpful for my profession: when I stand in front of the orchestra, I imagine exactly what kind of sound I want to hear from them, and I know—above all—exactly what I want with the strings, how it should sound, and what one should do technique-wise to achieve this.

My first work in the theater was more of an accident than actually planned. I took an opera workshop, which led to my first position as assistant conductor at a Stadttheater, where I stayed for a few seasons.

I had the good luck there to concentrate completely on conducting. After a few seasons in a professional theater, I jumped up to a bigger and better house in Germany as their *1. Kapellmeister*. It is no longer necessary to play piano as the *1. Kapellmeister* in a middle-to-large German theater. But you see, though, it has been a chain of fortunate circumstances that has helped me maintain my conducting career (almost ten years) without playing the piano.

You are presently finishing up your tenure as a Kapellmeister and your next step sometime in the near future will be *GMD* (*Generalmusikdirektor*) for a theater. Would you please describe these two positions, their differences, and what each does?

Thomas: The *GMD* (*Generalmusikdirektor/–in*) is the most important position in the music realm. The *GMD* is obliged to make all musical decisions: programming symphony concerts and opera repertoire; which people to hire and fires—soloists, chorus members, and orchestra members (with chorus and orchestra members, however, it is extremely difficult to fire them because German contracts offer tenure), plenty of boring and occasionally uncomfortable administrative duties to perform, rehearsal schedules to arrange; and vacation time to grant or sometimes deny.

The *1. Kapellmeister/–in* is—in the scheme of things—the assistant and advisor to the *GMD*. He or she is the second most important person in the theater. The *1. Kapellmeister/–in* takes over duties and powers of the *GMD* in case of absence, gives advice about musicians and singers, programming, conducts rehearsals for the *GMD*'s concerts and premieres, and then has his or her own studies and concerts. The *1. Kapellmeister/–in* sometimes takes over music theater (opera, operetta, musical) productions for the *GMD* after the premiere. Plenty of other positions are under the *1. Kapellmeister/–in*; *2. Kapellmeister/–in*, Studienleiter/–in (head coach) *Chorleiter/–in* (chorus director), and *Korrepetitoren* (coaches).

It can sometimes be quite stressful when the *GMD* "delegates" all the uncomfortable activities to *1. Kapellmeister/–in*, and the orchestra members vent all their frustrations to you about their lack of trust in the *GMD* (which they should naturally resolve on their own).

What is an audition like for both *Kapellmeister/–in* and *GMD*?
Thomas: Both auditions are somewhat alike. The process normally lasts two rounds, and each position has either a rehearsal or a performance for each round of auditions. The pieces for the *1. Kapellmeister/–in* position are naturally a bit less challenging in comparison to those for a potential *GMD*.

For a *1. Kapellmeister/–in* position, one must usually conduct the overtures to either *Die Zauberflöte* or *Die Fledermaus*. I have also had to conduct the opening to *Tristan und Isolde*, Beethoven's *5th Symphony* (first movement); Brahms' *3rd Symphony* (first movement); or Brahms' *1st Symphony* (fourth movement).

Auditions range from conducting performances of *La traviata* and *Rigoletto*, to *Il barbiere di Siviglia, Die Zauberflöte,* or *Cosi fan tutte*. Candidates for the *GMD* position often conduct performances of *Tannhäuser, Salome,* or *Der Rosenkavalier.*

What advice do you have for foreign conductors coming to Europe in the hopes of landing a *Kapellmeister/–in* position? What kind of experience and skills should they have?

Thomas:

Play the piano very well.

Speak German and Italian fluently.

Know the twenty most popular opera/symphonic scores well.

What do you say to the conductor who has little conducting experience and only wants to take a conducting position in the theater without *Korrepetitor* responsibilities?

Thomas: It does not exist. Sorry. Your only chance then is to try and assist someone.

What is the competition like for these positions?

Thomas: The competition is extremely high, as you might imagine. Brush up your networking skills.

Finally, part of your job is hiring singers, and you must hear an incredible amount of auditions. What are your observations about English-speaking singers? Where do we excel and where are we weak? Do you have any advice to pass along?

Thomas: My experiences are the following: all native English speakers are extremely professional with great work ethic. They come well studied to rehearsals, are very open-minded, and easy-going. They are always aware and are flexible.

But on the other hand they are keen on pleasing you, not appearing to make trouble or cause problems. One sometimes construes this as a lack of personality. I interpret it as part of the "hire and fire" cultural background; they cannot afford to say what they really think about a bad conductor or stage director, for example. They want the job so they keep their mouths shut. I find this unfortunate because I think debate and differing opinions are healthy in contrast to agreeing for the sake of harmony.

In auditions I observe that most Americans turn up very well dressed, quite often even "overdressed." Headshots come from expensive photographers—I can see the amount of time taken to appear "perfect"—bleaching teeth, photoshopping headshots, etc. While I understand that this is a difference in culture, it is not what I want to see. Rather, I prefer to see a natural, friendly aura instead of the "artificial" impression.

As for audition repertoire: In Germany, Austria, and Switzerland, all auditions are strictly held with the *Fachsystem* in mind, an important fact many foreign singers don't know. I recently heard an audition where a singer offered Blonde, Pamina and The Countess. These are three different *Fächer* and to the jury it seemed ridiculous. Before she even started to sing the jury had already decided to *not* take her seriously.

So pay attention and sing in only one *Fach*! Only sing something from another *Fach* if you think that is where your voice is going (i.e., lyric to lyric dramatic). Do not sing the big repertoire (i.e., Wagner and Strauss) too early, and often you will have to sing at least one Mozart aria. Above all, what I find most important is that you know who you are as a singer.

INTERVIEW 5 ~ Damon Nestor Ploumis, American/British/Greek buffo bass-baritone

If you mention the name Damon Nestor Ploumis (www.damon-nestor-ploumis.com) in any number of German-speaking theaters, there will inevitably be numerous people who will smile and start sharing Damon Ploumis stories with you. Damon is a true Renaissance man and a "character" in the most positive sense of the word. After having read at Cambridge, Damon graduated from Philadelphia's Academy of Vocal Arts and Zürich Opera's International Opera Studio, and then got his German start in the ensemble of Deutsches Nationaltheater Weimar. Since then, he has established a fruitful career—performing basso-buffo repertoire—in both German-speaking theaters as well as in numerous opera houses around the world, among them Finnish National Opera and Swedish Royal Opera. Damon is not only an absolute stage animal, but he is also an intelligent singing-businessman. He has also recently founded Lyric Opera Studio Weimar (www.lyricoperastudioweimar.com), a summer training program for singers that already has a proven track record of connecting young singers with *Fest* and *Gast* engagements in Germany. Below, he speaks about establishing a career as a guest in German-speaking theaters.

Damon, what would you say is the most important factor in establishing a healthy guesting career in the German-speaking theaters?
Damon: The most important thing is that you have to have a *niche*, because every house is going to have their own singers. In order for you to get hired as a guest, you must fill the *niche* that they need for that specific production.

What are they?
Damon: Anything in dramatic *Fach*. You could be a specialist in Baroque, and in my instance a basso-buffo/bass-baritone, specifically in the Rossini/Donizetti repertoire. The houses try to put their basses in the buffo repertoire, but often they are not comic and are unable to sing high enough. So in order to be able and go guest successfully—for more than just a season or two—you have to able to locate a *Fach* in which you become a bit known before you go guesting. This means the agents have to know that you are the guy [or girl] they can telephone when they need to fill your *niche*. This is also why I would say to any lyric baritone: do not try to make your career just as a guest [in Germany alone].

Would you say that this applies to all of the more-common *Fächer*, such as *Lyrischer Tenor* and *Lyrischer Sopran*?
Damon: All of them. You might get an occasional jump-in [*einspringen*], of course, if you are known for the role or if you based nearby and have done the role in the past couple of years. But in order to do it full-time you have to have a specialty.

We're talking if you are concentrating your career just in Germany, Austria, and Switzerland?
Damon: Right. The other houses abroad will hire according to what they need because they usually don't have the *Fest* system.

You came from AVA (Academy of Vocal Arts) in America, right?
Damon: I came from AVA. What I would suggest is, if you are trying to make the jump over from the U.S. to Europe, get yourself involved in some opera studio in Germany, just because enough agents will become acquainted with you that way.

Instead of getting a *Fest* position in a small theater?
Damon: Well, yes because with a *Fest* [in a smaller theater]—what can also happen is that they will drag you down into having to sing absolutely everything. With a studio you have a little bit more of a luxury because they treat you a little bit more gingerly—they treat you a little bit more like a student, quite frankly. But at the same time the agents are looking for fresh, new singers, and you can get more agents to pay attention to you if you are in an international opera studio. Starting off at a small *Fest*, unless you've already established what your specialty is going to be, you are going to end up having to sing *everything*.

You started out at the Opera Studio in Zürich. Do you think that gave you good footing to find a good *Fest* position?
Damon: Yes, because Zürich has the prestige. What I would say is this, although it has only been partially true in the case of my career: if you are going to go guesting, gain the confidence of a well-known and well-connected director and/or conductor.

And then?
Damon: And then what happens is that where they go, they bring you. Obviously then, you can branch out from there. Then you will have begun to make a name for yourself, and other theaters will call you up because you have performed the role already in good houses.

You have a number of working relationships with agents. What is your advice about them?
Damon: If you are just beginning out, agents have great value. But after that, if you are no longer a beginner [in Germany], the whole audition sequence is worthless—at least in my case I have found that it is worthless. [After you

have been working around a bit] they either take you because they know you or because someone has heard of you, or they won't take you. Most of the agents do not have enough clout to say, "this is so and so; I want you to take him." Very few agents have that influence. On the other hand, there are some smaller agents who work very hard. One, in particular, has done more than all of my other agents put together. Every agent is not going to work for every person. I happen to be in that little *niche*, and other agents who should be able to get me things because I am in that little *niche*, do not move on it. I find the agents in Germany are far too passive.

Would you recommend that singers contact theaters directly?
Damon: Yes. If they have a little bit of aggression—you actually do not have to be aggressive but you have to be consistent. I have found that a lot of times when an agent has said, "I cannot get you an audition there," or, "they're not interested," that when I end up calling the theaters directly, they end up hiring me.

But are you advocating not using agents for people just coming over for the first time?
Damon: No, because they would be totally unknown, they do not know the language and they do not know the system. For those just coming over I would say that you *do* need to work with agents, but do *not* expect them to get jobs for you.

But expect them to get auditions for you?
Damon: No. An agent in the German, Austrian, and Swiss realm consists of this: they are theater agents as opposed to personal agents, so they are working really for the theater rather than working for you. That is a key point to emphasize. Half of their salary from the singer's commission actually comes from the theater. So that means that they are more likely to be loyal to a theater who can give them three different contracts than to the singer who can give them only one contract. And this is why the agents are not aggressive enough. The agents have mixed loyalty, and in the long run I think that does not play very well for the singer. That is one reason there are constantly agents going out of business. If the agent is only getting 10% of a singer's fee which is €2,000 per night, they earn €200. But if the singer is getting only

€1,500 per night, that is only €50 less for the agent [€150 per night], and the agent still has the goodwill of the theater. I think agents think that way—I would if I were an agent.

And about negotiating directly with the theaters: what do you suggest to people who ended up writing the theaters, coming over for an audition tour, they did the audition and were offered a job?
Damon: Unless you're in a specialty *Fach*, such as a dramatic tenor or soprano or basso-buffo, you ought to take what you can get. I would suggest that you push the salary up between €200 or €300 per month. You're probably not going to get more than that. And an extra €200 per month is only about €2,000 per year. This is not going to bankrupt a theater. And if they do this for an entire ensemble, which might consist of ten singers, you're talking about the theater having to pay only €25,000 more per year. It is worth it to the theater to have the singers they want and pay a little bit extra.

Do you have any general advice to give?
Damon: Yes. The general advice is—pessimistically speaking—come over *not* expecting to get a job. Come over *not* expecting that the agents are going to be calling you up, because there are a million other singers. I know that sounds rather negative, but the truth is that if you are in a common *Fach*, the chances of your actually being called to go out to auditions are relatively slim. The agent might call you for one or two auditions, but if that does not pan out then they are not going to bother with you. Do not go home broken-hearted if you go home without a *Fest*. Rather, consider it an adventure where you got a taste for how things work over here and you learned some German.

And optimistically speaking…
Damon: What you and I perhaps do not realize is that we both came over and landed on our feet. I have people constantly calling me up from America wanting advice about coming over for an audition tour. They come over expecting that they are going to get auditions, of course, and nothing pans out. They end up singing for a few agents, waiting for auditions for a month or two, and then pack their bags and go home. It *is* predictable that if you are in a standard *Fach* and do not speak some German, they are going to favor

against you unless your voice is fantastic—and "your voice is fantastic" means that your voice has to be *different* and fantastic. You cannot just be: *I was at the top of my class at the conservatory.* You have to be able to differentiate yourself. Essentially, brace yourself; it is very competitive over here and many of you reading this are not going to go home with work. That being said the houses are full of North American singers so go for it!

INTERVIEW 6 ~ Robert Tannenbaum, American stage director and former Oberspielleiter (Chief Producer of Opera) of Badisches Staatstheater Karlsruhe

I first had the pleasure of working with American stage director, Robert Tannenbaum (www.robert-tannenbaum.com), when he directed me in a production twelve years ago. Since then, he has become not only a friend, but also a trusted advisor generously helping to guide me through my first years in Europe. Robert has been a frequent source of good advice, and he has helped my career immensely.

Since first coming to Germany in 1984, Robert Tannenbaum has successfully established himself as an in-demand stage director not only here, but also in North America. As well, he has held numerous artistic positions in German theaters, including General Director (*Intendant*) of Stadttheater Giessen from 1992 to 1996, and Chief Opera Producer (*Oberspielleiter*) for the Badisches Staatstheather Karlsruhe. Robert also maintains a busy freelance stage-directing schedule.

He was nice enough to sit down with me recently (for a four hour lunch) and speak with me about everything from directing in Germany, to *Fächer* and audition attire.

Robert, you direct productions in both Europe and North America. What are the similarities and differences?
Robert: Well, there is probably very little that is similar except that the opera is the same. But I think always that the simplest way to explain is that opera

in America is a decorative, cosmetic art form, and that opera in Europe is, emotionally and dramaturgically, an internally driven art form.

Does the staging take a more prominent role here (in Europe) than in America?
Robert: Whether it takes more of a prominent role is a secondary issue. In America the traditional way to do an opera is to duplicate the effect of the music visually for the audience. In Germany your talent is measured on your ability to illuminate parallel, complimentary levels to the piece and combine that with the basic first level of the piece. This is the primary issue.

When you are in an actual production, does it differ? How does it differ?
Robert: Let's put it this way: it depends. It depends if you are the sort of person who does it differently for America than for here. For example, when Herbert Wernicke—who was a very excellent and controversial German stage director—did his first production at the Met he used a completely different style. But that is generally not the case. Most quality German stage directors do not work in America. If you look at the whole list of top twenty German directors, none of them work in America.

Why?
Robert: Because Americans have a completely different idea of what opera is supposed to do. Opera [in America] is basically supposed to entertain you at a not-too-annoying level after you go to dinner.

And here it is supposed to provoke?
Robert: It is supposed to provoke, it's supposed to move you, it's supposed to educate you, it's supposed to make you angry, it's supposed to make you happy, and it's supposed to make you feel uncomfortable.

Does the audience expect this here?
Robert: Yes. When the audience goes to the opera here they always say, "What has the director done with it this time?" That's the expectation. But the other thing is that as a director, you're not a good director by the German

standard if all you do is illuminate what is already obvious in the opera.

They want to see something new?
Robert: Well, they want to see what I call the parallel and complimentary levels. It's interesting but for an American audience, if the opera looks like what they are hearing, they are happy. For the Germans, they want to see something that displays other levels of the piece; other textual levels, other subconscious levels, psychological, societal levels, political levels—there are many different approaches. But they are looking for what you can weave into the piece to make it fresh, new, and interesting.

The three words I always hear from my American colleagues are "Regietheater," "Eurotrash," and "Konzept." I always hear them with negative connotations. What do you think?
Robert: They are—for me—the way Americans protect their holy turf of doing opera like it belongs in a museum. And it is always easy, if you are uncomfortable with the religious, political, or sexual connotations of a production, you just call it *"Eurotrash."* It's a very easy way to wash over something very easily without discussing the issues behind it. And American opera is looking for something different because American opera is paid for by very rich, conservative people and their wives who are looking to entertain themselves with their money. So all they are really looking for is a vision of the world, which mirrors how they see life. Mr. and Mrs. Richard H. Moneybags III are not looking to give their money to an opera company in America so that the opera company can show them what's wrong with what they think about society, politics and religion. So American opera becomes this self-serving, *perpetuum mobile* where the rich wives hire the general directors who hire the staff who then produce the opera that the rich wives go to and then say to their husbands, "Oh isn't that lovely, dear. Let's go and have dinner now." So that's the whole cycle, and the cycle in Germany is different.

Opera in Germany is an art form and art is here to illuminate, challenge, educate and entertain. And it is a function of the government the same way that society should have schools and swimming pools, society should also have art.

But is it here to provoke?
Robert: It is definitely here to provoke.

And what about provoking just to provoke? Do you think it is a valid argument when people say there are directors out there who do this?
Robert: Well, this is just my personal opinion, but I always think it is much more interesting if you dig into the nature and content of the piece, and provoke through what the piece has to say. I think that is much more interesting. But there are many directors in Germany who make careers just by provoking outside of the realm of what piece actually has to say. I could say that is *not* my style and you could say you like it or you don't like it, but I think it is important to know that it *is* an approach in Germany that is valid and thought of as a fully valid way to look at producing opera... because it jumps outside of the box and because it creates interesting sub-textures, competing textures to what the music says. The whole idea that competing textures create a tension that is interesting is unknown in America... the whole idea of competing with the music in America is taboo. And in Germany it is expected... where you have other visual and thinking levels that are competing with the musical levels.

Where do you draw the line with your productions and with the actual concept?
Robert: Well, you know, part of it is your position in the market as a director... and there are directors here in Europe whose careers are indestructible.

You mean they can do anything they want?
Robert: They can do anything they want, they have a particular name, and they are hired for that name—there is no line and they can do whatever they want. But if you in are the sort of normal range of people like me who work for *Intendanten*, it depends very much on the *Intendant* for whom you are working. When I ran my own theater [Stadttheater Giessen] it was great because my artistic vision was my political vision, so I only had to please me. But in other situations you are always dealing with an *Intendant* who is either more or less conservative, or more or less involved in determining the

artistic level. I feel myself—in the theater I work in now—very free except with the taboo of, I would say, sex on stage—real, live sex. Also, defaming religion—I work in Southern Germany, which is quite conservative, so critical religious thought—I always do it but I always get into trouble for it. ... And in more conservative areas of Germany, if you highlight middleclass societal wrongs or middleclass societal taboos, you can get into a lot of trouble.

How so?
Robert: Because audiences in different parts of Germany are different. ... Audiences in the Northern part of Europe, in general, tend to be more open to more edgy types of thinking. If you're in more Catholic areas they tend to be less open, and so it's not true that all audiences in Europe are the same. The most conservative audience here is nowhere near as conservative as the audiences in America. ... Very Catholic parts of Bavaria—for example, Nürnberg and Augsburg—those audiences are nowhere near as conservative as an audience in... the Bible Belt in America, not even close. They're willing to accept so much more [in conservative, Catholic German cities].

I want to talk a little about your role in the theater. You are an *Oberspielleiter* (Chief Producer of Opera) and many people do not know what it is. In fact, it is on its way out as a position in the theater.
Robert: Imagine you have a theater—when you go to America you have an opera company and except for the two or three big opera companies the opera companies do two or three operas per season. Now, I'm in a city, which would be, let's say, comparable to city like Saint Louis. In Saint Louis they do four operas per season. We do twenty-five operas per season, and we do two hundred fifty performances a year of opera. So, my job is to make sure that—besides my own personal directing—to make sure that the artistic quality of the productions as they move away from their premiere remains high. And that's why [I work] with my staff of assistants, looking at the productions and getting involved personally, if I need to, to make sure that everything stays at the same high standard as it was on the day it came out at the premiere.

A lot of people do not realize, it's not as if you have a premiere on November 1, you play ten shows until December 1, and then you're done.
Robert: Right, sometimes more...

You're playing shows of the opera for the next two seasons, and it's easy for quality to slip.
Robert: Because there is not always time to rehearse the things properly when they come back, and you've got new people in the shows. ... My production of *Il Trittico*, which I did in 2002, is coming back in 2008 again. Now, what it's going to look like after six years...

Now, for a *Wiederaufnahme* (revival production) how much rehearsal time do you get?
Robert: On paper you might have two full weeks, but for *Trittico*... one third of the cast will have done it with me, another third of the cast will have done it with the assistant in the ensuing years, and another third of the cast will be brand new... two weeks is not a lot of time. ... Try in a German theater—where there is a performance every night or every other night—to get your cast of *Gianni Schicchi* together. Try to get your cast of *Gianni Schicchi* together for one rehearsal where everyone is there. ... It is an almost-impossible task.

At any given time in your theater, what is going on?
Robert: You know, at any give time a new production is being rehearsed, a revival is being re-rehearsed, and three other operas are running concurrently. We will very easily have a week where in a week you do *Parsifal, Puritani, Carmen, Hänsel und Gretel*, and *Magic Flute*.

And that's a normal week?
Robert: Normal week...

When you start a production with a singer, what do you want from them —what do you expect from them-from the first day of rehearsal?

Robert: Two things I expect: operas are not written about well-adjusted human beings. People choose subjects for operas because they are usually about flawed, interesting, conflicted characters. And I want someone who is willing to look at those sides of their personality and the personality of the character they are playing so they are willing to create something more than just the two-dimensional Disney figure. The other thing I am looking for, which is sometimes hard to find, is a singer who knows the difference between their personal life and the life of the character they're asked to play. So often you have a singer who says, "Well, I don't believe in this, so I'm not capable of playing that in a character you're asking me to play." So that's like saying, "I'm a painter. Brown makes me throw up. So, if you ask me to paint with brown, I won't paint with brown because I don't like brown." I want a singer who is willing— who is strong enough with their inner personality—to know the difference between who they are and what they believe in, and what the character they have to play... needs to believe in and do. That requires an open-mindedness that a lot of people don't have, period. ... But if you are a singer in Germany, you are an *artist*. I expect a singer to come with the open mind and the open heart of an artist.

From day one...
Robert: From day one, because it's the reality of opera in the German-speaking countries that director's view of the piece is the lighthouse for what we're going to do. That's just the way it is, and the director will probably see elements in the character that you will think are wrong or that you will think are superfluous—or you think are immoral, or you think are stupid. But if you've got a good director—even ones you don't like...

As a person...?
Robert: As a person or even if you don't... most directors in Germany are good directors... [I make a very skeptical face] the majority. Ok, can we agree with at least over 50%?

Yeah.
Robert: And they're going to have different ideas about this character than you do. I know as a director, when I'm faced with a singer who is open and arguing for his or her point of view, [it is] very different from someone who is

feeling threatened by the point of view that I wish for them to express about this character, and who is defending their "closed-ness."

That's very important to understand the difference between the two. A director here can smell it if a singer is closed or threatened.
Robert: Oh, right away. ... You smell it right away. And it is basically because, "I'm not homosexual, so I cannot play a homosexual character. The composer did not mean him to be homosexual." Yes and no. There are many operas where you can look at characters whose sexuality are quite nebulous. ... You have to—as an opera singer—be able to separate who you are, what you think is right and wrong, and the palette of emotions and experiences that a director will ask you to play.

Am I right in saying that this is expected in America, too, but the importance and the necessity of doing that here is much greater…?
Robert: Because the palette is so much broader. ... Nobody will ask you to do in America what they'll ask you to do in Germany, and it's some crazy stuff. For example, I had a colleague of mine years ago who was asked to give herself an abortion in *Macbeth* (Verdi) while she was singing the sleepwalking scene. This director believed that part of Lady Macbeth's trauma was that she was pregnant and that she did not feel—when she was in her sleepwalking state—that she didn't feel that she had a right to be a mother. Now, you may think that is stupid. I, as a director, have never done it that way but I can see that. I can definitely see it. ... There is definitely a possibility. ... As a singer in Europe, just because it does not seem like the overriding possibility to you does not mean you won't be required to do it.

And when you run up against a singer in rehearsals who, as you say, is not defensive but who is open to ideas and then comes to you and says, "Look Robert, I don't buy it. I don't believe it."
Robert: Well you know what happens… we'll usually end up getting into a conversation. And either—thru the talk—it will be clear to me that he's right, it will be clear to him that I'm right, or it will be clear to us both that we need something in the middle or something completely different. ... There are a lot of German directors who expect absolute obedience, and they say, "here is

where you stick your finger in your 'hmm-hmm.'" And all you have to say is, "to the knuckle or to the wrist?"

That is so true...
Robert: And that's all you're allowed...

But it's important to say, too, that this is not the norm.
Robert: Right, that's not the norm. ... That's really not the norm. But in most cases... it comes out one-third, one-third, one-third; the singers who come to me—it's either I explain to them why and they are able to do it, they're able to explain to me why it doesn't work and we go with their idea, and another third is that we come up with something different or something that's a combination of both.

But when these singers come to you who you can tell are defensive, and they say, "Uh, no," what then?
Robert: I am very lucky; I have gotten too old so that singers will no longer do that. When I was younger and was not the oldest person on the stage [they would do that], but now at fifty-one I am usually the oldest person. It's a great advantage; they don't do it anymore. They may go back in the cantina and say, "what is that baloney that I have to do here?" The other thing is that I'm watching. If it doesn't work, I'll change it. What you may see as a singer as a... marginal choice for a particular moment, may be the major driving force that this director wants to show. That will just be your job as a singer to know, *okay, I see where this could possibly be what he is saying*. But that's just the way he wants to focus the production.

And there are just some things that do not give?
Robert: Right. ... What I usually tend to do (laughing)... I've learned over the years to build things that I cannot live without into the sets and costumes so that they cannot do it any other way... American singers—because the theatres are all huge—all want to stand downstage, they want to be as close to the audience as they can be. And when you build a set that is open, the singers can always—when the director goes away, you know—cheat. I build my sets so the singers stand where I want them to stand and I like that. Why?

Not because I'm a prick, but because there is an overall visual element, and the overall visual aesthetic is my job. If that figure is at a particular spot in the set because of a particular combination between person and architecture, I will light it so everywhere else is dark except there. ... They'll be standing in the dark if they don't stand where I want them to stand.

But it's not a power play? It's just a...
Robert: Let's put it this way: it's a power play played with singers who don't have the capability to look at a production from the outside in. If they're capable of looking at a production from the overall picture inwards, they'll understand why you do things certain ways. But if they're only into, "my voice, my needs, my body, and my costume," then I just use my little tricks to make sure that they do what I need them to do.

I want to know your viewpoint—because you've certainly been in a million auditions for singers—what impresses you and what doesn't?
Robert: I am looking for an individual, interpretative artist. That is *all* I am looking for. I *assume* you have a good voice, I assume you're singing the right *Fach*, I assume your languages are okay, [and] I assume you're musically literate. Why am I assuming all these things? Because there are loads of people who have all of those talents but don't make it here in Europe.

Because?
Robert: Because they don't have that individual artistic interpretation. ... They're not a unique individual on stage with a unique point of view and a unique "something to say" when they sing and they perform.

You have spoken about this: whether good or bad—just an observation —that American music conservatories train the "perfect package."
Robert: The perfect, Teflon package...

And how does that go over here?
Robert: The minute I see it, the minute she walks in she's got on a teal blue dress cut below the knee. She's got on black shoes-either patent leather or

not. The hair is done basically for church and she sings Musetta. I know what I'm getting, it's over. You know, I've been auditioning people for over thirty years. The minute they walk in, I know what I am getting.

When they walk in, when do you say, "Okay, individual artist?"
Robert: It's sort of like sorting out the rotten tomatoes when you get them out of the field. The ones that are not going to work, you know right away. I'm open to everything, but when you get a singer who you can tell has spent more time learning audition techniques—a terminology that gives me hives—more than how to say something unique with their voice and their presence... when I see that, I know right away. For example, I don't think American audition dress and German audition dress is the same.

Elaborate on that...
Robert: Americans tend to dress for an audition like they would dress for Sunday church. In Germany, I think that a suit and tie is totally inappropriate and a sport jacket and tie is already... (makes a disapproving face). I'll buy shirt, pants, and sport coat open collar. I'm happier with clean, neat slacks, shirt, and sweater or no sweater.

The women, the debutante ball gowns...
Robert: No, no... not even that. ... I go as far as the church dress. If it's not something you wouldn't wear every day, I don't think it's appropriate for a German house audition. You always have to be neat, clean, and well groomed; you shouldn't come to an audition in jeans. But a pants outfit is great. I would say what a woman would wear on a casual Friday in a no jeans, no tank-top office, would be the right thing. So it might be a dress, it might be a pantsuit, it might be a nice pair of pants and blouse, it might be a skirt and a blouse, but Americans generally come overdressed to auditions.

We've spoken before about *Fach* and *Fächer*. Talk a little about that.
Robert: The thing is, the German *Fachsystem* is designed to take into account cultural differences in vocal color taste, which are not the same as in America. For example, if you look at this concept of vocal color for the *Fach Dramatischer Koloratursopran*: Lucia, Violetta, and Queen of the Night are

all dramatic coloraturas. Now on the international stage each of those is a totally different voice. For example, Germans tend to like Donna Anna a lot lighter than Americans do. They tend to cast a much lighter voice as Micaëla than Americans do. ... In Germany very often, Micaëla will not be Mimi. Mimi will very often be a Susanna voice in Germany. It's a matter of taste. You know what I love? If you want to know about all of that, go look at all the recordings in German language of the Italian operas back from the 50's. Anneliese Rothenberger sang Butterfly and that was a really light, lyric coloratura voice. It's just different taste.

That being said, I still think singers should stick to their *Fach*, and the thing that always happens here that I think is a very big mistake, is that singers think *the theater is smaller; I can up my Fach one gear*. Wrong, because of the following and this is very important: when the orchestras get smaller in Germany they do not get proportionally smaller. What happens is the string sections get smaller and the noise making instruments stay the same—the winds and the brass. So what happens is that you're in a situation where *Bohème* in a "D" house—where the orchestra is forty-five people—and you think it is more transparent to sing through than a *Bohème* in an "A" house. It's not true. So, a lot of Americans singers want to sing what they want to sing and not what their voice is made to sing. And a lot of people think, *oh, I'll go to Europe because the houses are smaller and there they'll like my voice for this*. That is just not true.

And about *Fach* and flexibility...
Robert: You see, that's the other thing. The theatres in Germany—to a greater extent than the theatres in Austria and Switzerland—have gone through a period of what I like to call "financial consolidation." There is not as much money around anymore, so the theatres have to save money. And where theatres used to have loads of singers and they could have one or two of everything, they cannot do that anymore. So, theatres are today—in a moneysaving move—letting people sing outside their *Fach*, purposely.

When a singer comes to an audition, is he or she offering things outside of *Fach*?
Robert: That will also happen very often. Because, for example, a true dramatic coloratura is useless in a *Fest* contract to a medium-sized opera

house because they don't have enough operas... what *are* the roles of a true dramatic coloratura? Donna Anna [on an] international scale. If it's an Italian color voice, maybe something like *Puritani*... there's not enough of that stuff going on. So, if you happen to have been born with a dramatic coloratura voice and you go audition, they will want you to sing some lyric coloratura stuff, they'll want you to sing some lyric soprano stuff. ... It's just a given of the market; there are more average lyric-sized voices than bigger voices. The bigger and heavier the voice gets, the fewer people there are. So, you will find many women who are—for an International standard, a 3,500-seat house—a Susanna, who come to Germany and who are asked if they will sing Mimi, or asked if they will sing Marie in *The Bartered Bride*. And we're basically talking about a Susanna for a 3500-seat, regional American opera house. And a real Mimi will be asked often to sing *Tosca*.

And the singers coming here singing one *Fach* who are asked to sing another *Fach*... should they remain flexible to that idea?
Robert: You have to know your voice very well. There's no use to going beyond the limit of your voice unless you're fine with singing four years and then losing your job. If you're okay with that, fine. ... It happens *so* much. The landscape in Europe is filled with ex-American singers still living over here, not being able to sing anymore, all over the place. So you have to know what your voice can do. For somebody who is intelligent and whose voice is basically an Adina, she can sing Musetta if she's intelligent about the way she does it. A girl who is a creamy-voice light lyric who would sing a good Ilia or a good Susanna—if she's smart, she can probably get through *Bohème*.

You just have to weigh: *how much do I want the job? Should I wait? Will a house that's bigger and will listen with more international ears—will I have a better chance there?*

You have to be really intelligent and you have to listen to people you really trust, and it's sometimes just walking a tightrope knowing, "okay, can I do this, should I do this, is this okay?"

For people who do have an idea of their voice but who understandably do not know where it fits into the system here, whom do they speak with?
Robert: That is a very good question. There are very few people around who

really know. Good agents really know... American and European. Many houses have a *Studienleiter* (head coach) who has a good ear and knows about this stuff. ... Unfortunately a lot of people really don't have that much experience with how much sound really comes out of that pit in that opera in a real, living theater space. Here's a perfect example: *Gianni Schicchi*. I cannot tell you how many Barbarinas and Susannas come up and audition with *O, mio babbino caro*. They have no idea [how thick the orchestration is]. If people come in and ask me, I will tell them right off. If they ask me about their voice and repertoire, I will tell them exactly what I think and what I think they should be doing and not be doing.

One opera that always comes up—and I think it's a great example of how people have different tastes in North America and Europe—is *Die Zauberflöte*, specifically Tamino, Pamina, and Queen of the Night.
Robert: Let's talk about Tamino. Because I think on the regional scene [in America] there is very little German opera done. People will put either a lyric Italian voice, a lyric French voice in there, and sometimes will put in a character tenor, depending upon who is listening. But in the bigger theatres, generally the guy who sings Rodolfo will be asked to sing Tamino, or the guy who sings Faust will also bring Tamino.

Here there are two schools: there is the *Heavy Tamino School* and there is the *Light Tamino School*. There are people here who go back to who the big Taminos were... guys like Richard Tauber who also sang *Lohengrin*. So, on the international scale you will have *Jugendliche Heldentenöre* singing Tamino because *Jugendliche Heldentenöre* are rare. The smaller the house goes, you will tend to have character voices singing Tamino.

And you don't mean light lyric Fentons?
Robert: No. I mean Pedrillos singing Tamino. And a lot that has to do with... it's a culture thing. ... Americans tend to like voices with more overtones, richer sounds. Germans tend to like what they call *Edleklänge*, which people —who know about International opera style—they're talking about silver voices. For example, Pilar Lorengar: silver voice. Americans tend to like gold voices, which means rounder, creamier, more Italianate and French sounding voices. Now the problem is that when you get to theaters that are smaller and who cannot afford people like this, then the *Edlerklang* means character

voices with very little vibrato and very little carrying power. So you will very often get someone who in America would very often sing just character stuff, singing a Tamino or Belmonte here [in the smaller houses]. I've heard Belmontes here who are basically voiceless, in the smaller theaters, because you can't get Gösta Winbergh stamped out seventeen times.

And that goes for Pamina, too?
Robert: That goes for Pamina, too. For example, in many theaters the Pamina is also Susanna, and I do not see Pamina and Susanna as having the same voice.

Then it's because of the necessity in the theater…
Robert: Right, and also because they can get more of what they think this *Edlerklang* is with a Susanna than they can out of a Marguerite. Now, Marguerite is actually closer to the right voice for Pamina than for Susanna. But you will rarely see that here.

And the Queen of the Night? If you have the high notes?
Robert: You can be a soubrette, you can be a lyric coloratura. … As long as you've got an F, they want to hear it. In the smaller and medium houses, that is. When you get to the larger, regional houses—let's say Hannover and upwards—they want a real dramatic coloratura. So, if you are a real dramatic coloratura and you really have Queen of the Night in your voice, the agents will also send you to the houses that are looking for that. … If you've got the high notes, then you too can be Norina and sing Queen of the Night in Braunschweig, no problem!

A lot of people have told me, "I'm a soprano and I went over there and I sang repertoire for agents that showed I have high notes. Then they asked if I had Queen of the Night, and I said 'no.'" But basically if you have high notes, bring Queen of the Night?
Robert: Bring Queen of the Night knowing what your limits are.

In regard to which houses you should sing it in?
Robert: Right, exactly.

The advice you once gave me was great: market yourself a little differently and then push your career forward singing different repertoire in much better theaters.
Robert: This is really important because the thing is that... the German-speaking countries are dying for true buffo and character singers. Okay, you blow into one bottle and you get one sound. You blow into another bottle and you get another sound. What you get is what you get and what your body gives you. What you have is what you have, and what happens is that most people who have a good technique but have a buffo voice go for the lyric jobs. So then what happens is that the system here is completely devoid of well-trained singers with a good technique who sing character and buffo repertoire. So, what am I talking about? For tenors, Pedrillo. For the basses, not to sing Sarastro but instead singing... operetta. You see it mostly with tenors because there are so few tenors.

How, then, are these people supposed to know that they are singing the wrong *Fach*?
Robert: Well, if the only theaters that want to hear you sing this stuff are the small theaters, you're probably in the wrong *Fach*. If only Coburg wants your Mimi, you're probably Susanna. ... Listen to your colleagues. ... Singers need good advice from people they trust.

With sopranos it's always less about "character" versus "first *Fach*". It's always they sing a *Fach* too heavy—one to two *Fach*s too heavy. With mezzos, there's the "Mercédès mezzo" and there's the "Carmen mezzo," and they're two different things. And if you think that even though you were born with a Mercédès voice you are going to come to Germany and sing Carmen—yeah, you might sing Carmen in a small house. But if you were born to sing Mercédès and born to sing Second Lady, then go sing Mercédès in Munich and forget about Carmen. Because places like Munich and Frankfurt are dying for a good Mercédès, a good Marcellina, a good Second Lady, and a good Dryade in *Ariadne*... desperate. But everybody's trying to be something else. [It's a question of] knowing what your voice is. ... Sit on the stage in a *Sitzprobe* when you are in an apprentice program and listen to what is coming out of the orchestra when your colleagues are singing. When you're an apprentice in Lake George and there's a *Sitz* of *Bohème,* go up there and listen to what's coming out of that orchestra...

The orchestras here don't always play quietly. They want to play out.
Robert: That's another important point, this is *really* important. There is a different German orchestral sound than an Italian-American orchestral sound. ... The German orchestral musicians are trained to play in traditional German concert orchestras that play symphonic repertoire. They learn a technique of using their instrument that is particularly German. For example, American woodwind players usually don't get jobs in Germany. American brass players have a very hard time because their technique is different; they have a softer, less-aggressive technique, and they have a very hard time getting jobs over here. So what that means is that most of the time you are playing with an orchestra in the pit that is used to playing Bruckner symphonies and would rather play Bruckner symphonies than play *Lucia*. So you will very often get a situation where the first oboe will be as loud and as present as a singer on stage. ... And don't expect them to quiet down, because that's their *Klangkonzept* ("sound concept"). They've been taught that it is right for their job.

Now, American opera orchestras—America is more flexible—when they play in a symphony orchestra they play with a symphony sound. When they play in an opera orchestra, they play with an Italian sound. They create that carpet of sound over which the voices can bloom. German orchestras do not do that *anywhere, ever*. But who are you going to blame for that? They're trained [German symphonic orchestras] a certain way to make a certain sound because that is the traditional German symphony orchestra sound, and to ask them to not play that way is to kind of ask them to not be who they are. ... So as a singer you're usually dealing with a symphony orchestra in the pit, and that's a huge difference.

You have been in the system in Germany for twenty-three years, so you have seen it before the Berlin Wall came down and now with what is a German economic recession. Everybody knows the theaters are in trouble. Where is everything going?
Robert: Where is it now? ... It's the same way German companies—for

example, German washing machine makers no longer build their washing machines in Germany. They build them in Poland, because in Germany they have to pay their workers €2,000 a month, whereas they can pay their workers €500 in Poland. And because of the way life is in Poland, €500 a month is fine. So, all those singers from all those Eastern European countries come here, are used to a different standard of living, are used to a different pay scale, and are willing to sing for less. So, those of us who come from the Western countries and have a different living standard are at a disadvantage, because the opera houses that are all starving for money, will hire the cheaper solution very often. ... It's that simple: they'll hire the cheaper solution.

Where is it going to go? Well, it's anybody's guess because the German theater system is constructed with intertwined contracts that are not cancelable. You can't say, "well, we don't like the chorus contract so we're going to change it." That chorus contract was worked out in the 50's, it is part of the whole socialized democracy system here..., which is part of the theater system, and they're all tied together. So, you will never get a theater system here in German composed of freely negotiated contracts, *ever*. So what happens is the following: you have these contracts. The government says, "we don't have the money." The theaters then say, "Sorry, these people are all on contract and we can't fire any of them." They come up with just enough money to squeak by. ... I think the German theater system is going to be like a patient with a diabetic foot hobbling along on crutches—I think—for many decades to come. You can't change it; it's an intertwined system that's impossible to change.

What it means for American singers is that the whole 70's/80's idea —*if you're not making it in America, go to Europe*—is over, it's absolutely over. You have to be as good here. The reasons now to come to Europe are different; the reasons now to come to Europe are because you can sing past thirty-two. No matter what they tell you in America, I don't care. Unless you are Debbie Voigt, you will be the star of regional opera from the time you get out of school until the time you hit your early thirties, and then you will never hear from them [American regional opera theaters] again. You will have to have a plan B.

You mean, if you don't jump up into the international houses?

Robert: Right, and there are only a couple of people who do that. So, the only place of having a better chance of jumping to the international houses and having a career past the age of thirty-five, is to come to Europe. And that is the reason now to come to Europe. Your quality has to be as good as in America.

Last question: what's your advice? Who should come over here and who should not?
Robert: If you're not good enough to make it in America, don't come here because you won't make it here either. If you want to sing past thirty-something, come here. If you think living in a foreign culture is an adventure, come here. If you think living in a foreign country means missing all the great American things you have to have in your life, don't come here. It's interesting because in Germany opera is called *Musiktheater*, not "opera." If you are interested in using your talents to create that special combination of Music Theater, come to Germany. If you want to go on stage in a pretty dress and just sing loud, stay in America.

INTERVIEW 7 ~ *Helene von Orlowsky, Swedish Künstlerische Betriebsdirektorin (Director of Artistic Administration) for Austria's Landestheater Linz*

Helene von Orlowsky was born in Sweden and received her musical training as an opera singer at the Mozarteum in Salzburg, after which she embarked on a successful opera career. After taking a maternity leave, Helene returned to the Kepler Universität in Linz for Culture Management. This led to her second career in Arts Administration, which began at Stadttheater Gießen. She was formerly the *Chefdisponentin* at Stadttheater Pforzheim and Theater Lübeck, and since 2006 she has been the *Künstlerische Betriebsdirektorin* at Landestheater Linz. Helene loves old films (particularly those with W.C. Fields, Bustur Keaton, and The Marx Brothers), she has a sharp wit, likes french fries with mayonaise, and hates my dog.

You are The Director of The *Betriebsbüro* (Director of Artistic Administration) at The Landestheater Linz in Austria. Can you please explain your job responsibilities?

Helene: Planning and disposition, as well as plenty of meetings. I take a leading role in multi-year planning of opera, drama, ballet, children's' and teen theater. For the long term, I oversee subscription series planning, and rehearsals and performances throughout the season. Each month I also decide which additional performances, readings, extra events (such as gala concerts and guest performances) should be added to the Theater's calendar. As well, I schedule the free days for performances and take part in monthly planning meetings. Every week I prepare the weekly plan for the theater, consider particular needs for rehearsals, and make necessary changes to accommodate emergencies.

    I am responsible for arranging and keeping records of auditions, communicating with singers and agents, and maintaining a list of contacts. I also search for and engage guests for productions, as well as guests to fill in for indisposed cast members. I work out many of the details of contracts with guest and *Fest* artists. I oversee the consideration of vacation permission slips that artists turn in, approve (or deny) them, and archive them. I prepare the singer disposition for individual performances throughout the month and plan the production calendar (when, where, who, who is not available, working rehearsals, final rehearsals, technical rehearsals, and free days). I also make arrangements to hear auditions in other places besides Linz, such as New York City.

    That's not all! I am in constant contact within the theater with colleagues and other departments, often as the "go between" between the higher echelon of the theater and those working underneath, so to speak. I communicate with organizations that visit the theater, the ticket office to see how productions and particular performances are selling, and communicate directly with Ensemble members. I am often responsible as the leading person in the theater during performances, and am always available for that inevitable emergency. And most of all, of every everything I put out: proofread, proofread, proofread, proofread, proofread...

Helene, I had no idea! I must say that I am quite impressed. It seems to me as if your position is the neck of the theater that holds the head up!

What kind of role to you play in casting for the theater? And also for scheduling?

Helene: I am always a part of the politics of casting and give my opinions and advice, not only at auditions but also in long-term casting decisions. The final decision, of course, comes from the *Intendant*. I am, however, in charge of the guest artists who jump in for indisposed cast members. I also constantly consider the burdens of singers.

I want to ask your opinions not only about singing, but also about stage abilities and looks. When you are sitting in the house listening to auditions, what do you want to hear? What will turn you off? How quickly is a first impression made with you?

Helene: Good question. I like the American way; how they come as uncomplicated and friendly when they are on stage. Personally, I take more time for an assessment [of an auditioning singer]. A singer can grow and get better after the first burst of energy, or also sing themselves tired. I like to hear singers who offer arias within their *Fach* (when a tenor sings for Pedrillo, for example, he should not offer Belmonte, too). Do offer repertoire in German. P.S. I hate it when women drink from a water bottle on the open stage. That turns me off. I think that people should go to the wings if they need to get a drink of water, but perhaps this is just my opinion.

Now, how about stage presence and looks. A particular issue for Americans—as we all know—is that, well, Americans can be "sizable" singers. What do you say to those who are overweight? Does it affect your decision-making process?

Helene: The way a singer looks definitely plays a role. The singer's physical figure must fit with their *Fach*, and overweight singers definitely have bad chances. What we see on stage definitely plays a role, true? The days when singers could look like cement mixers are gradually disappearing.

Another component then comes into the mix [no pun intended] and one that cannot be learned: charisma. Stage animals with charisma that radiates will always have that advantage over others. This phenomena is intangible and is difficult to adequately clarify...

When a singer goes to audition, he or she should pay attention to have appropriate clothing that is at least tasteful. I prefer to see woman with make-up, but when they come in evening gowns, I find it overdressed. Keep the hair out of the face. Thin mezzi can wear pants (if they're dapper).

Age is somehow a big issue for many. You once mentioned that you do ask singers' age. Can age somehow for against a singer?
Helene: Naturally, we ask singers their age, and when they come to audition they are obliged to write their birthdate on the forms. It makes a dishonest impression when a singer covers up his or her age.

What about stage presence. What do you want to see and/or experience in an audition? What makes a strong impression and what makes a negative impression?
Helene: Too much action is not desirable (unless you're specifically asked to do so in an audition, what can occasionally happen). Our *Intendant* does it sometimes to see how a singer moves on stage and how he or she responds to direction. It is great art when the singer embodies just as much scenic expression that the content of the aria or the scene unambiguously comes across. One can train this, but when you are nervous sometimes there is a possibility of stiffening up.

Am I correct in saying that you accept *Unterlagen* (publicity materials) primarily—or only—from agents? If so, why is this?
Helene: Exactly [note: this means *do not* send your materials directly to Landestheater Linz.] The agents come to me with their proposed candidates. So many singers believe that they are the "perfect" person for the role, and in many cases they are not only *not* qualified for the part, but also not for an audition in general. My agents receive a vacancy profile from me stating what we need, how much (approximately) we are able to pay, and what kind of singer we need. When it regards a guest contract, we also mention the production performance dates, if they are already decided.

Do you want recordings with publicity materials? If so, DVD, CD, Youtube?
Helene: I personally collect no recordings because I have no time to listen to them. In other theaters it may very well be otherwise. Sometimes we listen to arias on the Internet, but the singers will definitely have to come here and audition. Materials should be precise and clearly arranged. I personally do

not give much credit to printed review quotes; they are chosen from singers themselves. Materials (include a photo with them) should ideally be in German and only in English in case of emergency. Never send materials in other languages.

You and I have spoken often about agents, and you have mentioned that you have some with whom you enjoy working. What do you like about the agents with whom you work?
Helene: Agents are all different. I have chosen my agent partners because they are flexible, matter-of-fact and not pushy. When we do not like a singer, I am not going to argue over it for long. It is important that an agent send singers of a certain *niveau*, that their artistic capabilities speak to us and what we need. [The Agents] need to understand the limitations of what we can pay and not want to haggle; there will almost never be a "dream fee." They need to be precise and work quickly. All the agents with whom I work fulfill these criteria. They know what we need and know that we are under a tight timeline.

Then there are some with whom I work against my will, but that is neither here, nor there. Here is a very interesting question: who is the customer of the agent? The singer or the theater? Who does the agent really serve? This is not so easy to define.

What are some things that agents do—or that singers should look out for—that give you a negative impression?
Helene: It depends on how they present themselves. One should watch out when then agents wants money up front and makes a a disinterested impression. But there is a lot of chemistry involved with whom one feels he or she is in good hands and whose professional advice is appreciated. It is also wise to ask around and speak with other singers about who is serious and who is trustworthy. It's like with doctors; some of them are competent and some of them are incompetent, and in between are so many. One notices it sometimes when it is all too late. An aggressive agent (I have experienced two or three with whom I quickly terminated our working relationship) can cause big damage.

When singers are deciding with what agents they want to work, what do you suggest?

Helene: They can always begin with the ZBF [now the ZAV]. In Munich they are extremely competent and friendly, and it does not cost anything.

There is no doubt that the *Fest* System is much different from the stagione system of the English-speaking world. This can be a shock to us Anglo-Saxons. What expectations should we have and what expectations should we leave at the *Bühneneingang* (stage door) of the theater?

Helene: I think that the American approach and motivation really sets a good example. Americans are very collegial (some Scandinavians [disclaimer: Helene is Swedish!] are unfortunately the opposite...) Most Americans learn German very well; it is really very important to do so.

In 2010/11, what is the *Mindestgehalt* (minimum salary) for an *Anfänger/-in* ("beginner") soloist in Austria?

Helene: I believe it is €1600 per month. In Austria, singers also receive fourteen months of pay per year as well as a tax reduction. They also receive extra pay for too-few free days, Sunday rehearsals, rehearsals to set in last-minute cast members, and rehearsals in the afternoon. Germany has almost none of that any more.

How does it work for contract renewals with soloists? In Austria, by when must the theater tell a singer if his or her contract is extended for the next season? When must the singer either accept the offer or quit?

Helene: In Austria, the theater has until January 31 to fire a singer for the next season. The singer then has until February 15 to accept or decline the offer. In Germany, the theater has until October 15th and the singer must respond by October 31st. The length of the contract is negotiable. If the singer wants out of his or her contract early, the theater has to be OK with it. Otherwise the singer could be responsible for a paying a fee.

How has the economic recession affected the *Fest* opera system?

Helene: And how! The opera house in Flensburg is going to be closed, Würzburg is—as far as I know—at the tipping point, and things are not going so well in Wuppertal. Culture funding is being cut more and more during this financial crisis.

As for negotiating a contract with the theater, what do you advise?
Helene: You may do it yourself or through an agent. If it goes through an agent, the singer and the theater each pay 3% of the singer's gross income for two years (or 6% for one year if the singers wishes). [ZAV] takes no commission. One should also make sure that fourteen days of paid "guesting vacation" be written into the contract (though permission to take guest engagements must be allowed by the theater). Normally it is approved. Provisions for singing extra performances no longer exist in Linz, and I fear that they are falling by the wayside, as well, in Germany.

And as for renegotiating you contract once you have been at the theater, what do you advise?
Helene: It is always a question of good communication with the theater, and particularly with the Intendant. Singers can communicate their wishes but should remain, at least, moderate. But you know, in show business it is always a question of your market worth, or offers and demand for singers. The more in-demand a singer is, the higher the salary demands go. But don't forget: the market is getting tighter and tighter, and most singers are expendable (horrible, no?). One should carefully consider quitting a *Fest* engagement. It can naturally go well but "it takes balls to do it" (as my old friend from Texas always said. She was really cool!)

I know many singers who want to combine *Festing* with Guesting. How realistic is this and what do you suggest?
Helene: It can be an issue... There is the theoretical possibility to set a *Fest* contract to low guest conditions. Then there would be more freedom to take guest engagements. We really do it as the exception here in Linz. Normally a singer needs to be present and ready for action here.

In bigger houses it is possibly somewhat more frequent. But again it depends on how in-demand the singer is. There are situations where a theater says, *we will say, "Yes" to everything just to keep this* singer, but this is really a dream situation.

Ok, *FACH*. How important to you and Landestheater Linz is it that singers perform only in one *Fach*?
Helene: We will often cast people out of their *Fächer*. But it is important that one does not singer of his or her *Fach* for an audition. Soubrettes should not

sing Violetta and Lyric Tenors should not sing Rodolfo. That usually awakens impatience and displeasure in the audition jury.

Many singers believe they have larger voices than they actually have because they think that the bigger *Fächer* are more attractive. When a singer is in an engagement, he or she may certainly try out roles in a new *Fach*. With the understanding of the theater, they are sometimes able to officially study them with the musical staff and sometimes even receive performances. Of course, caution is always advised; one can sing themselves out faster than one can blink. And a damaged voice is irreversible.

Finally, You and I have spoken often about NYIOP, and we even had lunch when you were in NYC for them (remember those Hamburgers we ate at Old John's across from Merkin Hall?!). What do you think of NYIOP? Do you hire—or have you ever hired—from the NYIOPs?
Helene: NYIOP is not bad! Every time I hear astounding voices there and remarked (as I have often mentioned) at how professional and friendly the singers are on the audition stage. We have just engaged a sensational dramatic soprano (whom I heard in New York) for Leonora in *Il trovatore* next season as a guest. She had to come to Linz, though, to audition, and she was stunning and got the job! In the meantime, I have recommended her to two other agents. She came again and, recommended by one of these agents, sang for and received another engagement in in Saarbrücken!

The singers from NYIOP, of course, need to come here and audition. It costs a lot of money and the theater only pays for the cost of a hotel. Because of that, I also try to help and recommend singers to agents and theaters. I had two tenors here in March from NYIOP. Unfortunately, neither sang as well as they had in New York and did not get the job.

But what do you do? There is not another way to do it. Two other candidates whom I invited to Linz and really wanted to introduce to the theater decided not to come. OK, I have to accept that. I know from other engagements that have come through NYIOP, that David Blackburn does his job well. Last year I was [at NYIOP] in Bologna and June NIYOP will take place in Vienna. I am going, of course. But as you see the auditions are not always in America.

Helene, any more advice?
Helene: My God, we could go on and on for four hours. However, I need to get back to setting the subscription series.

Helene, thanks so much for doing this. I really appreciate it.
Helene: No, thank you! Send a greeting to your future wife and give your dog a kick from me [they don't get along].

INTERVIEW 8 ~ *Alma Wagner (not her real name), German mezzo-soprano*

I chose to interview the Berlin-born mezzo-soprano, "Alma Wagner," for many reasons. However, there is one path that she has taken that is to be emulated: she is a success story of how one can use the German *Fest* system to build experience and a foundation to establish and expand a career. After completing her Masters degree at a top North American music university, she made her way back to her native Berlin and eventually to a *B size* house in Germany, where she had her first *Fest* contract. After a couple season there, a season and a half *Fest* in an *A size* house, and a breakthrough second place award and Wagnerian Prize at a large, international competition, Alma can now safely say that she enjoys a thriving international career at some of the biggest houses in Europe. Of course, this is the very short version of her biography. In particular demand for her Wagner interpretations, among others, Alma was kind enough to spend some time speaking about her path through the *Fest* system, as well as her opinions on other matters.

I want to talk to you about what is going on in the *Fest* system these days, the economy, and how you think it is affecting the opera system here in Germany. Do you agree that things have changed a lot in the past ten years here?
Well, at least the last eight years that I have been working here.

You've have worked your way up and out of the *Fest* system. In fact, you were *Fest* for only two seasons. Is that correct?
I was actually *Fest* for two and a half seasons in B house., one and a half in A house., and then I was freelance in between and have been again for the past season and a half.

And in [A house] they let you go a lot [for other guest engagements]?
Yes, because I was smart about negotiating that contract.

The idea of you coming back over to Germany [after finishing your degree at a top university in North America]—was that always the plan for you?

Alma: There really never was an alternative since I obviously did not have an American Green Card, and there were very few American young artist programs that I could have applied to as a non-US or Canadian citizen. I think Merola may have been the only one at the time that I could have done.

    I could have moved to New York and started doing auditions there, but I would not have been legally allowed to work. That was not an option I wanted to explore. I also knew that at the time the chances of getting work were far better in Germany.

When you came back to Germany, what was your intention? Was your intention to freelance or was your intention to get started through a *Fest* engagement?

Alma: I think I was basically looking for a *Fest* engagement. Had I gotten some freelance work, I would have gladly done so. But I think I wanted to go *Fest*—as much as I actually knew about it at the time, which wasn't as much since I had been away at college in foreign countries for seven years – and the best place for me starting out would be a medium or smallish house to try out several roles and get my feet wet.

And you got at least seven or eight new roles in your first two seasons?

Alma: Yes, exactly. I certainly found out what it's like to be a slave to a theater!

But what you did that is not typical and that I want to bring up, is that you branched out from the *Fest* system [to other countries]. You managed to successfully use it to propel your career forward.

Alma: Yes, and I think a lot of that had to do with the fact that I had the courage to go freelance. In fact, my first contract began not as a two year contract (which is the norm), but as a one-and-a-half year contract. I started midseason and for some reason they only gave me the season-and-a-half contract, which I was happy to do. I think I could have had it longer, but my agent said, "You can wait a bit to decide if you want to extend the contract. Let's just see how it goes." I think she thought we would then be able to negotiate a pay raise, or something like that. And after the first half of that season, I told the theater that I was not going to renew.

Why not?
Alma: I was quite happy with all the roles that I was doing in those first eighteen months, but I wasn't so keen on a few people working there, like the *Operndirektor*, for example. And I felt that I would have a good chance of getting some freelance work, if I started doing auditions.

So what came first, the chicken or the egg? Did you say to yourself, "I have enough guest work, so I am going to go ahead and do this." Or did you unbuckle your *Fest* seatbelt and jump off the cliff?
Alma: I jumped! In October I said, "I'm telling you now officially that I am not renewing, just so if something comes up I am free to go legally." [When a singer officially gives notice to end a *Fest* engagement, the theater is legally obliged to let the singer accept other auditions.] Actually, a number of my colleagues did the same thing that fall—I think five of us. And all five of us ended up staying for one more season. In the spring, [B house] had done lots of auditions and had not found people they liked enough to fill our spots. So, they negotiated with each one of us. While I had spent nice time there and was quite happy working there, I knew that my happiness and success was not necessarily dependent on staying there. And so I got them to raise my paycheck by about €300 per month. At the time I was earning the least amount of all the people *Fest* in the ensemble, even though I was singing almost one hundred shows per season and doing some of the major roles, including Carmen. I figured that if they really wanted me to stay, they might as well make it worth my while and pay me what they were paying most of the others that were at my experience level. In the end they did!

Your agent essentially negotiated a contract for you where you were one of the least-paid, yet hardest working people in the theater. Is that right?
Alma: [My agent] never came to see me in performance... when we first negotiated the contract, some of the roles that had been set for me... for example, when we first negotiated the contract, I was going to sing the role of Mercedes. But in the spring, they still had not found someone to sing Carmen. They were thinking of finding a guest, and I went to the GMD at the

time (who is a wonderful conductor and now making a big career). I went to him and said, "I have sung the arias. Why don't you just listen to me and see if you could consider that." I did an *Arbeitsprobe* (working rehearsal) with him and then he said, "I don't know. Let's see." So, we did another rehearsal with the tenor who was singing Don José in his office, and then another one in the big rehearsal studio. Then the GMD actually decided he thought *I was ready to sing it*. It was a great chance to be able to try out that role, which is such a big core of my repertoire. I had just turned twenty-eight years old and sang thirty-one performances [of *Carmen*] in two seasons.

Tell me, what is it like singing *Carmen* at the *Generalprobe* (final dress rehearsal) and *Premiere*, and your *Carmen* at the thirty-first performance?

Alma: It's a world of difference. First of all, you grow vocally by the mere number of performances you do and by becoming less nervous about it. Also with all the other singing you are doing in-between even though it's exhausting—either it kills you or makes you stronger. In my case it made me stronger and gave me more control over certain areas of my voice that were still developing.

On the front end of *Carmen* performances, was it ever going through your mind, *my God. I've got 31 performances of Carmen*!?

Alma: No, because you're young and stupid and you don't realize how much you're working. We opened it in September, and in October I had seven *Carmen* performances. Some of them were even away in different theaters, on tour. We always had rehearsals in the mornings. I never had the day off when I had a performance that night — nothing like it was in [A house] where they are quite nice about things like that. You just slave through it, and at the time I didn't even realize that it was all quite a lot. I was just enjoying the fact that I could sing this role. It was a beautiful production; we had a wonderful director who gave me various inspiring feedback after almost every performance. It made me really change a lot of things throughout the process of developing this character. So, [the development] didn't stop; it evolved… something very exciting and something that I have not found with a lot of directors lately.

Your path after [B house]… were you thinking that you needed to move up within the *Fest* system, since a traditional way to go is to move up to a larger house?

Alma: There weren't a lot of auditions that I had in my last year in [B house]. I had an audition in a few A houses and at some smaller ones for guest contracts. There were not a lot of openings in the *Fach* that I would eventually be. I think, in a way, I was lucky to get my first job. [When I sang for my first agent], she said, "I won't be able to place you in a house; you're not really what they're looking for. You're not the lyric pants role mezzo." And I thought, well there must be something that I can sing! I can't just wait around for another five years.

But I just took the step. I had nothing coming up but said I will go ahead and freelance. I had a year of unemployment pay and knew that something would come up. I didn't know why I believed that, but I just did! I got a guest production in a B house and had some concerts in Berlin. I ended up having some jump-ins and also did the last four shows of a *Carmen* in an A house in the East, where the Carmen had gotten sick indefinitely. As it turned out, I was working quite a bit, but I also had some time to work with my voice teacher, which—I think—was very essential for me at the time; I was able to work on the repertoire that was very important to me.

The second year of freelancing, I decided to do a few more competitions since I had literally nothing else lined up yet. I was thirty-one and there weren't that many left for me to do. But I thought I'd give it one more try since I had never been too successful before I started working. I often made the semi-finals or the finals, but I never got a prize. I didn't have much to lose this time around, and perhaps it would finally be my time. It seemed that I suddenly had a [repertoire] package together that people would see me in and thought I did especially well in. I was semi-successful in getting into finals where artistic directors offered me jobs, or winning prizes and I got connections to agents and other artistic directors.

And these are in other countries?

Alma: Yes. I did one in France where the artistic director of an opera house in the South of France was on the jury. He offered me an Emilia in *Otello*. And then I did the [one of the largest in the world] competition—the third time I was doing it. I had done it twice before and gotten into the semi-finals. I had always thought it was a very nice experience and a very nice atmosphere. I figured, one more try, who knows. This time I made the finals and won Second Prize, The Wagner Prize, and another prize.

And that opened things up.
Alma: It did. It got me a gig at [a big Spanish theater] and [big management]. And even though I went on to my second *Fest* engagement afterwards, I already had some international work that prepared my career path into freelancing later. Also, it linked my name to the Wagner repertoire; something I was lucky enough to explore during my subsequent *Fest* engagement, and which has since become my calling card in many ways.

You have really branched out, meaning to markets outside the German-speaking world. I was under the impression back when I was in college that it was possible to come over to Germany and have a fruitful career just singing in Germany.
Alma: And even just at one house!

What do you think about that now?
Alma: It's no longer possible. I have seen it with many colleagues—some in smaller towns and some in Berlin—who have been in a house for ten, twelve, or thirteen seasons, and then do not get their contracts renewed.

And what's the significance of that?
Alma: Because otherwise, they'd be *unkündbar* (tenured) [after fifteen seasons]. [Not being renewed] used to happen much more with actors than with singers, and singers were just better off. But this is no longer. It's especially hard—especially for a soprano in her early or mid-forties who has been singing successfully in one house for many years. She suddenly gets the boot and now has to go find a *Fest* job or guest work. This is really hard. Many [theaters] all want singers young and cheap, but with twenty years of experience.

And have you noticed that fees have either stagnated or gone down?
Alma: Yes, absolutely. As I told you, when I started in [B house] I had the lowest fee which I think was €1,995 [per month]. But my colleagues who came after—the one who came and basically took my spot— got €1,800 [per month]. And I know some of the coaches who started later in [B house], and

they started out with almost the bare minimum of €1,600 [per month]. I don't know how they live off that.

It's ridiculous.
Alma: Yes. This was all under a new *Intendant*, I might add. So, at the time I felt that I was lucky to have been paid as I much as I was. And I know that in the East there are many colleagues who earn less than those in the West, in many cases. But then again, in the East you have far more colleagues that have been in the same theater for many years; in the former GDR you got into a theater and had a contract for life.

Theaters want the young, cheap people?
Alma: Often, not always. But I am seeing it more and more. I know of singers out auditioning for *Fest* jobs because they want to leave the job they have now or because they do not have one right now. But they are hearing that a theater wants a "beginner." Sometimes the roles are not really "beginner" roles, but if the theater is saying that they want a "beginner," they are basically saying, "*we're not going to pay you shit.*"

I'm just really lucky that I am singing dramatic mezzo/contralto repertoire, because they don't have that many of them around and not always *Fest* in a house.

Where do you see things going with the *Fest* system here?
Alma: I think it's in flux—it's changing. I think [theaters] have to find a better way of doing things. What I hate is that they have older people in the ensemble who *are unkündbar* (tenured) and do not find work for them. Or they put them in only one show or in an *operetta* where they only have a speaking part, which I find very disrespectful. Obviously, they are sometimes no longer up to the vocal challenges of some things, but they are often just kind of dropped.

I recently heard of a story about a woman who sings at [one of the largest opera houses in Germany]. When she first started, she was singing the big, starring roles. Eventually, it got less and less and less. In the end, they offered her some kind of compensation to quit completely, or else she would be used as something like a stage manager—something completely different. She finally quit somehow and now teaches.

What kind of shape was she in again?

Alma: I heard her just a few years ago and thought that she was still in great shape. She was in her mid-fifties, I think. The last thing I heard her in was in *Der Rosenkavalier* and I thought it still sounded pretty good. I am *sure* there were things she still could have sung.

I have seen that a lot, too, where we have "older" colleagues in their fifties or sixties, and they can still really sing!
Alma: Indeed. We had one in [B house]. He had been there for over 25 years, and before he retired he wanted to do one more dream role. So, they mounted *Die tote Stadt* for him. He was amazing. Since then he's retired but still comes back as a guest for certain things.

In the grand sense of things, do you think the *Fest* system can hold up? I know it is a very general question...
Alma: I'm not sure. I cannot say either way. I think, though, it can hold up if they make some changes. How exactly those changes will be implemented and what exactly they will be, I haven't thought enough about. I don't think it will survive in its present state for terribly long... houses are starting not to plan seasons ahead using the ensembles they have anymore. Lots of houses are having to cut budgets, while others are having to think about doing more of a *stagione* type of season.

Things will have to change eventually, but I would find it very sad if the *Fest* system were dismantled and singers had to always travel around the country to get jobs. The best work that I have done in theaters has often been because the people had been working together for many seasons—knowing each other's strengths and weaknesses, building a piece as an ensemble together, including the director and conductor. I really hope the *Fest* system survives, but like most things it will have to change to do so.

12 ZWÖLF

NYIOP: Never Heard of Them? Where Have You Been?

Interview with David Blackburn, CEO, founder of NYIOP, Artistic Consultant for Teatro Communale Bologna, and (as of 2010) Director of Artistic Operations for Palm Beach Opera

If you are an American opera singer and do not know what NYIOP (www.nyiop.com) is, where have you been? NYIOP is known as either an enhancement to a European audition tour, or as an alternative. I have never done NYIOP and have received no kinds of benefits—tangible or intangible—for this interview. I receive a number of questions, however, regarding them. Here is what I know for sure: I have many friends and colleagues working over here or who have worked over here, specifically because they were hired *directly* from NYIOP. That is, simply put, the proof that NYIOP is a legitimate, effective business, and one revolutionizing the way European house auditions are done. They deserve their own chapter in this book. Furthermore, since the first edition of *What The FACH?!* was published in

2007, NYIOP and its co-founder and CEO, David Blackburn, have both steadily grown into an established force in the business. He has built a solid reputation with his creativity and honesty.

I first met David Blackburn in 1994 when he sang what still remains for me as one of the most thoughtful, unique, and memorable recitals I have ever experienced (in his former career as opera singer). In fact, I still have the little blue program folded up in my library. I knew right away—here is guy who certainly thinks outside of the box. It is no surprise to me that David has cultivated the idea of NYIOP into what it is today. I hear a number of comments about NYIOP—some true and some fantasy—so I wanted to hear it from the horse's mouth, so to speak. I managed to track down David for a lengthy interview in 2007 to explain NYIOP process and also hear his thoughts and advice for American singers. I also had the chance re-connect with him in March 2010 to discuss changes in the opera world, as well as how NYIOP has changed and grown over the past few seasons.

David, you deal with a great number of *Intendanten*, casting directors, and members of theater KBB. What general impressions do you hear from them about American singers?
David: What I got at the beginning was a lot of—Americans were plastic and they were generic, they had very good training but no real soul or heart. One thing I've noticed also being a singer is that in the U.S. there is so much focus on technique and just making sound, and moreover making loud sound or sounds with "core." The European casting directors hear that as basically shouting at them. What an American voice teacher will say is "keeping core in your sound," sounds to a European as having no nuance and making loud noise. They [European casting directors] *do* recognize that Americans are the best trained in the world—there is no doubt about that. It's just a matter of the nuance.

The European casting directors also tend to think that—and I know this is horrible—Americans get mad about the fact that so much emphasis is put on how someone looks in Europe, and they think that just complaining about it is going to make a difference instead of just realizing that in Europe how you act and what you look like is equally and sometimes more important than how you sing. And that's something that the Americans get mad about, but they haven't quite made peace with the fact that that's just how it is.

Now, what about weight?
David: It is almost impossible for overweight people to be hired in Europe. That is kind of the reality, and writing about that is hard.

When you mean "overweight," do you mean obese, morbidly obese?
David: Morbidly obese, certainly; I think if you are in a difficult *Fach* to cast or do certain roles that are hard—if you can sing the Dyer's Wife [*Die ägyptische Helena*] then your size does not matter. In Europe, because they put so much emphasis on how someone looks and how they are on stage, especially in the German *Fest* system, they would rather hire someone who is less of a singer than someone where they don't like how they look. I've seen that happen many times. In fact, I know several opera houses that call themselves "musical theater" houses; not opera houses, which means they focus on the direction much more openly...

Than just the sound of the singer...
David: I can say that of all the *Intendanten* I work with in Germany—in the German system—I am counting about four or five whom I know where voice is really their main focus. For the rest of them, it is *Regietheater* [director's theater].

Can you give a percentage of the number of theaters who come to the NYIOPs] and hire singers?
David: Well I can say that of the theaters that have come to New York, we generally make a rule that if a theater comes once and doesn't hire someone, we'll invite them one more time. If they don't hire someone after two times, we simply don't invite them again because it's obviously not useful for them. That is for all except the very biggest houses. Obviously when Paris, Barcelona or Amsterdam comes, it's a higher bar to get hired. Therefore, if in two or three years someone develops into getting hired by Paris, then it's still useful to have the company come. One casting director [name withheld—from one of the five largest opera houses in the world] told me flat out he will never hire someone before hearing them three times over several years. Period.

So they aren't going to be hiring directly from these auditions?
David: Sometimes they do. When Paris was in New York last time they gave out five or six contracts.

You probably know thousands of singers. What kinds of conceptions or misconceptions do they have going into the NYIOPs?
David: The ones that we tend to get most often is that lots of people—of course everybody has problems with the fee—I would have had problems with it if I was a singer. What many people don't understand is what we actually pay. ... This isn't money were sticking in our pockets. We are paying for a hotel, flight and hall in New York, and each of these auditions costs roughly $20,000 USD *before* we ever put anything in our pocket. Hotel rooms in New York are over $300 USD per night right now for our discounted rates. So a lot of people tend to think that somehow I've become wealthy on it.

  The other thing that is a difficulty and it is just sad... the singers tend to get upset that everyone who comes, because [the singers] are paying a fee, [the theaters] should be able to and *should* write contracts on the spot, instead of [the singers] realizing that some people can't. Some *Intendanten* can offer contracts on the spot and do. Some offer contracts all the time. Other houses can't and don't, or can but they won't. Once the theater signs that contract, especially with a *Fest* contract, they owe you as much as you owe them, and therefore they sometimes must hear you in their theater to make sure you sound ok.

Does that go for guest contracts, as well?
David: It depends on what they are looking for—it depends on the contract. I think if it's a difficult role and they need it soon, then the theater can take more chances. At the same time, I think some people don't realize that when they do this audition, if they get invited to an additional [house] audition, they kind of sell short the usefulness of this; someone who casts in that house has already taken an interest and invited them over. It is not even unusual—how many times you do two or three auditions for the same house, even in Germany? So the difference is that you've got people who either don't have an agent or people who have an agent who doesn't deal in Europe. They come to do our audition, they spark some interest and they get invited to go over and

sing another [house] audition. If they don't have an agent, they've basically gotten thru and gotten an audition they never would have gotten—ever—if they didn't have a European agent.

And they were invited to do a house audition for something specific, as well?
David: Yeah, exactly. And when it's all said and done they don't have to pay a 10% commission because the houses *love* to contract directly with singers. Then the singers don't pay a commission, either.

If somebody says, "I want to work in the *Fest* system," would you make a blanket statement out saying, "then the NYIOPs are for you?"
David: No, I wouldn't actually. Here's the way I think about it: if you want to do an audition tour and if you've got the money, it's a hell of an experience. You get to see Europe, you learn how these companies work, and you get to contact people. It's an enormous pain in the ass, as I am sure you know; you have to find out whom to sing for in the house—not just write the *Intendant*—and they also have to be hearing people. They have to want to hear you. It's easy to go to Europe, bankroll two months there, have five auditions none of which turn into anything and it's easy to spend a month there and have no auditions—or to sing for Haase, Seitter, and Neill Thornborrow [German and Austrian agents], they send you on one or two auditions, only to never hear anything from them again. It's also possible to go there, sing for one person, and they say you have a job for two years.

I would say that if somebody, based really anywhere, wants to find out if they are really marketable in the German *Fest* system before they go bankroll a big audition tour, then it's [doing the NYIOPs] a useful thing. The main reason why we created the NYIOPs was that most of the people the *Fest* houses heard were the people (the Americans) who didn't have jobs. They were the people who could afford to spend two months doing a tour, whereas the ones who were working constantly in the United States didn't really have time for that. And with the NYIOPs, they [European houses] could really come over and hear the rest of what was in the American system, because it was convenient. There are a lot of really good, young singers who go over there [to Germany, Austria, and Switzerland] and do audition tours. But if somebody needs a Scarpia, they're not going to find a young, wandering

Scarpia. If they come to New York they can hear three or four, because Scarpias are not sitting around without work.

Also, I would say that what the NYIOPs are most useful for (and I hope I'm not pricing myself out of business!) is for young singers who want *Anfänger* (beginner) contracts, for established singers who have enough résumé behind them to be marketable as a guest, for singers singing obscure or odd repertoire, and for very individual artists. So that's what it's most useful for.

Ok, here's the difference: you do an audition tour and take away the major things like you pay a fortune. You might not get anything if you get over there. With the NYIOPs it's a much surer shot. You get an audition and I promise you that the people you are singing for are the ones making the decisions, or at least one of the people making the decisions. I don't bring over janitors or garbage collectors. ... I've had over one hundred thirty houses come for the auditions.

So you would say a good majority of the houses in Germany, Austria and Switzerland have come for the NYIOPs?
David: Yes, I can say that the ones who haven't come are easier to say... one house in Switzerland... and two houses in Austria. Of all the houses in Germany, there are only four who have not come to New York. Only one theater in Germany has said they are not interested in this process, and with the other three it has to do with timing issues.

Ok, what do you say to the person who says, "I want to get a Fest job so I am just going to do the NYIOPs. If I don't get a *Fest* from the NYIOPs, I guess it means that I just cannot get a *Fest* job"?
David: The first thing I would ask is... what repertoire they're singing plus the basic information of how old they are and what their experience is, and realistically if they are any good. I should just be honest with that. If they sing a NYIOP audition, they should write the houses and find out what people thought of them. If everyone in the entire place were basically saying you were not satisfactory, then I would say it depends on which houses were there. I would say that if it's a cross section—if you sing for Düsseldorf, Deutsche Oper Berlin, Stuttgart, Hamburg [all large, international German

theaters], and nobody's interested, maybe it's just the wrong level of houses for you. But if you sing for Görlitz, Erfurt, Saarbrücken, Bonn, and Hamburg [a cross-section of regional and international German theaters] and nobody's interested, then there's a problem. I would say that if you do an audition or two with us with like-sized houses and each house has a bad impression of you, then it might not work out for you—then you might not be the taste the theaters are looking for. Singers who sing the NYIOPs are welcome to contact us to see if there was any feedback from the houses. We may have a general idea of how your audition was received.

Where is the NYIOP going in the future?
David: NYIOP make really no money. That's the sad thing. I make a very modest living, and I flew one hundred twenty thousand miles last year for it. I got married, moved to Europe, and I work with a couple houses as a casting agent. The auditions will continue in New York but they will probably scale back to a couple times a year. So that means a couple times a year in New York, once a year in Berlin, and once somewhere else in the world.

Do you think the NYIOPs and a European audition tour compliment each other?
David: I think that's exactly right. If somebody has limited funds, I would encourage them to do a NYIOP audition before they go and do an audition tour, because you can at least gather information. Too many singers flail about not thinking that this is a business and that you have to count to become an accountant. They don't try to gather information and focus their efforts, and that's where a NYIOP *can* help. If you have limited funds, obviously NYIOP is the choice. If you have a lot of money, I would still say that your best bet is to do a NIYOP and then follow up with every house that was there since now you have personal contact in some capacity. And then do your audition tour on that.

Since we spoke last (in 2007), what has changed for you personally and professionally?
Since we last spoke I have taken a job as [artistic consultant] for the Teatro Communale Bologna and their young artist program there—the Scuola

dell'Opera Italiana, and a couple other big European theaters on an unofficial basis. Beginning next season I will also be the Director of Artistic Operations at the Pam Beach Opera.

What has changed with NYIOP is that we have moved to doing even more sessions in Europe — [for the big project each summer] it has been in Berlin, last year it was in Bologna, this year it will be in Vienna at Theater an der Wien. Each year it looks like we will be moving to a different major theater in Europe. I am doing a project now in Napoli, as well as a project for singers looking for *Fest* positions at Deutsche Oper Berlin. What singers are asking me increasingly is if I can bring this whole German audition process to Germany. So, this will be the first time we have tried it, and if it works out we will keep doing it.

Since better houses are coming to the auditions, I am no longer having to make deals with the bigger agencies to get singers into the auditions. As the level of singers has gotten higher and more people are getting hired, I have been able to gradually let these agreements go. And hopefully by next year no deals will be made.

Here's the big question: the economy. How is it affecting the opera scene in Europe? Have you noticed anything?
Yes, I have noticed it a lot. The way that [the economy] has affected things is that I have noticed fees dropping significantly. The last country to drop their fees was Spain, but they seem [to be bottoming out] now. Italy is a nightmare. The other way that I have noticed it affecting theaters is that they plan later. You know, you've got major theaters that simply have not planned next season yet. And that is the nature of what is happening with that.

13 DREIZEHN

All in the Family: Life in an Ensemble

Life in an ensemble is not only extremely busy, but also a constant challenge for multi-tasking and pacing skills. It can be a great joy or you're worst nightmare. Since the publication of the First Edition of *What The FACH?!*, I have decided to my leave my last *Fest* position behind, and have entered other exciting areas of the operatic world. However, a normal week as a *Fest* singer is still what it has always been: performing three contrasting operas in repertoire, a gala concert on the weekend, and a *Sitzprobe* of a world premiere opera. Whether you are *Fest* or freelance, role preparation is always at the forefront, as well as auditions and oratorio concerts.

Intendant, colleagues, and atmosphere

Your experience in an ensemble will be influenced by numerous variables: *Intendant/–in*, colleagues, the overall atmosphere in your theater, your amount of free time, and the city in which you live (there are huge differences between Berlin, Dessau, and Innsbruck!). While some factors about *Fest* engagements remain constant (i.e. performing operas in repertoire, modest pay, relative stability, etc.), it is a mistake to take one person's experience—yes, even mine—and assume that this is the way in every *Fest* ensemble. With some factors you just have to take the plunge and have faith it will be all right.

My first few months living here were certainly the most difficult. I had to work especially hard just to appear linguistically competent in rehearsals, I had no friends to speak of, and I was miserably homesick. As much as I wanted to assimilate into German life, I found it difficult and frequently frustrating. My first Christmas came just three weeks after beginning my first *Fest* engagement. I erroneously assumed that since my new colleagues knew I was here alone and I had nobody with whom to celebrate Christmas, somebody would have a little pity for the new kid and I would at least receive an invitation to somebody's home. I did not receive an invitation, however, and spent Christmas Day wandering around the city trying to pass the time. That was absolutely the worst day I have had here, and if you move here, you are bound to have a few of these days. Those days will pass into distant memory and life here will get not only easier, but also more enjoyable and fulfilling.

One of the most important variables of life in a theater is the atmosphere (*die Stimmung*). As a member of the ensemble, you are a member of a large family (my last *Fest* theater, for example, employed over five hundred people full-time). You will see the same people every day so a positive attitude in the theater makes a difference. If people say "hi" to each other in the hallways, this is a very good sign. You would be surprised how many theaters I have been to where I have seen thirty people in my first ten minutes through the front door and everybody just looks the other way—that's a bad sign.

I have often gotten the impression that there is a constant game of "pass the buck/it's not my job" going on in theaters here. Of course, not with everybody, but with some. While I am not certain as to why, I do have some good theories: These theaters, as I have already mentioned, are pumping out hundreds of shows each year and the stress level is very high. This sometimes leads to personnel either feeling or actually being overwhelmed. I believe, as well, that this overwhelming feeling has been exacberated by budget cuts and an indefatigable demand put upon the theaters by the municipalities (and the public) to produce, produce, produce. In addition, each person has a specific job with specific responsibilities, and the word "flexible" is not always associated with German culture! What is my point? You may sometimes be frustrated as you try to navigate the beaurocratic maze of a theater. Do your best to find the person directly responsible for helping resolve whatever particular challenge you are facing, and do not expect help above and beyond what that particular person believes is in his or her job responsibility. But if you find an advocate or two in the theater to be there for you (and there are those), use them and appreciate them.

There is a saying in German that *"der Fisch stinkt vom Kopf"* ("the fish stinks from the head"). The *Intendant/–in* sets the tone for how any theater is run. Good bosses inspire confidence in their leadership, their understanding of opera guide the artistic mission of the company, and they have respect for artists and their craft. Bad bosses are overwhelmed by the resposibilities of the job, do not inspire confidence in their abilities, and sit in the captain's chair (or in the lifeboat) of a sinking *Titanic*. If you think about it, there are over one hundred theaters in the German-speaking world, they all have multi-million Euro budgets, and it is a gigantic challenge for each theater to find a competent leader who not only has savvy business and political acumen, but also a love for artists (in opera, drama, ballet, and orchestral music), an understanding/empathy for what we do, and a knowledge of these art forms with the ability to effectively carry out a vision.

It makes a positive difference in the atmosphere and daily life of a theater when the *Intendant/–in* cares about his or her artists, actually understands how to run a theater, and makes tangible steps to show this, such as actually coming to performances and speaking with artists backstage after performances. This attitude is contageous as it spreads down the food chain and has a potentially positive effect on the way a theater is run.

Life in a *Fest* theater is a constant grind, and some days you may feel like a hampster on a wheel. But whatever happens, the show always goes on! A typical couple days in the theater might begin with an orchestra dress rehearsal for *Don Giovanni* in the morning, a performance of *Les Contes d'Hoffmann* in the evening, and then a performance of *Aida* the next night. Although it differs from theater to theater, singers are often entitled to one or two days off per week, although this is not always adhered to. Check with your employees' representative (*Betriebsrat*) for clarification of the rules. It may also be that if you do not receive your entitled free days or your entitled amount of free time between rehearsals, you may receive extra compensation. Again, check with your *Betriebsrat*.

In my first *Fest* engagement, I once worked twenty-one days in a row, was scheduled for my twenty-second day, and finally just told them, "no, I am taking today off." If you are considering regular trips back to America, do not hold your breath. Getting home will be likely only if the theater is dying to have you, if you have a very good agent, the theater is flexible and understanding, or your schedule is not too demanding. I was always fortunate to have good relationships with the folks in the KBB, who bent over backwards to let me go for other obligations.

I would like to share a story that may contradict some things I have already written and will also show the empathy of which theater personnel are capable. During my second season here I learned (during one of my performances) that my father just had a heart attack and needed emergency bypass surgery. I had no choice but to finish the show because there were no immediate flights to the U.S., and I then immediately spoke to the KBB about going home. Their answer was simple and without strings attached: I should go to America and they would take care of finding a guest to cover my performances. I was floored by their understanding and compassion. Fortunately, all turned out well and I was grateful to have my theater's support during a difficult time.

Where to start festing and when to jump ship?

I wish I had just one answer to this question, but it is different for each and every singer. (I will take a moment now, however, to step up on my soapbox and preach.) When you enter into a *Fest* engagement or even into the path of working your way through the German-speaking *Fest* system as a *Fest* singer, guest singer, or both, I **strongly** suggest that you have a carefully planned—yet flexible—long-term vision of how you want your career to progress?

Think very carefully before you accept a *Fest* engagement at a house whose *niveau* and reputation is lower than the theaters in which you are working; once you enter into this system as a *Fest* singer, you will quickly discover that—to some degree—you carry your theater's name on your résumé either as a mark of prestige or as a scarlet letter.

If you are already working as a guest in theaters here and abroad, and you receive an offer to take a *Fest* engagement here, analyze carefully the kind of exposure (press, the opera world, etc.) you want and need, and then figure out if that particular *Fest* engagement will help you along. Yes, you certainly want the repertoire and experience that come along with a fixed engagement here, but you also want career momentum if you wish to carry you career further.

Which is why I say the following in no unequivocal terms: do not trust a theater to decide what is best for you—neither for your voice nor for your for artistic and career goals. Do not fall under the misguided idea that the opera world revolves around your particular *Fest* theater (as so many people do), and know if or when it is time to move up and out of your theater and/or the *Fest* system.

How long should you be a *Fest* singer? For each singer it is different, but you should always be in close touch with the kind of artistic work you are doing while under contract. Yes, there is much to it that is fulfilling, and you will almost certainly have the possibility to grow as an artist and singer. However, should you feel that the theater is taking more from you than you are investing, it's time to go. Either go to another theater, or freelance. I have seen theaters consume artistic souls of singers, and "sad" does not begin to describe it.

Da du da Sie!

As you are certainly (I hope) aware, the German language has both an informal version of the singular "you" (*du*) and a formal version (*Sie*). Trying to figure out which version to use is often difficult, even for the natives, and the rules are somewhat different in a theater than they are in "real life." Unfortunately, there is no definite way to solve this riddle, but I will do my best.

The general rule of thumb is this: if there is some kind of clear differentiation between two individuals, such as age or rank in the theater wher one person appears to be in a superior position to you, you should begin with *Sie*. It is then the choice of the party who is more senior to offer the *du*. Whoever offers the *du* first is usually confident that either he or she is of higher status, or confident that the use of du will not be a big deal. (It's kind of like two dogs peeing on a fire hydrant, and the one who pees last wins.)

When dealing with your *Intendant/–in*, senior theater people, and theater personnel with whom you have limited contact (ushers, business office people, etc.) stick to *Sie*. Sometimes a *du* is offered, sometimes it is just understood that you will *du* each other, and sometimes a *Sie* is just the best way to go. You will slowly learn to appreciate this custom, as it keeps a unique civility to workplace interactions. As well, you may certainly appreciate the value of staying on *Sie* with your *Intendant/–in* since it will afford you a polite personal distance, handy particularly during renegotiations.

All bets are off when you go to rehearsal and deal with other folks behind the scenes, such as technical crew and stage door personnel. On the first day of rehearsal, I generally *Sie* the stage director and conductor. More often than not I stay on *Sie* with the Maestro and immediately go to *du* with the stage director. I often let the stage director offer the *du* to me first, however. If the conductor is closer to an equal, such as a house conductor, we will probably already be on *du*. Are you confused yet? The only time I have ever been on *Sie* with a singer was if the singer was older and we did not know each other, or if it was someone very famous and very unfriendly. Singers almost always go immediately to *du*. In Austria, Switzerland, and Southern Germany, I have noticed that people *du* each other much more freely (no snickering, please). When in doubt, either follow somebody else's lead, or ask. You're an *Ausländer/–in*, for Tom Cruise's sake! You will know, too, that your Germanic integration is working according to plan the first time a stranger inappropriately *du's* you and you are offended.

Illness and vacation

There are formal processes for everything in the theater and two of the most important are for when you are sick (*Krankanmeldung*) and for vacation (*Urlaub*). Do not come to rehearsals when you are sick. Call the KBB to let them know of your malady and then either stay home or go to the doctor. If you are sick for one more than one day or have to cancel a performance because of illness, you will need a confirmation of illness from the doctor (*Krankenschein*) to give to the theater. However, some theaters now require that you have that doctor's note starting on the first day of illness. You will certainly meet plenty of colleagues who, when they feel a little tired or are sick of working with a certain director, will call in sick.

Frankly, this irritates me and I find it unprofessional. Fortunately, Americans and other English-speaking singers are not known for calling in sick and we are not known to exploit this loophole.

When you want to leave the general geographical location of your theater you will need to go to the KBB and fill out a vacation request (*Urlaubsschein* or *Urlaubsgesuch*). This is done not only so the theater can keep track of you, but also so you are covered under insurance while you are away. If you do not fill out an *Urlaubsschein* and you then travel away and get in an accident, you will not be covered by insurance. Then you have serious problems. If you call in sick or do not fill out an *Urlaubsschein* and then leave to sing another engagement, you have even bigger problems. A colleague once did this and the theater responded by revoking all of his vacation (for other jobs) for the remainder of the season. They could have actually fired him. Don't play around with this.

Musical preparation and stage rehearsals

When you are assigned a role to perform in a production the theater often gives you a piano score (*Klavierauszug*), which you must return after the production. They also help you prepare the role with their musical staff. Depending on the quality of your music staff, you will either want to prepare the role with them or run far, far away to a coach outside of the theater. The music staff is accustomed to pounding out notes for singers because, as you will see, some of your colleagues take advantage of the system to let these coaches actually teach them the roles. Coming unprepared to musical rehearsals is tacky, unprofessional, lazy, and a hundred other negative adjectives. Unfortunately, this practice is pervasive, so do not let yourself be lured by the temptations of laziness and procrastination. Do your grunt work before you show up for a coaching—the coaches will appreciate it and your reputation for being well prepared will spread around the theater.

Be memorized when you get to stage rehearsals, even if many of your colleagues may not be. This should go without saying, but I will still mention it: translate your text so you understand every single word. You will look like a complete idiot if you get to the first day of stage rehearsals for *Die Zauberflöte* in Germany and you do not know what the hell you are singing.

Stage directors are all about production concept (*das Konzept*) and at the first stage rehearsal (*Konzeptionsgespräch*) the stage director and design team will present their *Konzept* (or lack thereof) to the cast. The stage director in the German-speaking world is very high in the theater food chain, something you will realize when you read your first set of reviews; the majority of each review will address the *Konzept,* and if you are lucky, the last paragraph or two will mention a few singers. You are certainly familiar with many infamous European concepts: *Entführung* with real prostitutes, Planet of The Apes *Rigoletto,* and the list goes on. Whatever you do, do not tell a director they have no *Konzept.* I once thought I was complimenting my director by saying, "I really like your vision; you have absolutely no *Konzept* —rather, you are just telling the story." That was apparently a big insult and the end of good times on that show.

The average length of rehearsals here is between four and eight weeks, though most of my productions have rehearsed for around six weeks. One of the advantages of working here is that you will start rehearsing on stage relatively early in the process, so there will be no shock of production week when everyone is scrambling to get their bearings in the theater. The other great advantage is that you will have buckets of time to rehearse with the orchestra. In addition to one to three orchestra musical run-thrus (*Sitzproben*), you will also have three to five orchestra stage rehearsals with minimal staging (*BO* or *Bühnen–Orchester–Proben*), which are essentially stage rehearsals/run-thrus with orchestra. Then comes the piano dress rehearsal (*KHP* or *Klavierhauptprobe*), orchestra dress rehearsal (*OHP* or *Orchesterhauptprobe*), and then final dress rehearsal (*GP* or *Generalprobe*). If you are fortunate, you will get a day off between the *GP* and opening night. Sometimes I get one or two days off, while occasionally I have gone straight thru to opening night without a break, once for thirteen days. Time off between the *GP* and premiere depends on how organized your theater is, and if they actually respect and understand your needs as a singer. There are plenty of variations on the production process, but the above provides you with a reliable framework of what to expect.

There are disadvantages to rehearsing for so long, as well. Singers and conductors sometimes come unprepared because they think they can "learn on the job," so to speak. This causes the process to be somewhat painful. The biggest disadvantage I have experienced, though, is suffering under a director who does not know how to pace six weeks of rehearsal, and this happens much more often than it should. Sometimes the director does not know what he or she wants, and sometimes the director has never directed before and has no idea how to conduct rehearsals (seriously...). Sometimes, as well, the director insists on rehearsing for every second allowed, and the production is an over-rehearsed, limp show on opening night.

I have commited virtually every mortal and venial sin on stage (thanks, Catholic school for repeatedly driving home the point between the two...). I have committed multiple murders, executed people, raped, participated in orgies, had sex in a clown costume, masturbated, masturbated in a clown costume, snorted cocaine, given plenty of Hitler salutes (they somehow never go over well with the audience), sung my character's big aria while walking on a treadmill (why, I have no idea...), and I was recently in love with a middle-aged, very heterosexual singer of my same sex for twenty performances. We got married at the end of the show.

I have been involved in a number of extraordinary productions with talented directors who are interested in seeing what I have to offer instead of just shoving their *Konzept* down my throat with no questions asked. Some of the heinous acts described above came from wonderful productions with directors whom I adore. You will just have to be open to new (and often immoral!) ideas during the staging process. Keep an open mind to different dramatic ideas, be ready to diplomatically hold your ground if you think something does not make sense (and you can explain why *and* offer intelligent alternatives), and get ready to get half-naked for your big aria!

Plays well with others

For better or for worse (as I have already written), you are part of a large family. I have enjoyed the feeling of working with the same colleagues in a number of productions. It adds to the security when other stressful factors are present (i.e., performing new roles, opening night, etc.). The feeling can be quite similar to the collegiality of a young artist program as it was my last *Fest* theater. You also have the opportunity to sing beside some wonderful, more-experienced colleagues who are full of sage advice.

When colleagues work in such close proximity together for long periods of time, there are sometimes conflicts. Whether it is a lazy, undiplomatic colleague, the *Studienleiter* who seems to have perfected mediocrity, or the friendly experienced colleague who comes to rehearsals unprepared, thereby forcing you to rehearse the scene over and over, you will work with all kinds of different people. Get ready for it and be prepared. This is true, however, with everything in life and part of being a *Fest* singer is learning how to be a diplomat, as well. Before you even think about opening your mouth to confront a colleague, just remember that you will be working with this particular colleague in a number of shows for at least the rest of this season, if not the next. One of the biggest challenges of working with the same group of artists is that you may feel your artistic creativity stagnate. Keep a very close eye on this and do everything you can to avoid repeating your same bag of acting tricks.

A final note about productions: in some theaters the roles are double cast (*doppelbesetzt*). If you do the math, you will realize that sometimes you will be in the first cast (*Erstbesetztung*), and sometimes you are going to be in the second cast (*Zweitbesetzung*). Being in the first cast certainly has it's advantages; you often get more rehearsal time, the director (depending on the director, of course) pays more attention to the *Erstbesetzung*, and the *Erstbesetzung* sings the premiere performance, thereby receiving many—if not all—of the reviews. But if you are first cast in this show, you may very well be second cast in the next show. Do not expect to always sing in the first cast and when your time comes to take one for the team, be a good colleague. I have watched a few colleagues overtly and covertly jockey to be in the premiere cast for every production, and this has—without fail—created bad blood. Singing first *and* second cast is just part of life in a *Fest* ensemble. If you are second cast, just remember that you are still on stage and that you are still performing the role.

Stability

Being a member of a *Fest* ensemble provides a singer with financial security unheard of in the rest of the world. You know how much money you will make for the next season, two, or even three, and you can plan accordingly. Guest work—both concerts and opera—is financial gravy, and you will even have some paid vacation time to work as a guest and for actual vacation, as well! The list goes on and a *Fest* engagement can be a very smart career move.

CONCLUSION

Veni, Vidi, Vici

So, there you have it. As with everything in life, there is more than one side to every story and opinions are like noses; everybody has one. I have had both good and bad experiences in Europe, and have made an earnest attempt to present both sides. Working and living here is not for everyone; it takes courage to hop on a plane and start auditioning here with no guarantees of work.

But if you are one of those many people who have said to me, *I would love to come do an audition tour and work in Europe*, start saving your money, figure a way out to make it happen, and get over here. Take the chance and get on a plane. You will never know unless you actually try. I would enjoy hearing from you. Please feel free to send your comments, questions, complaints, and suggestions to Philip@what-the-fach.com, visit us at www.what-the-fach.com and follow us on Twitter at @WhatTheFACHbook.

Toi toi toi for your audition tour!

PHRASE BOOK AND DICTIONARY

The Very Basic

Hello	*Guten Tag, Hallo* (in Germany); *Grüß Gott* (Austria, Switzerland, and Bavaria)
	Servus (informal in Austria and Southern Germany)
	Ciao
Goodbye	*Tschüs* (informal), *Auf Wiedersehen, Auf Wiederschauen* (Formal, also used commonly in Austria)
	Ade (informal in Switzerland)
	Servus (informal in Austria and Southern Germany
	Ciao
Please	*Bitte*
Thank you	*Danke schön*
Excuse me	*Entschuldigen Sie* or *Verzeihung* (that's very polite)
Where is...?	*Wo ist...?*
I would like...	*Ich möchte...* or *Ich hätte gerne...*
My name is...	*Ich heiße...* or *mein Name ist...*

Publicity

Publicity materials	*die Unterlagen* or *die Bewerbungsunterlagen*
Resume/CV	*der Lebenslauf*

Reviews	*die Kritiken*
Biography	*die Biografie*
Agent	*die Agentur*
Letter	*der Brief*
Cover letter	*das Anschreiben*
Note	*die Nachricht* or *die Notiz*
Regional theater	*Landestheater*
City theater	*Stadttheater*
State theater	*Staatstheater*
National theater	*Nationaltheater*

For the Résumé

Nationality	*Nationalität*
Address	*Adresse*
Permanent address	*Festanschrift* or *Ständige Adresse*
Fax	*Fax*
Telephone	*Telefon*
Mobile phone	*Handy*
Mobile phone number	*Handynummer*
Opera roles	*Opernpartien*
Opera performances	*Opernaufführungen*
Roles	*Rollen*
As Cover	*als Nebenbesetzung* or *als Cover*
Youth Performances	*Kindervorstellungen*

World Premiere	*Uraufführung*
Opera Studios/Young Artist Programs	*Opernstudio/s*
Education	*Ausbildung*
Concert Performances	*Konzertauftritte*
Recitals	*Liederabende*
Voice Teacher	*Lehrer/–in*
Stage Directors	*Regisseure*
Conductors	*Dirigenten*
Coaches	*Korrepetitoren*
Competitions	*Wettbewerbe*
Grants	*Stipendien*
Awards	*Preise*
First Place	*1. Preis* or *Erster Preis*
Second Place	*2. Preis* or *Zweiter Preis*
Masterclasses	*Meisterkurse*
Roles ready to perform immediately	*Rollen parat*

Musical Terminology

Piano	*das Klavier*
Voice	*die Stimme*
Vocal chords	*die Stimmbänder*
Piano vocal score	*der Klavierauszug*
Upbeat	*der Auftakt*
Measure	*der Takt*

Edition (e.g. *Tannhäuser* Paris and Dresden editions)	*die Fassung* (e.g. *Tannhäuser Pariser und Dresdner Fassung*)
Publisher (e.g., Schirmer, Ricordi, etc.)	*der Verlag*

In the Theater

Places in the Theater

Entrance	*der Eingang*
Stage door entrance	*der Bühneneingang*
Elevator	*der Aufzug* or *der Lift*
Stairs	*die Treppe*
Staircase	*das Treppenhaus*
Floor/Story (in a building)	*der Stock* or *das Stockwerk*
Door	*die Tür*
Artistic administration office	*das KBB, das Künstlerische Betriebsbüro*
Warm-up room	*der/die Einsingraum/–räume, der/die Überaum/–räume,* or *der/die Probenraum/–räume*
Coaching room	*das Korrepetitionszimmer*
Stage	*die Bühne*
Orchestra pit	*der Orchestergraben*
Rehearsal stage	*die Probebühne*
Rehearsal room	*der Proberaum*
Props table	*der Requisitentisch*
Emergency exit	*der Notausgang*
Exit	*der Ausgang*

Chorus room	der Chorsaal
Dressing room	die Garderobe
Makeup room or just "makeup"	die Maske
Business Office	das Verwaltungsbüro
Costume shop	die Schneiderei
Men's costume shop	die Herrenschneiderei
Women's costume shop	die Damenschneiderei
The Cantina (employee café)	die Kantine
Lobby	das Foyer
Auditorium ("the house")	der Zuschauerraum
Balcony	der Balkon
First-, Second-, Third balcony	1., 2., 3. Rang
Side balcony	der Seitenrang / die Galarie
Box (in the auditorium)	die Loge
Stage box / Proscenium box	die Proszeniumsloge
Row (in the auditorium)	die Reihe
Standing room	die Stehplätze
Cloak room	die Garderobe

Places and Actions on Stage

Stage	die Bühne
Backstage	der Bereich außerhalb der Szene or Backstage
Rearstage	die Hinterbühne
Sidestage	die Seitenbühne

Downstage	*die Vorderbühne* or (when giving directions) *nach vorne*
Upstage	*hintere Bühne* or (when giving directions) *nach hinten*
Sightline	*die Sichtlinie*
Entrance	*der Auftritt*
To exit	*abgehen*
"Go."	*"los"*
"Stop."	*"halt"* / *"stop"*

People in the Theater

General Director	*der/die Intendant/–in*
Music Director	*der/die Generalmusikdirektor/–in* or *GMD* (shortened)
Chief Conductor	*der/die Chefdirigent/–in*
Director of Opera	*der/die Operndirektor/–in*
Chief Producer of Opera	*der/die Oberspielleiter/–in*
Director of Artistic Administration	*der/die Künstlerische Betriebsdirektor /–in*
Director of The Rehearsal Department	*der/die Chefdisponent//–in*
Chief Financial Officer	*der/die Verwaltungsdirektor/–in*
First Assistant Conductor	*1./Erster Kapellmeister /–in*
Second Assistant Conductor	*2./Zweiter Kapellmeister /–in*
Head Coach	*der/die Studienleiter/–in*
Chorus Director	*der/die Chordirektor/–in*
Conductor	*der/die Dirigent/–in*
Stage Director	*der/die Regisseur/–in*

Assistant Stage Director	*der/die Regieassistent/–in*
Stage Manager	*der/die Inspizient/–in*
Prompter	*der Souffleur/die Souffleuse*
Coach	*der/die Korrepetitor/–in*
Employees' Representative	*der Betriebsrat*
Ensemble Spokesperson	*der/die Ensemblesprecher/–in*
Stage hog	*die Rampensau*

Activities in the Theater

To warm up (vocally)	*Einsingen*
To practice	*Üben*
Rehearsal	*die Probe*
Rehearsal for all soloists involved in the production	*Probe für alle beteiligten Soli* or *Probe für alle bet. Soli*
Rehearsal from/according to the announcement	*Probe nach Ansage*
Stage directions (coming from director during rehearsal)	*die Regieanweisungen*
Musical coaching	*die Korrepetition*
Conception meeting	*das Konzeptionsgespräch*
Costume fitting	*die Anprobe*
Costume change	*der Umzug* or *der Kostümwechsel*
Stage rehearsal with orchestra (without costumes and makeup)	*die BO* or *Bühnen–Orchester–Probe*
Makeup time	*die Schminkzeit*
Running Order	*die Szenenfolge*
Running time / Playing time	*die Vorstellungsdauer*
Scene change	*der Szenenwechsel*

Scene shift	der Umbau / die Verwandlung
Piano dress rehearsal	die KHP or Klavierhauptprobe
Orchestral dress rehearsal	die OHP or Orchesterhauptprobe
Final dress rehearsal	die GP or Generalprobe
Performance	der Auftritt (your personal performance) or die Vorstellung (the entire performance)
Opening night	die Premiere
Intermission	die Pause
Curtain Call	die Applausordnung
Applause	der Beifall / der Applaus

Miscellaneous in the Theater

Moustache	der Schnauzbart/der Schnauzer/der Oberlippenbart
Beard	der Bart
Sideburns	die Koteletten/der Backenbart
Wig	die Perücke
Music stand	das Notenpult
Announcement	die Ansage
Daily-, Weekly-, Monthly schedule	der Tages-, Wochen-, Monatsplan
Single cast	die Einzelbesetzung
Double cast	die Doppelbesetzung
First cast	die Erstbesetzung
Second cast	die Zweitbesetzung

New production	*die neue Produktion*
Revival production	*die Wiederaufnahme*
Repertory	*der Spielplan / das Repertoire*
Vacation	*der Urlaub*
Vacation request	*der Urlaubsschein or das Urlaubsgesuch*
Calling in sick	*die Krankanmeldung*
Doctor's sick note	*der Krankenschein*
Atmosphere	*die Stimmung/die Atmosphäre*
Concept	*das Konzept*
Union	*die Gewerkschaft*
Director's theater	*das Regietheater*

Phrases to Use Before Your Audition

Where is the stage door entrance?	*Wo ist der Bühneneingang?*
I am auditioning today.	*Ich singe heute vor.*
Where can I find a warm-up room/artistic administration office?	*Wo finde ich ein Einsingzimmer/das KBB?*
Go straight ahead. At the end of the hallway take either the stairs or the elevator to the 3rd floor. When you get off, turn right, go through the double doors, and the KBB will be the 2nd door on the left side. [and you think I am joking. Just wait...].	*Gehen Sie weiter geradeaus. Am Ende des Korridors nehmen Sie entweder die Treppe oder den Aufzug in den dritten Stock. Wenn Sie aussteigen, gleich rechts, durch die Doppeltür, und das KBB ist die zweite Tür von links.*
Please fill out this information form.	*Bitte füllen Sie dieses Formular aus.*
Might you have a pen?	*Haben Sie zufällig einen Kugelschreiber?*

I will give it (the pen) right back.	*Ich gebe ihn gleich zurück.*
You do not need to fill out an information form.	*Sie brauchen kein Informationsformular auszufüllen.*
Could you please give me a confirmation letter (for my taxes)?	*Könnten Sie mir eine Bestätigung für das heutige Vorsingen geben?*
My train is at 16:00 O'clock. Would it be possible to audition earlier?	*Mein Zug fährt um 16:00 Uhr. Wäre es möglich, früher für Sie vorzusingen?*
Where do we meet before the audition?	*Wo treffen wir uns vor dem Vorsingen?*
Will you pick me up here?	*Holen Sie mich hier ab?*
Should I wait here or just come to the stage/rehearsal room?	*Soll ich hier warten oder einfach zur Bühne/ Probebühne kommen?*
Excuse me. How do I find the stage?	*Entschuldigen Sie. Wie finde ich zur Bühne?*
Thank you for your understanding.	*Vielen Dank für Ihr Verständnis.*

Phrases to Use During Your Audition

Could you please walk backwards a little?	*Können Sie bitte ein bisschen zurück/nach hinten gehen?*
What would you like to begin with?	*Womit möchten Sie beginnen/ anfangen?*
Let's hear "Un bel dì."	*Lassen Sie uns "Un bel dì" hören.*
What else did you bring today?	*Was haben Sie noch mitgebracht?*
How long have you been in Germany/ Austria/ Switzerland?	*Seit wann sind Sie in Deutschland/Österreich/der Schweiz?*
Can I take a quick sip of water?	*Darf ich kurz einen Schluck Wasser trinken?*
May I take a short pause?	*Darf ich kurz eine Pause machen?*
How long are you staying in Germany?	*Wie lange bleiben Sie in Deutschland?*

Do you have a few minutes to speak with us after the audition?	*Haben Sie nach dem Vorsingen noch ein paar Minuten Zeit, um mit uns zu sprechen?*
Could we possibly speak English?	*Könnten wir vielleicht Englisch sprechen?*
We would like to engage you.	*Wir möchten Sie gerne engagieren.*

On the Telephone

ALWAYS start a phone conversation by announcing your name.

Hello, my name is Helmut Mustermann. Could you please connect me with the KBB?	*Hallo. Mein Name ist Helmut Mustermann. Könnten Sie mich bitte mit dem KBB verbinden?*
Hello, my name is Angela Merkel. I am calling to confirm my audition on December 4th.	*Guten Tag. Mein Name ist Angela Merkel. Ich rufe Sie an, um mein Vorsingen am vierten Dezember zu bestätigen.*
Hello, my name is Stefan Raab. You called me yesterday about an audition.	*Guten Tag. Mein Name ist Stefan Raab. Sie haben mich gestern wegen eines Vorsingtermins angerufen.*
Hello, my name is Helmut Mustermann. I have an audition with you next week. I am calling you with regards to a hotel room and would like to know if you know of a hotel where I could get the theater discount.	*Guten Tag. Mein Name ist Helmut Mustermann und ich singe nächste Woche für Sie vor. Ich rufe Sie wegen eines Hotelzimmers an und wollte mich erkundigen, ob Sie ein Hotel kennen, wo man einen Theaterpreis bekommen kann.*
I have a cold and unfortunately must cancel my audition.	*Wegen einer Erkältung muss ich mein Vorsingen leider absagen.*

In Sickness and in Health

Sick	*krank*
Sore throat	*Halsschmerzen*
Sinus infection	*Nebenhöhlenentzündung*
Headache	*Kopfschmerzen*
Stomach ache	*Magenschmerzen/ Bauchschmerzen*
Diarrhea	*Durchfall*
Cramps	*Krämpfe*
Urinary tract infection	*Blasenentzündung/ Harninfekt/ Harnwegsinfektion*
Bot flies	*Botfliegen*
Pharmacy	*Apotheke*
Night/weekend/ emergency hours	*Notdienst*
Ear, Nose, and Throat Doctor/ENT	*HNO* or *Fachärzte für Hals-, Nasen-, und Ohrenkrankheiten*
General Practitioner	*Facharzt/–ärztin für Allgemeinmedizin*
OB/GYN	*Facharzt/–ärztin für Frauenheilkunde und Geburtshilfe* or *Facharzt/–ärztin für Gynäkologie*
Dentist	*Zahnarzt/–ärztin*
Office hours	*die Sprechstunde*
Extremely urgent	*sehr dringend*
Hospital	*das Krankenhaus*
ENT emergency room	*HNO-Ambulanz*
Emergency room	*die Notaufnahme*

Contracts

Negotiating	*verhandeln*
Agreement	*die Vereinbarung / das Übereinkommen*
Contract	*der Arbeitsvertrag*
Fixed contract	*der Festvertrag*
Guest contract	*der Gastvertrag*
Jumping in	*einspringen* (v.), *das Einspringen* (n.)
Standard German stage contract for soloists	*Der Normalvertrag (NV) Bühne Solomitglied*
Beginner's contract	*der Anfängervertrag*
Ms. Schmidt will be employed as a soloist with the occupation term dramatic mezzo soprano, and roles according to individuality.	*Frau Schmidt wird als Solomitglied mit der Tätigkeitsbezeichnung Dramatischer Mezzosopran und Partien nach Individualität eingestellt.*
Roles contingent upon agreement	*Partien nach Absprache*
Fee/pay	*die Gage*
Limit for number of performances	*die Abendbegrenzung*
Extra per-performance fee for performances over the pre-agreed number	*das Spielgeld*
Salary	*das Gehalt / die Gage / der Lohn*
Gross income	*das Bruttogehalt* or *das Bruttoeinkommen*
Net income	*das Nettogehalt* or *das Nettoeinkommen*

Bureaucracy: Permits, Money, and Taxes

To register with local authorities	*anmelden*
Registration form	*das Anmeldungsformular*

WHAT THE FACH?!

To be registered	*angemeldet*
Bureau/Office	*das Amt*
Registration office	*das Einwohnermeldeamt*
City office (often inside the city hall)	*das Bürgeramt*
City hall	*das Rathaus*
Foreigner's office	*das Ausländeramt* or *die Ausländerbehörde*
Unemployment office	*die Agentur für Arbeit*
Residence permit	*die Aufenthaltserlaubnis* or *die Aufenthaltsbewilligung*
Work permit	*die Arbeitserlaubnis*
Unlimited work and residence permit	*die unbefristete Arbeits- und Aufenthaltserlaubnis*
Officially approved translation (of a birth certificate)	*die beglaubigte Übersetzung (der Geburtsurkunde)*
Police certificate of good conduct	*das Polizeiliche Führungszeugnis*
Income tax classification card	*die Lohnsteuerkarte*
Tax category or classification	*die Steuerklasse*
Bank account	*das Konto* or *das Bankkonto*
Bank transfer	*die Überweisung*
Health insurance	*die Krankenkasse* or *die Krankenversicherung*
Public health insurance	*die Gesetzliche Krankenkasse*
Private health insurance	*die private Krankenversicherung*
Children's money	*das Kindergeld*
Paid maternity leave	*die Karenz* or *der Schwangerschaftsurlaub*
Nursing home insurance	*die Pflegeversicherung (PV)*
Social security	*die Rentenversicherung (RV)*
Reunification (East/West Germany) tax	*der Solidaritätzuschlag (SolZ)*

Unemployment insurance	*die Arbeitslosenversicherung (AV)*
Church tax	*die Kirchensteuer (KS)*
German Theatrical Pension Fund	*die Bayrische Versorgungskammer (BVK)*
Catholic Church	*die Katholische Kirche*
Protestant Church	*die Evangelische Kirche*
Culture tax	*die Kultursteuer*
No church tax	*konfessionslos*
Agent commission	*die Agenturgebühren*
Filing taxes	*die Steuererklärung*
Accountant	*der/die Steuerberater/–in*
To deduct taxes	*von der Steuer absetzen*

Transportation

Train	*der Zug*
Wagon	*der Wagen*
Seat	*der Sitzplatz*
Reservation	*die Reservierung*
In a large wagon	*im Großraumabteil*
In a small (six-passenger) wagon	*im Abteil*
From	*von*
To (specific geographical location, i.e. Hamburg)	*nach*
Arrival	*die Ankunft*
Departure	*die Abfahrt*
Main train station	*der Hauptbahnhof (HBF)*

WHAT THE FACH?!

Train station	der Bahnhof
Non-smoking seat	der Nichtraucherplatz
On the aisle	am Gang
By the window	am Fenster
Dining car	der Bordwagen/Bordbistro
"Has anyone gotten on board?" (said by train personnel)	"Ist jemand zugestiegen?" / "Zugestiegen?"
"Our dining car may be found in car number thirty-four." (said by train personnel)	"Unser Bordbistro befindet sich im Wagen Nummer vierunddreizig."
Train connection	die Verbindung
Train platform	das Gleis
To get in/get on board	einsteigen
To get off/get out/exit	aussteigen
I would like a one-way ticket to Nürnberg.	Ich möchte einen Fahrschein —nur Hinfahrt—nach Nürnberg.
Where do I need to change trains?	Wo muss ich umsteigen?
I would like to reserve a non-smoking seat on the aisle.	Ich möchte einen Nichtrauchersitzplatz am Gang reservieren.
Bicycle	das Fahrrad
Bicycle path	der/die Fahrradweg/–e
Fare dodger	der/die Schwarzfahrer /–in
Traffic jam	der Stau

Finding an Apartment

Real estate	*Immobilien*
Newspaper	*die Zeitung*
Advertisement/Classified ad	*die Anzeige*
Apartment for rent	*Wohnung zu vermieten*
Apartment wanted	*Wohnung gesucht*
Rental contract	*der Mietvertrag*
Rental confirmation	*die Mietbestätigung*
Apartment with roommate/s	*die Wohngemeinschaft* or *WG*
Room	*das Zimmer*
Bedroom	*das Schlafzimmer*
Living/Family/Great room	*das Wohnzimmmer*
For a commuter (e.g. not in the apartment on the weekends)	*für Pendler geeignet*
Kitchen	*die Küche*
Bathroom	*das Badezimmer*
Storage room	*der Abstellraum*
2 rooms, kitchen, bathroom	2 ZKB *(Zimmer, Küche, Bad)* or in Eastern Germany 2 RKB *(Raum, Küche, Bad)*
2 rooms, kitchen, bathroom, balcony	2 ZKBB *(Zimmer, Küche, Bad, Balkon)* or in Eastern Germany 2RKBB *(Raum, Küche, Bad, Balkon)*
Ground floor	EG *(Erdgeschoss)*
Second floor (what Americans call the 3rd floor)	2. OG *(Obergeschoss)*
Room for loft apartment	DG *(Dachgeschoss)*
Sublet	*die Zwischenmiete*

Sublettor wanted	*Zwischenmieter /–in gesucht*
Tenant wanted to take over a lease	*Nachmieter /–in gesucht*
Fitted kitchen	*EBK (Einbauküche)*
Square meter and describes the size of the apartment.	*qm or m² (Quadratmeter)*
Cold rent; i.e. rent without utilities and extra costs	*KM (Kaltmiete)*
Extra costs; i.e. garbage disposal, street and house cleaning costs, as well as heating and water costs	*NK (Nebenkosten)*
Warm rent; means rent plus all utilities except TV, Internet, and Telephone	*WM (Warmmiete)*
Quiet time	*die Ruhezeit*

Miscellaneous

Cigarette store	*der Kiosk/Tabak* (in Austria)
Turkish flat bread with meat, onions, lettuce, and yogurt sauce	*der Döner*
Coffee and cake	*Kaffee und Kuchen*
Superficial	*oberflächlich*

WEB SITES AND DOCUMENTS

Embassies and Consulates General

Germany

German Embassy in The United States	www.germany.info
German Embassy in Canada	www.ottawa.diplo.de
German Embassy in The United Kingdom	www.london.diplo.de
German Embassy in Australia	www.germanembassy.org.au
German Embassy in New Zealand	www.wellington.diplo.de
German Embassy in South Africa	Pretoria.diplo.de

Austria

Austrian Embassy in The United States	www.austria.org
Austrian Embassy in Canada	www.bmaa.gv.at
Austrian Embassy in The United Kingdom	www.bmaa.gv.at
Austrian Embassy in Australia	www.bmaa.gv.at
Austrian Consulate in New Zealand	www.bmaa.gv.at
Austrian Embassy in South Africa	www.aussenministerium.at

Switzerland

Swiss Embassy Main Web Site	www.eda.admin.ch

Foreign Embassies in Germany

American Embassy in Berlin	tel+ 49 (0)30 2385 174 http://berlin.usembassy.gov
Canadian Embassy in Berlin	tel+ 49 (0)30 20312 0 www.dfait-maeci.gc.ca
British Embassy in Berlin	tel+ 49 (0)30 20457 0 www.britischebotschaft.de/en/
Australian Embassy in Berlin	tel+ 49 (0)30 88 00 88 0 www.germany.embassy.gov.au

New Zealand Embassy in Berlin	tel+ 49 (0)30 20621 0 www.nzembassy.com
South African Embassy in Berlin	tel+ 49 (0)30 22073 0 www.suedafrika.org

Foreign Embassies in Austria

American Embassy in Vienna	tel+ 43 (0)1 31339 0 http://vienna.usembassy.gov
Canadian Embassy in Vienna	tel+ 43 (0)1 531 38 3000 http://geo.international.gc.ca
British Embassy in Vienna	tel+ 43 (0)1 71613 5151 www.britishembassy.gov.uk
Australian Embassy in Vienna	tel+ 43 (0)1 506 740 www.australian-embassy.at
New Zealand Consulate-General in Vienna	tel+ 43 (0)1 318 8505 www.nzembassy.com
South African Embassy in Vienna	tel+ 43 (0)1 320 6493 www.saembvie.at

Foreign Embassies in Switzerland

American Embassy in Bern	tel+ 41 (0)31 357 7234 embasshttp://bern.usembassy.gov
Canadian Embassy in Bern	tel+ 41 (0)31 357 3200 http://geo.international.gc.ca
British Embassy in Bern	tel+ 41 (0)31 359 7700 www.britishembassy.gov.uk
Australian Consulate-General in Geneva	tel+ 41 (0)22 799 9100 www.geneva.mission.gov.au/
New Zealand Consulate-General In Geneva	tel+ 41 (0)22 929 0350 www.nzembassy.com
South African Embassy in Bern	tel+ 41 (0)31 350 1313 www.southafrica.ch

Visa Applications and Essential Documents

Shengen Visa Application in Germany
(www.what-the-fach.com/pdfs/German-Visa-Application.pdf)

Germany Residency Permit Application
(www.what-the-fach.com/pdfs/Germany-Residence-Permit-Application.pdf)

German Declaration
(www.what-the-fach.com/pdfs/Germany-Residence-Permit-Declaration.pdf) ~ must accompany your residency permit application

Austrian Residency Application
(www.what-the-fach.com/pdfs/Austrian-Residence-Permit-Application.pdf)

Explanation of Austrian Residency Permit Application
(www.what-the-fach.com/pdfs/Explanation-of-Austrian-Residence-Permit-Application.pdf)

Opera Studios / Young Artist Programs

Deutsche Oper Berlin
(www.operafoundation.org) ~ The American Berlin Opera Foundation offers an annual stipend to a singer for the Deutsche Oper Berlin. The singer receives advanced training and performs roles on the Opera's productions. For this, this recipient receives $15,000 USD, a round-trip plane ticket, and honorarium for roles performed.

Deutsche Oper am Rhein, Düsseldorf
(www.rheinoper.de) ~ Junges Ensemble Rheinoper

Oper Frankfurt
(www.oper-frankfurt.de) ~ Opernstudio

Staatsoper Hamburg
(www.staatsoper-hamburg.de) ~ Das Internationale Opernstudio der Hamburgischen Staatsoper

Oper Köln
(http://www.buehnenkoeln.de) ~ Opernstudio

Staatsoper Mainz
(www.staatstheater-mainz.de) ~ Junges Ensemble

Bayerische Staatsoper, München
(www.bayerische.staatsoper.de) ~ Das Opernstudio Der Bayerischen Staatsoper

Staatstheater Nürnberg
(www.staatstheater-nuernberg.de) ~ Internationales Opernstudio Nürnberg

Opernhaus Zürich
(www.opernhaus.ch) ~ Internationales Opernstudio IOS

Recommended Reading, Publications and Documents

Deutsches Bühnen Jahrbuch or "*DBJ*"
(www.buehnengenossenschaft.de/dtbuehnenbuch.htm) ~ This book, published annually, is a necessary addition to your library. It contains important information and statistics about every theater in the Germany, Austria, and Switzerland. A directory of agents may also be found at the back of the book. *Note*: You are billed for this book and must pay with a bank transfer. From non-German bank accounts, make payments to the following account number: BIC HASPDEHHXXX, IBAN DE 23 2005 0550 12821274 79 (Account holder name: Bühnenschriften-Vertriebs-GmbH, Sonderkonten "Deutsches Bühnen Jahrbuch"). Send a Euro check to:Bühnenschriften-Vertriebs-GmbH, Postfach 13 02 70, D-20102 Hamburg.. They do not take credit cards.

Handbuch der Oper
(www.amazon.de) ~ By Dr. Rudolf Kloiber (Also known as "The Kloiber"). Along with the *Deutsches Bühnen Jahrbuch*, the *Handbuch der Oper* is an essential addition to your library. It lists *Fächer* and associated roles, as well as synopsis for operas. Before each opera synopsis, they list the roles, their *Fächer*, and whether they are considered small, middle, or leading roles. Alles auf Deutsch.

Guide to Operatic Roles & Arias
(www.amazon.com) ~ By Richard Boldrey. This book is also an excellent resource and

cross-indexing reference for *Fächer*. Unlike the *Handbuch der Oper*, *Guide to Operatic Roles & Arias* lists numerous operetta roles and arias.

Genossenschaft Deutscher Bühnen-Angehöriger or "GBDA"

(www.buehnengenossenschaft.de) ~ The labor union for stage workers in Germany. In addition to the *DBJ* (see above), this site is a useful resource to purchase other documents such as copies of standard theater contracts. They accept no credit or debit cards. To pay for purchases from a foreign bank account, use the banking codes on the previous page under "Handbuch der Oper."

New Theatre Words (*Northern Europe*)

www.theatrewords.com ~ This fantastic book has a comprehensive listing of virtually every theater word (technical and not technical) in twelve different languages. ISBN 91-63005666-6

Transportation Websites

Airline Search Sites

Airline Consolidator

(www.airlineconsolidator.com) ~ Web site selling consolidated airfares originating in the USA and Canada. These friendly folks often have prices cheaper than any of the popular search engines.

Expedia

(www.expedia.com) ~ Popular online travel agent

Kayak

(www.kayak.com) ~ Meta search engine for airline tickets. This site searches virtually all of the online sources for airline tickets and shows you price comparisons. Tickets may originate in North America *and* Europe

Mobissimo

(www.mobissimo.com) ~ Meta search engine for airline tickets. This site searches virtually all of the online sources for airline tickets and shows you price comparisons. Tickets may originate in North America *and* Europe

Orbitz

(www.orbitz.com) ~ Online discount travel site.

Travelocity

(www.travelocity.com) ~ Popular online travel agent

Wegolo

(www.wegolo.com) ~ The leading European search engine for discount airlines

European Airline/Discount Airline Search Sites

Billiger Fliegen

(www.billiger-fliegen.de) ~ German site for inexpensive flights

Billiger Reisen

(www.billiger-reisen.de) ~ German site for inexpensive flights

Flylc

(www.flylc.com) ~ Search engine for European discount airline flights

Opodo

(www.opodo.de) ~ Popular German site for inexpensive flights

Which Budget

(www.whichbudget.com) ~ Web site comparing cheap flights in Europe

Discount European Airlines

Air Berlin

(www.airberlin.de) ~ Serving all of Europe. Numerous connections from Berlin

BMI

(www.flybmi.com) ~ Airline connecting mainland Europe with Great Britain.

Brussels Airlines

(www.brusselsairlines.com) ~ Numerous connections in Germany and Austria, and throughout Europe

DBA

(www.flydba.com) ~ In connection with Air Berlin, DBA offers numerous connections within Germany and to other countries throughout Europe.

Easy Jet

(www.easyjet.com) ~ Offers service throughout Europe. Connections from many German cities to elsewhere in Europe. However, no connections between German cities.

German Wings

(www.germanwings.com) ~ Offers numerous connections between German cities, as well as connections throughout Europe.

Germania Airline

(www.germaniaairline.de) ~ Limited connections throughout Europe and within Germany. Strangely enough, plenty of connections to Moscow.

HLX

(www.hlx.com) ~ Discount service throughout Europe

Jet4you

(www.jet4you.com) ~ Serving France, Brussels, and North Africa (should you land that audition in Algiers)

Ryan Air

(www.ryanair.com) ~ Cheap, *cheap* flights throughout Europe. Airports are often out of the way, *especially* Frankfurt Hahn Airport. Frankfurt Hahn Airport is *not* Frankfurt International Airport. It is closer to Luxembourg than it is to Frankfurt, but cheap as hell. Watch out for extra costs, especially for luggage.

Sky Europe

(www.skyeurope.com) ~ Central European-based airline. Numerous flights from Vienna but no service in Germany. Nice planes, leather seats, good service.

Sterling

(www.sterling.dk) ~ Danish airline serving much of Western and Central Europe

Wizzair

(www.wizzair.com) ~ Airline serving all of Europe. Many routes in Central and Eastern Europe. Planes are putrid shades of purple and pink.

Traditional European Airlines

British Airways

(www.britishairways.com) ~ Very good service. They're British, after all.

Lufthansa

(www.lufthansa.de) ~ *The* German Airline seemingly serving every location. Though not "discount," they often have €99 roundtrip specials worth checking into.

KLM

(www.klm.com) ~ Dutch airline with friendly service. And you will probably travel through my favorite airport in the world, Amsterdam's Schiphol Airport.

Singapore Airlines

(www.singaporeair.com) ~ Arguably the best service in the world

Eurailpasses, Train Travel, Hotels, and Travel/Health Insurance

Rail Europe

(www.raileurope.com) ~ Official site for Eurailpasses. Acquaint yourself with the many different options available.

STA Travel

(www.statravel.com) ~ Excellent site. Reseller for Eurailpasses and German Rail Passes, among others. They also sell reasonably priced travel health insurance.

Deutsche Bahn

(www.bahn.de) ~ Official Site for the often-on time, overpriced German train system.

ÖBB

(www.oebb.at) ~ Official site for the even more mostly-on time, reasonably priced, Austrian train system.

WEB SITES AND DOCUMENTS

SBB

(www.sbb.ch) ~ Official site for Switzerland's Rail System

Mitfahrgelegenheit

(www.mitfahrgelegenheit.de) ~ Shared auto Web site connecting drivers looking for passengers, and vice versa. Often cheaper than a full-priced train ticket.

Hotel Reservation Service

(www.hrs.de) ~ The only service I ever use to book hotels for auditions. If you are going to an audition, also call the KBB to see if they can arrange a room at a hotel they use. They will usually be happy to oblige. The room may also be very close to the theater.

Local Public Transportation Web Sites

Berlin	www.bvg.de	**München**	www.mvv-muenchen.de
Dresden	www.dvbag.de	**Nürnberg**	www.vgn.de
Düsseldorf	www.vrr.de	**Stuttgart**	www.vvs.de
Frankfurt	www.rmv.de	**Vienna**	www.wienerlinien.at
Hamburg	www.hvv.de	**Zürich**	www.vbz.ch
Mannheim	www.vrn.de		

Apartments

Craigslist	www.craigslist.com
Immobilienscout	www.immobilienscout.de
Mitwohnzentrale	www.mitwohnzentrale.de
MWZ	www.mwz.de
Mr Lodge	www.mrlodge.com
Wg-gesucht	www.wg-gesucht.de
Zwischenmiete	www.zwischenmiete.com

Mobile Phone / Handy Providers

	E Plus	**O2**	**Vodafone**
Germany	www.eplus.de	www.o2online.de	www.vodafone.de

Austria	Aldi www.aldi.de	Blau www.blau.de	Netto www.netto.de
	Orange www.orange.at	**Tele Ring** www.telering.at	**Yesss** www.yesss.at
	Drei www.drei.at		

Practice Spaces

The following are practice spaces in a few major cities. I have chosen these cites because so many agent auditions take place and they often have no place for you to warm-up (*einsingen*).

CITY	PRACTICE SPACE	HOURS
Berlin	**Theaterhaus Mitte** www.thbm.de info@thbm.de Koppenplatz 12 Tel +49 (0)30 28 04 19 66 Nearest Transit Stops: U Rosenthaler Platz, U Weinmeister Straße, S Hackescher Markt and S Oranienburger Straße	M-F: 10 AM–10 PM Sat/Sun: 10 AM–6 PM
Düsseldorf	**Steinway Haus Heinersdorff** www.heinersdorff.de info@heinersdorff.de Kronprinzenstraße 97 Tel +49 (0)211 300 6 300	M-F: 10 AM–8 PM Sat: 10 AM–4 PM
München	**Movimento München** www.movimento-muenchen.de info@movimento-muenchen.de Neuhauser Straße 15 Tel +49 (0)89 26 01 82 82 On the pedestrian mall in central München between Marienplatz and Stachus. Entrance in the KULT-Passage across from Michaelskirche.	Hours vary Call for exact hours Daily: 9 AM–11 PM

WEB SITES AND DOCUMENTS

Wien	**Klaviergalerie Wendl & Lung**	M-F:
	www.klaviergalerie.com	9 AM–7 PM
	office@wendl-lung.com	
	Kaiserstr. 10	Sat:
	Tel +43 (0)1 524 15 68	9 AM–5 PM
	Located just two blocks from Vienna's Westbahnhof	
Zürich	**Jecklin Musikhaus**	M-F:
	www.jecklin.ch	9 AM–6:30 PM
	info@jecklin.ch	
	Rämistraße 30/42	Sat:
	Tel +41 (0)44 253 77 77	9 AM–4 PM
	Centrally located in Zürich. Fifteen minute walk from the Hauptbahnhof.	

Audition Websites

NYIOP

(www.nyiop.com) ~ New York International Opera Auditions. Fantastic business organizing auditions for singers with European theaters.

Theater Jobs

(www.theaterjobs.de) ~ Excellent site (in German) for audition information, freelance singing engagements, music theater auditions, pianist and conductor positions, and chorus positions. There is a subscription fee but if you are looking for any of the above positions, it is well worth the fee. Constantly updated with vacancies.

Stage Pool

(www.stagepool.com) ~ Casting site in German and Scandinavian

German Language Schools

Goethe Institut

(www.goethe.de) ~ Offering German language instruction in over eighty countries worldwide. This site is also a useful resource for all things German.

Berlitz

(www.berlitz.com) ~ Well-regarded language school

Middlebury College German Program for Singers

(www.middlebury.edu) ~ Well-regarded German program in America for singers

Rosetta Stone

(www.rosettastone.com) ~ Self-study language courses

Banks and Money Transfer Service

Germany	**Deutsche Bank** www.deutsche-bank.de	**Postbank** www.postbank.de
Austria	**BAWAG** www.bawag.at	**Bank Austria** www.ba-ca.com

XETrade

(www.xetrade.com) ~ The best way to transfer money internationally. Once you get set up (it takes a few days), you pay no transfer fees if you transfer to banks in the U.S. or Canada.

Internet

Skype

(www.skype.com) ~ The world's best internet telephoning and instant messaging program and a perfect way to keep in touch for free with friends and family back home while in Europe.

Jiwire

(www.jiwire.com) ~ Comprehensive worldwide listing of wireless hotspots

Taxes and Finance fun

Bayrische Versorgungskammer

(www.versorgungskammer.de) ~ The retirement fund for German Theater Employees

Bundesministerium der Finanzen Deutschland

(www.bundesfinanzministerium.de) ~ Almost everything you need to know about German Taxes.

Finanzamt

(www.finanzamt.de) ~ German Tax Collectors

Austrian Federal Ministry of Finance

(http://english.bmf.gv.at/taxation/_start.htm) ~ Very informative site in English helpful for explaining the Austrian tax system.

Steuer von A bis Z

(www.what-the-fach.com/pdfs/Germany-Tax-Booklet.pdf) ~ Informative booklet in German about Germany's specific taxes.

Austrian Tax Book 2007

(www.what-the-fach.com/pdfs/Austrian-Tax-Booklet-2007.pdf) ~ Informative booklet in English about paying taxes in Austria. Unfortunately, only for 2007.

Social Services ~ Retirement, Health Insurance, and Kindergeld

German Ministry of Labor and Social Affairs

(www.bmas.bund.de) ~ Everything you want to know (in English) about your social services in Germany

German Social Services Book

(www.what-the-fach.com/pdfs/German-Social-Services-Book.pdf) ~ This fantastic document (in English) explains all of your social benefits in Germany, including retirement and *Kindgergeld*.

Krankenkassentarife

(www.krankenkassentarife.de) ~ One-stop comparison-shopping for all health insurance plans in Germany. Prices vary by company and your geographical location.

Merkblatt Kindergeld

(www.what-the-fach.com/pdfs/Germany-Kindergeld-Booklet.pdf)

Important Changes to Kindergeld

(www.what-the-fach.com/pdfs/Important-Changes-to-Germany-Kindergeld-for-2007.pdf)

Miscellaneous Websites

New Forum for Classical Singers

(www.nfcs.net) ~ Online forum for classical singers. See the "Europe Forum" for information about working in Europe.

Operabase

(www.operabase.com) ~ Comprehensive Web site for worldwide performance schedules, plus theater, agent, and artist information.

OperaCue

(www.operacue.com) ~ This German-based business prepares and translates your publicity materials into German for agents and theaters. Owned and operated by a veteran of German opera, Delia Tedeschi knows what catches the eye of administrators and agents, and works with you to create appealing materials at an affordable price.

LEO English-German Dictionary

(dict.leo.org) ~ Online English-German dictionary

Google Translate

(translate.google.com) ~ Online translation Web site. While not perfect, it is the best free translation site I have yet to find.

Expatica

(www.expatica.com) ~ A useful Web site for ex-patriots living and working in Europe. Good resource for FAQs about life here.

WEB SITES AND DOCUMENTS

How To Germany

(www.howtogermany.com) ~ Web site for ex-patriots living in Germany

Toy Town Germany

(www.toytowngermany.com) ~ Online forum for native English speakers in Germany

RESOURCES

Prescription and Nonprescription Medication

The following list is of common drug names—both generic and brand name—and their equivalent in Germany. Names will vary for Switzerland and Austria, as well. You may find all of these drugs at the pharmacy (*Apotheke*), where the pharmacists are generally helpful, patient, and friendly. Here is my disclaimer: If ever in doubt, always consult a doctor of Pharmacist for advice. I am not a doctor and cannot be responsible (don't even try to sue me) if you you were supposed to take an antibiotic, but were stupid enough to mistake it with a horse tranquilizer.

This list was compiled with the very generous assistance of my future brother-in-law, the very gracious, charming, handsome, Danish, Dr. Christpoher Schäfer. Christpoher is a brilliant doctor, gourmet chef, and history buff. He is also an eligible bachelor (ladies... ?).

Christpher also stresses the importance of consulting a doctor for medication. Also, he wishes that I share the following information: import of medications from the US/overseas is forbidden, and you need a EU confirmation ("pill passport") when you travel with medications. It can be issued by your doctor or your pharmacy. For indepensable drugs you need to get a writtten confirmation from the doctor perscribing them. Do not order drugs or food supplements online from overseas, since the shipments will be confiscated by Customs in Germany. Many food supplements are illegal in Europe since they contain substances which are considered performance enhancing. Finally, there is an other culture in Europe concerning the use of painkillers, anxiety medication, and sedatives. Europeans are more reluctant to admit they use these medications. It is important to mention that one should share this information only with people who can be trusted. There is no difference between Europe and America, however, concerning confidentiality when you address health care professionals.

RESOURCES

American Name	Active Ingredient	German Name	Prescription Needed?
Antibiotics			
ZMax, Zithromax	Azithromycin	Azithromycin, Azibact, AZI-TEVA, Azithrobeta, Ultreon, Zithromax	YES
	Erythromycin	Erythromycin, Ery-500-1A Pharma, Infectomycin, EryHEXAL, Erythro-CT, Sanasepton, Paediathrocin	YES
Amoxil, Polymox, Trimox, Wymox	Amoxicillin	Amoxicillin, Amoxi-Lich, Amoxi-CT, Amoxi-Sandoz, Amoxipen, Amoxi-Tablinen, Amoxi-saar, Amoxi-Wolff, INFECTOMOX, Amoxibeta, AmoxiHEXAL, AmoxiHefa, Jutamox, Amoxypen <u>Be aware:</u> There are several other products combining amoxicillin with clavulanic acid and fluconazcole	YES
Antihistamines			
Benadryl	Diphenhydramine	Diphenhydramin, Dormutil, Halbmond-Tabl., Hevert-Dorm, nervo OPT, Sediat, Sedopretten, Sleepia, Vivinox, Emesan, Dormocaps, Dolestan, Dormutil, Sediat, Hermodorm, Dorm	NO

American Name	Active Ingredient	German Name	Prescription Needed?
Claritan	Loratadine	Loratadin, !LORA BASICS, Lisino, Livotab, Lobeta, Lora-Lich, LORA-PUREN, Loraclar, Loraderm, Loragalen, Loragamma, Loralerg, Lorano, Loratadura, Vividrin, Lora-ADGC	NO
Zyrtec	Cetirizine	Cetirizin, Cetalerg, Ceterifug, Ceti TAD, Cetiderm, cetidura, cetil, CetiLich, Cetirigamma, Cetirlan, Reactine, Zetir, Zyrtec, Reactine	NO
Tavist	Clemastine	Tavegil	NO
Clarinex	Desloratadine	Aerius	YES
Xyzal	Levocetirizine	Xusal, Xyzal	YES
Allegra	Fexofenadine	Fexofenadin, Telfast	YES

Cold Medication

American Name	Active Ingredient	German Name	Prescription Needed?
Sudafed	Pseudoephedrine	Reactine Note: It is a mix with ceterizine	NO
4 Way Fast-Acting Nasal Spray	Naphazoline	Rhinex	NO
Afrin Nasal Spray	Oxymetazoline/ Xymetazolin	Em-eukal, Nasivin, Wick Sinex, Otriven, Nasenspray K, Nasenspray E, Nasenspray AL, Endrine, Olynth, Imidin, Nasic, Snup Nasenspray, Nasenspray Sandoz	NO
Mucinex	Guaifenesin	Fagusan, Wick Husten Löser, Lontussin duplex	NO

RESOURCES

GERD (Acid Reflux)/Heartburn

American Name	Active Ingredient	German Name	Prescription Needed?
Axid	Nizatidine	Not registered.	
Pepcid	Famotidine	Famotidin, FADUL, Famo, Famobeta, Famonerton, PEPDUL Pepcid, Pepciddual	YES / NO
Tagamet	Cimetidine	Cimetidin, Azucimet, Cime, CIME-PUREN, Cimebeta, Cimehexal, CimLich, duraH2, Gastroprotect, Sigacimet, , H2-blokker-ratiopharm	YES
Zantac	Ranitidine	Ranitidin, !RANITIDIN BASICS, Azuranit, Junizac, Phamoranit, Ramitab, Ran Lich, Rani, Rani-nerton, RANI-PUREN, Raniberl, Ranibloc, Ranicux, Ranidura, Ranimerck, Raniprotect, Ranitic, Ranitidoc, Sostril, Zantic	YES
Prilosec	Omeprazole	Omeprazol, Antra, Buscogast, Gastracid, OME-nerton, OME-PUREN, Omebeta, Omegamma, OmeLich, Omelind, OMEP, Ome-Q, Omeloxan, OmeHennig, Ulcozol, Ulnor, Omedoc	YES
Prevacid	Lansoprazole	Lansoprazol, Agopton, Lanzor, Lansogamme, Lanso TAD, Lansox, Lanso-Q	YES
Aciphex	Rabeprazole	Pariet	YES
Protonix	Pantoprazole	Pantoprazol, Pantozol, Rifun, Pantopra-Q, Pantorc, Zurcal, Gastrozol	YES

American Name	Active Ingredient	German Name	Prescription Needed?
Pain Medication			
Motrin, Advil, Nuprin	Ibuprofen	Ibuprofen, Contraneural, Dolgit, DOLO-PUREN, Esprenit, Ibu, Ibu Eu Rho, Ibu KD, Ibu-acis, ibu-Attritin, Ibu-ratiopharm, Ibubeta, Ibuhexal, Ibumerck, Ibuphlogont, ibuprof, ibuTAD, Imbun, Jenaprofen, Opturem, Parsal, Schmerz-Dolgit, Spalt, Liqua, Tabalon, Eudorlin, Aktren, Dolormin, Nurofen, Ibubeta, Optalidon Ibu, IBU-ratiopharm Lysinat, Tispol IBU-DD, Pfeil Zahnschmerz-Tabletten, Dismenol N, Ibudolor, Migränin	YES/No (depends on strength and size of pack)
Tylenol	Acetaminophen In Europe: Paracetamol	Paracetamol, ben-u-ron, Captin, Contac, Enelfa, Fensum, Grippostad, Mono Praecimed, Paracetamol, PCM-Hemopharm, Sinpro, Togal, Thomapyrin*, Saridon*, DayMed*, , Vivimed*, Rubiemol, Prapaed, Paedialgon, Doregrippin*, Neuranidal N*, ParaCetaMol, Temagin*, Optalidon* *These products contain other substances like codeine, ephedrine, acetylic salicylic acid	NO
Aleve	Naproxen	Naproxen, Proxen, Dolormin, Aleve, Prodolor	YES

RESOURCES

American Name	Active Ingredient	German Name	Prescription Needed?
Other fun drugs			
Ciala	Tadalafil	Cialis, Adcirca	
Norvasc	Amlodipine Besylate	Amlodipin, Norvasc	
OxyContin	Oxycodone	Oxygesic, Oxycodon, TARGIN	YES
Paxil	Paroxetine	Paroxetin, Euplix, Oxet, Paroxat, ParoLich, Paroxalon, paroxedura, Seroxat, Tagonis	YES
Percocet	Oxycodone with Paracetamol/ Acetaminophen	Not registered	
Meticorten, Sterapred, Sterapred DS	Prednisone	Prednison, Lodotra, Decortin, Predni Tablinen	YES
Prozac	Fluoxetine	Fluoxetin, Fluctin, Fluneurin, Fluox, FLUOX-PUREN, FluoxeLich, Fluoxemerck, Fluoxgamma, Fluxet, Fysionorm, Fluoxe-Q	YES
Seroquel	Quetiapine	Seroquel	YES
TOPAMAX	Topiramate	Topiramat	YES
Ultram, Ultram ER	Tramadol	Tramadol, TRAMADOL BASICS, Amadol, Jutadol, Tial, TRADOL-PUREN, Trama, Trama-Dorsch, Tramabeta, Tramadoc, Tramadolor, Tramadura, Tramagetic, Tramagit, Tramal, Tramundin	YES
Viagra	Sildenafil	Viagra, Revatio	YES
Vicodin	Acetaminophen and Hydrocodone		
Wellbutrin	Bupropion	Zyban	YES

American Name	Active Ingredient	German Name	Prescription Needed?
Xanax	Alprazolam	Alprazolam, Cassadan, Tafil, Xanax	YES
Zoloft	Sertraline	Sertalin, Gladem, Zoloft, Sertra-ISIS, Sertra-Q	YES
Lexapro	Escitalopram	Cipralex	YES

National Holidays for 2011

The following are holidays for Germany, Austria, and Switzerland. Please note that the holidays listed are only those observed nation-wide, with a few exceptions. Although December 24th and 31st are not officially holidays, stores close early. If you can avoid traveling on or around these days, it is a wise decision.

NATIONAL HOLIDAYS

Holiday	Date	Country/Countries
New Year's Day/*Neujahrstag*	January 1 annually	Germany, Austria, Switzerland
Epiphany/*Heiligen Drei Könige*	January 6 annually	Germany (Bayern, Baden-Württemberg, Saxon Anhalt)
Good Friday/*Karfreitag*	April 22, 2011	Germany, Austria (partial closing), Switzerland
Easter Monday/*Ostermontag*	April 25, 2011	Germany, Austria, Switzerland
May Day/*Tag der Arbeit*	May 1 annually	Germany, Austria, Switzerland
Ascension Thursday/*Christi Himmelfahrt*	June 2, 2011	Germany, Austria, Switzerland
Pentecost Monday/*Pfingstmontag*	May 24, 2010, and June 13, 2011	Germany, Austria, Switzerland

NATIONAL HOLIDAYS (Continued)

Holiday	Date	Country/Countries
Corpus Christi/*Fronleichnam*	June 3, 2010, and June 23, 2011	Austria
National Day/*Nationalfeiertag*	August 1 annually	Switzerland
Assumption Day/*Maria Himmelfahrt*	August 15 annually	Austria, Germany (only Bayern and Saarland)
German Unification Day/*Tag der Deutschen Einheit*	October 3 annually	Germany
National Day/*Nationalfeiertag Österreich*	October 26 annually	Austria
Reformation Day/*Reformationstag*	October 31 annually	Germany (east only)
All Saints Day/*Allerheiligen*	November 1 annually	Germany (partial closing), Austria
Immaculate Conception/*Mariä Empfängnis*	December 8 annually	Austria
Christmas Day/*Erster Weinachtstag*	December 25 annually	Germany, Austria, Switzerland
Boxing Day/*Zweiter Weinachtstag*	December 26 annually	Germany, Austria, Switzerland

Sample Résumé *(Jenny Smith is a figment of my imagination)*

JENNY SMITH
Lyrischer Koloratursopran

(Photo of your head shot here)

Nationalität: Amerikanerin

Adresse	**Ständige Adresse**
Hauptstr. 22	890 Broadway, Apt. 5
D-04040 München	New York, NY 10024 U.S.A.
Handy: +49 (0)160 759 54389	Handy: +001 646 555 1212
E-mail: jennysmith@jahoo.com	

OPERNPARTIEN

Adina	*L'elisir d'Amore*	Vancouver Opera	2010
Lucia	*Lucia di Lammermoor*	Portland Opera	2009
Norina	*Don Pasquale*	Orlando Opera	2007
Manon	*Manon*	Idaho Opera	2006
Olympia	*Les Contes d'Hoffmann*	Florida Grand Opera (Opernstudio)	2006
Zerbinetta	*Ariadne auf Naxos*	Juilliard Opera Center	2005
Barbarina	*Le nozze di Figaro*	Jonestown Opera	2004
Giannetta	*L'elisir d'Amore*	Bob Jones University	2003
Zerlina	*Don Giovanni*	Bob Jones University	2002

WETTBEWERBE

1. Preis	Roswell Annual Vocal Competition	2006

Regisseure	Jim Bob, Sarah Palin, Jimmy Joe Smith	
Dirigenten	Rick Smith, John Jones, Bristol Palin	
Korrepetitoren	Suzie Smith, James Jones, Glenn Beck	
Ausbildung	Juilliard Opera Center ~ Abschluss *Performance Certificate*	2005
	Bob Jones University ~ Bachelor Abschluss in *Vocal Performance*	2003

Form Letters

Helmut Mustermann
123 Smith Street
New York City, NY 10001

Frau Dr. Helga Schmidt
Theateragentur Helga Schmidt
Hauptstr. 222
D-30983 Berlin

01 September 2010

Sehr geehrte Frau Dr. Schmidt,
ich bin *Kavalierbariton* und würde gerne für Sie vorsingen. Ich bin ab dem 2. Oktober 2010 in Deutschland und werde bis zum 13. Februar 2011 bleiben. Anbei schicke ich Ihnen meine Unterlagen sowie eine CD. Ich freue mich, von Ihnen zu hören.

Mit freundlichen Grüßen,
Helmut Mustermann

Resources

Helmut Mustermann
123 Smith Street
New York City, NY 10001

Frau Dr. Helga Schmidt
Theateragentur Helga Schmidt
Hauptstr. 222
D-30983 Berlin

01 September 2010

Dear Dr. Schmidt,

I am a Kavalierbariton and would like to audition for you. I will be in Germany starting October 2, 2010, and will stay until February 13, 2011. Enclosed I am sending you my publicity materials as well as a CD. I look forward to hearing from you.

Sincerely,
Helmut Mustermann

Form E-Mails

Sehr geehrte Frau Dr. Schmidt,

ich bin *Kavalierbariton* und habe Ihnen vor drei Wochen meine Unterlagen geschickt. Ich wollte Ihnen mitteilen, dass ich seit gestern in Deutschland bin. Sie können mich jederzeit unter folgender Handynummer erreichen: 0175 555 55 555.

Mit freundlichen Grüßen,
Helmut Mustermann

Dear Dr. Schmidt,

I am a Kavalierbariton and sent you my publicity materials a few weeks ago. I am writing to let you know that I arrived in Germany yesterday. You may now reach me on the following mobile number: 0175 555 55 555.

Sincerely,
Helmut Mustermann

Sehr geehrte Frau Dr. Schmidt,

vielen Dank für Ihre E-Mail. Gerne singe ich am 23. Oktober für Sie vor und möchte den Termin hiermit bestätigen.

Mit freundlichen Grüßen,

Stefan Raab

Dear Dr. Schmidt,

Thank you very much for your e-mail. I am able to audition for you on October 23rd, and I would like to confirm the appointment.

Sincerely,

Stefan Raab

Sehr geehrte Frau Dr. Schmidt,

vielen Dank für Ihre E-Mail und Ihre Einladung zum Vorsingen. Leider kann ich diesen Termin nicht wahrnehmen. Ich würde jedoch gerne zu einem Ihrer nächsten Vorsingtermine kommen. Ich freue mich, von Ihnen zu hören.

Mit freundlichen Grüßen,

Stefan Raab

Dear Dr. Schmidt,

Thank you very much for your E-mail and invitation to audition. Unfortunately, I am unable to sing for you on that particular day. If possible, I would happily come to your next day of auditions. I look forward to hearing from you.

Sincerely,

Stefan Raab

ZAV Audition Invitation E-Mail

Sehr geehrter Herr Raab,

für ein Vorsingen in der ZAV-Agentur Hamburg, Kreuzweg 7, 20099 Hamburg schlagen wir Ihnen folgende Termine vor:

    15.02.2011 - 15:30 Uhr

    12.03.2011 - 14:30 Uhr

Bitte teilen Sie uns möglichst bald mit, für welchen Termin Sie sich entschieden haben (Tel.: 010 - 28 11 15 17) oder per Mail:

angela.merkel@arbeitsagentur.de. Bitte bereiten Sie 5-6 Opern-/Operettenarien vor, darunter mindestens 1 Arie in deutscher Sprache. Leider können wir für dieses informative Vorsingen keine Reisekosten erstatten. Kosten für den Korrepetitor entstehen Ihnen nicht. Für ein Engagement an einem deutschsprachigem Theater sind Grundkenntnisse der deutsche Sprache unerlässlich.

Mit freundlichen Grüßen
Frau Angela Merkel

Dear Mr Raab,

We propose the following dates for an audition with ZAV-Agentur Hamburg, Kreuzweg 7, 20099 Hamburg:

    02.15.2011 – 3:30 PM

    03.12.2011 – 2:30 PM

Please let us know as soon as possible, for which day you have decided (Tel: 010 – 28 11 15 17) or by E-mail:

angela.merkel@arbeitsagentur.de.

Please have 5-6 opera and/or operetta arias ready, with at least one selection in German. Unfortunately, for such an informative audition we cannot reimburse your travel expenses. However, you will incur no cost for a pianist. For an engagement in a German speaking theater, it is essential to have knowledge of the German language.

Sincerely,
Frau Angela Merkel

Opera and Concert Agents

Agents in Germany

Konzert-Direktion Hans Adler
Auguste-Viktoria-Str. 64
http://www.musikadler.de
E-mail: info@musikadler.de
Phone: +49 30 89 59 92-0
Fax: +49 30 82 63 520

Agentur Klein *(Antonia Klein)*
Hanselmannstr. 11
D-80809 München
http://www.agenturklein.de
E-mail: aklein@agenturklein.de
Phone: +49 89 45 57 99 31
Fax: +49 89 45 57 99 42

Künstleragentur Seifert *(Elisabeth Seifert, Sebastian Seifert)*
Postfach 38 02 57
D-14112 Berlin
http://www.agentur-seifert.de
E-mail: mail@agentur-seifert.de
Phone: +49 30 83 19 03 86
Fax: +49 30 83 19 03 88

Künstleragentur Wrage *(Stefan Wrage)*
Rothenbaumchaussee 1
D-20148 Hamburg
http://www.agentur-wrage.de
E-mail: info@agentur-wrage.de
Phone: +49 40 41 86 56
Fax: +49 40 410 46 68

Alexander Vassiliev Künstlervermittlung
Am Kirchplatz 4
D-79241 Ihringen
E-mail: agentur@vassiliev.eu
Phone: +49 7668 908 398
Fax: +49 7668 908 398

Allegro Artist Management
c/o Boris Orlob management
Jägerstrasse 70
D-10117 Berlin
http://www.allegroartist.com
E-mail: allegro@allegroartist.com
Phone: +49 30 20450839

Agence Massis Opéra *(René Massis)*
Martin-Luther-Strasse 63
D-60389 Frankfurt
http://www.amo-massis.com
E-mail: amo@amo-massis.com
Phone: +49 (0)69 48 00 56 78
Fax: +49(0)69 43 05 86 71

ArnoldMusic Management & Consulting *(R. Arnold)*
Harweg 13
47239 Duisburg
http://www.arnold-music.de
E-mail: info@arnold-music.de
Phone: +49 (2151) 94 03 28
Fax: +49 (2151) 41 97 11

Artista International Künstlermanagement *(Franziska Hunke)*
Kyffhäuserstraße 3
D-10781 Berlin
http://www.artistainternational.com
E-mail: mail@artistainternational.com

Künstleragentur Augstein & Hahn *(Helge Rudolf Augstein, Stefan Hahn)*
Tal 28
D-80331 München
http://www.augstein.info
E-mail: mail@augstein.info
Phone: +49 89 260 24 333
Fax: +49 89 260 24 344

Konzertagentur Marianne Böttger *(Marianne Böttger)*
Dahlmannstr. 9
D-10629 Berlin
http://www.boettger-berlin.de
E-mail: agency@boettger-berlin.de
Phone: +49 30 324 85 27
Fax: +49 30 323 11 93

Theateragentur Belcanto
PF 810171
D-81901München
http://www.theateragentur-belcanto.de
E-mail: info@theateragentur-belcanto.de
Phone: +49 89 125 910 45
Fax: +49 89 125 910 45

BelcantoArtist *(Saverio Suarez-Ribaudo)*
Isartalstraße 26
D-80469 München
http://www.belcantoartist.de
E-mail: belcantoartist@yahoo.de
Phone: +49 (89) 78 07 16 52
Fax: +49 (89) 78 07 16 51

Lore Blümel Opern- und Konzertagentur
Heiglhofstrasse 49
D-81377 München
http://www.lore-bluemel.de
E-mail: bluemel@bayern-mail.de
Phone: +49 89 859 38 64
Fax: +49 89 859 37 59

Bühnen- und Konzertagentur Marianne Böttger
Dahlmannstrasse 9
D-10629 Berlin
http://www.boettger-berlin.de
E-mail: agency@boettger-berlin.de
Phone: +49 30 324 85 27
Fax: +49 30 323 11 93

Berliner Opern- und Konzertagentur *(B. Jennifer Bredtmeyer)*
Barbarossastr. 5
D-10781 Berlin
http://www.bokab.de/
E-mail: Bredtmeyer@bokab.de
Phone: +49 30 21 969 181
Fax: +49 30 21 697 70

Boris Orlob Management
Jägerstrasse 70
D-10117 Berlin
http://www.orlob.net
E-mail: info@orlob.net
Phone: +49 30 20 45 08 39
Fax: +49 30 20 45 08 49

Resources

Konzertbüro Andreas Braun
Sülzgürtel 86
D-50937 Köln
http://www.konzertbuero-braun.de
E-mail: braun@konzertbuero-braun.de
Phone: +49 221 9 420 430
Fax: +49 221 9 420 431 9

Hannagret Bueker Agentur für Musiktheater und Konzert
Fuhsestrasse 2
D-30419 Hannover
http://www.buekervoice.de
E-mail: mail@buekervoice.de
Phone: +49 511-271 69 10
Fax: +49 511-271 78 73

CADEMI Artists Management *(Carmen de Miguel)*
Neugrabenweg 22A
D-66123 Saarbrücken
http://www.cademi.eu
E-mail: demiguelcarmen@aol.com
Phone: +49 68 19 58 04 88

CAMI - Columbia Artists Management GmbH
Albrechtstr. 18
D-10117 Berlin
http://www.cami.com
E-mail: info@cami.com
Phone: +49 30 20 64 80 78
Fax: +49 30 20 45 34 80

CICADA. con Agentur & Management *(Volker Piefke)*
Gubener Straße 3b
D-10243 Berlin
http://www.cicada-con.de
E-mail: info@cicada-con.de
Phone: +49-(0)30-29 00 1335
Fax: +49-(0)30-29 00 5897

CMC - Cecilia Music Concept GmbH *(Franz-Georg Stähling)*
Brauweilerweg 183
D-50933 Köln
http://www.cecilia-cmc.de
E-mail: staehling@cecilia-cmc.de
Phone: +49 221 800 00 70
Fax: +49 221 800 00 71

CVM Künstler Management *(Wolfgang Gruber)*
Herrenwiesstrasse 7C
D-82031 Grünwald
E-mail: wg@semic.de
Phone: +49 179 205 00 91

Konzertdirektion Fritz Dietrich GmbH
Sigmund-Freud-Str 1
D-60435 Frankfurt am Main
http://www.konzertdirektion-dietrich.de
E-mail: info@konzertdirektion-dietrich.de
Phone: +49 69-54 45 04
Fax: +49 69-54 84 107

Dietrich Eberhard Gross Künstleragentur *(Dietrich Gross)*
Eschenweg 19
D-61440 Oberursel
http://www.grossagentur.de
E-mail: d.e.gross@grossagentur.de
Phone: +49 6172 934144
Fax: +49 6172 934145

Elke Wiemer Künstleragentur

Exerzierstraße 9
D-13357 Berlin
http://www.agentur-wiemer.de
E-mail: mail@agentur-wiemer.de
Phone: +49 30 46 60 78 03
Fax: +49 30 46 60 78 17

Konzertagentur Erika Esslinger

Spittlerstrasse 6
D-70190 Stuttgart
http://www.konzertagentur.de
E-mail: esslinger@konzertagentur.de
Phone: +49 711-344-0
Fax: +49 711-344-11

Agentur Garbrecht *(Evelin Garbrecht)*

Fretzdorfer Weg 6
D-14165 Berlin
http://www.agentur-garbrecht.de
E-mail: egarbrecht@web.de
Fax: +49 30 80 49 58 27

Karl-Erich Haase - Theateragentur e. K. *(Ingrid Raffeiner)*

Nymphenburger Straße 154
D-80634 München
E-mail: info@theateragentur-k-e-haase.de
Phone: +49 89 33 31 62
Fax: +49 89 34 26 74

Artists Management Hartmut Haase

Aalgrund 8
D-31275 Lehrte
http://www.artists-haase.de
E-mail: artists@t-online.de
Phone: +49 5175 95 32 32
Fax: +49 5175 95 32 33

Theateragentur Heidi Schäfer *(Heidi Schaefer)*

Glauburgstraße 83
D-60318 Frankfurt am Main
http://www.santuzza.de
E-mail: hs@santuzza.de
Phone: +49 69 28 33 47

Herwald Artists Management *(Thomas Herwald, Matthias Widmaier)*

Strasse d. Roten Kreuzes 64
D-76228 Karlsruhe
http://www.herwald-artists.com/
E-mail: info@herwald-artists.com
Phone: +49 721 947 39 39
Fax: +49 721 947 39 37

H&H Kuenstleragentur Leipzig-Muenchen *(Wolfgang Hoyer)*

Brandvorwerkstrasse 78
D-04275 Leipzig
http://www.hh-kuenstleragentur.de
E-mail: hoyer@hh-kuenstleragentur.de
Phone: +49 341 301 83 18
Fax: +49 341 391 86 11

H&H Kuenstleragentur Leipzig-Muenchen *(Gerhard Huettl)*

PF 90 05 62
D-81505 Muenchen
http://www.hh-kuenstleragentur.de
E-mail: huettl@hh-kuenstleragentur.de
Phone: +49 89 69 70 89 99
Fax: +49 89 69 73 76 37

Resources

Hilbert Artists Management
Maximilianstrasse 22
D-80539 München
http://www.hilbert.de
E-mail: agentur@hilbert.de
Phone: +49 89 290 747-0
Fax: +49 89 290 747-90

Konzertdirektion Hoertnagel Berlin GmbH
Oranienburger Straße 50 D
D-10117 Berlin
http://www.hoertnagel.com
E-mail: agentur@hoertnagel.com
Phone: +49 30 30 88 770
Fax: +49 30 30 88 77 33

Opernagentur Inge Tennigkeit
Humboldtstr. 60
D-40237 Düsseldorf
http://www.tennigkeit-ag.de
E-mail: opera@tennigkeit-ag.de
Phone: +49 211 516 00 60

Karsten Witt Musik Management Gmbh
Leuschnerdamm 13
D-10999 Berlin
http://www.karstenwitt.com
E-mail: info@karstenwitt.com
Phone: +49-30-616 921 925
Fax: +49-30-616 921 101

klartekst: Anne-Kathrin Seibel *(Anne-Kathrin Seibel)*
Berlin
http://www.klartekst.eu
E-mail: aks@klartekst.eu

Michael Kocyan Artists Management
Alt-Moabit 104a
D-10559 Berlin
http://www.kocyan.de
E-mail: artists@kocyan.de
Phone: +49 30 31 00 49 40
Fax: +49 30 31 00 49 84

Konzertdirektion Schmid *(Hans Ulrich Schmid, Cornelia Schmid)*
Königstrasse 36
D-30175 Hanover
http://www.kdschmid.de
E-mail: mail@kdschmid.de
Phone: +49 511 366 07 60
Fax: +49 511 366 07 34

Natalie K. Kreft, Artists Service & Promotion
Pellenzstraße 8
D-50823 Köln
http://www.kreftartists.de
E-mail: kreftartists@web.de
Phone: +49 221 55 00 246
Fax: + 49 221 55 00 247

KünstlerSekretariat am Gasteig
Rosenheimer Str. 52
D-81669 München
http://www.ks-gasteig.de
E-mail: team@ks-gasteig.de
Phone: +49 89 4448879-0
Fax: +49 89 4489522

WHAT THE FACH?!

Theateragentur Kühnly *(Michael Kühnly)*
Wörthstr. 31
CITY?
http://Agentur-Kuehnly.de
E-mail: Kuehnly@aol.com
Phone: +49 711 780 27 64
Fax: +49 711 780 44 03

KulturKontor Regine Dierse *(Regine Dierse)*
Kollwitzring 9
D-22115 Hamburg
http://kulturkontor.de
E-mail: mail@kulturkontor.de
Phone: +49 40 35 71 93 80
Fax: +49 40 35 71 93 82

Leuwer Artists Management *(Barbara Leuwer)*
Adam-Berg-Str. 6
D-81735 München
http://www.leuwerartists.com
E-mail: mail@leuwerartists.com
Phone: +49 89 6809 4452

Lore-M. Schulz International Artists Management
Zittelstr. 8
CITY???
http://www.lore-m-schulz.com
E-mail: artists@lore-m-schulz.com
Phone: +49 89 308 70 92
Fax: +49 89 308 70 93

Luetje Artist Management *(Martin Gregor Lütje, Kristin Rennack)*
Kalckreuthstraße 16
D-10777 Berlin
http://www.luetjeartist.com
E-mail: gregor@luetjeartist.com
Phone: +49 30 544 93 407
Fax: +49 30 544 93 408

Konzertdirektion Martin Müller *(Martin Müller)*
Uhrs Knäppken 8
D-59320 Ennigerloh-Ostenfelde
http://www.kdmueller.de
E-mail: info@kdmueller.de
Phone: +49 2524 26 34 80
Fax: +49 2524 26 34 81

Künstleragentur Matthias Gentzen *(Matthias Gentzen)*
Klenzestrasse 44
D-80469 München
http://www.matthias-gentzen.com
E-mail: gentzen@aol.com
Phone: +49 89 57 08 66 77
Fax: +49 89 57 08 66 75

PR-Managemant artist communication
Heinrich-Zille-Str. 19
D-15711 Zeesen (bei Berlin)
http://www.mennicken-pr.com
E-mail: info@mennicken-pr.com
Phone: +49 3375 524 98 77
Fax: +49 3375 524 98 79

noName artists management *(Jost Miehlbradt)*
Klaus-Groth-Str. 38
D-20535 Hamburg
E-mail: nn.artists.management@gmx.de
Phone: +49 40 25 49 87 01

Resources

Personal Artists Management David Molnár
Palais Kolle Belle
Kollwitzstrasse 26
D-10405 Berlin
E-mail: david-molnar@t-online.de
Phone: +49 30 4171 78 08
Fax: +49 30 41 71 78 09

Musica Management GmbH
Neubauerstr. 4
D-65193 Wiesbaden
E-mail: marcus.carl@opernagent.de
Phone: +49 611 23 868 11
Fax: +49 611 23 868 10

MusiKado GmbH
Franz-Marc-Str. 4
D-50999 Köln
http://www.musikado.com
E-mail: musikado@musikado.com
Phone: +49 221 357 94 67
Fax: +49 221 357 94 68

Opera in viaggio, Kultur & Management *(Ulrich Hentze)*
Charlottenstraße 16
D-30449 Hannover
http://www.kmuh.de
E-mail: kulturkonzert@web.de
Phone: +49 511 123 66 55
Fax: +49 511 123 66 14

Opera-Connection Alste & Mödersheim
(Erkki Alste, Guido Mödersheim, Stephan Reineke)
Leibnizstrasse 94
D-10625 Berlin
http://opera-connection.com
E-mail: info@opera-connection.com
Phone: +49 30 31 99 66 88
Fax: +49 30 31 80 97 39

OPERN-AGENTUR Kursidem & Tschaidse & Herzl
(Manuela Kursidem, Elene Tschaidse, Tamara Herzl)
Tal 15
D-80331 München
http://www.opern-agentur.com
E-mail: kursidem@opern-agentur.com
Phone: +49 89 291 61 661/2
Fax: +49 89 291 61 667

Orfeo Artist Management *(Daniela Spering)*
Mönchsgüterweg 4
D-50999 Köln
http://www.orfeo-artist-management.de
E-mail: info@orfeo-artist-management.de
Phone: +49 2236 38 13 40
Fax: +49 2236 38 19 96

Theateragentur Luisa Petrov
Glauburgstr. 95
D-60318 Frankfurt a.M.
E-mail: LuisaPetrov@web.de
Phone: +49 69 597 03 77
Fax: +49 69 597 48 08

PR2classic
Kreuznacher Str. 63
D-50968 Koeln
http://www.pr2classic.de
E-mail: office@pr2classic.de
Phone: +49 221 38 10 63
Fax: +49 221 38 39 55

Theateragentur Bernhard Preuss
Georgstraße 38
D-30159 Hannover
E-mail: agentur-preuss@gmx.de
Phone: +49 511 470 77 12
Fax: +49 511 898 17 32

Prima Fila Artists *(Federico Tondelli)*
Postfach 950145
D-81517 München
http://www.primafila-artists.com/
E-mail: info@primafila-artists.com
Phone: +49 160 95 04 12 15

Opern- und Konzertagentur Therese Renick
Wenkerstr. 7
D-40470 Düsseldorf
http://www.opernagentur-renick.de
E-mail: t.renick@opernagentur-renick.de
Phone: +49 211 15 77 57 72
Fax: +49 211 66 96 72 81

Gudrun Rohrbach Personal Artist Mgt
Sierichstrasse 99
D-22299 Hamburg
E-mail: grohrbach@arcor.de
Phone: +49 40 48 81 47
Fax: +49 40 46 09 53 05

Agentur Sigrid Rostock
Eugen-Schönhaar-Straße 1
D-10407 Berlin
http://www.agentur-sigrid-rostock.de/
E-mail: sigridrostock@web.de
Phone: +49-30-4257514
Fax: +49-30-4239136

Agentur Salinas Musik GmbH *(Mireya Salinas)*
Laehr'scher Jagdweg 2
D-14167 Berlin
http://www.salinasmusik.com
E-mail: office@salinasmusik.de
Phone: +49 30 4472 4170
Fax: +49 30 4472 4171

Katrin Schirrmeister
Münchner Philharmoniker
Kellerstr. 4
D-81667 München
E-mail: info@katrin-schirrmeister.de

Stefan Schmerbeck Artist Management
Knöbelstr. 10b
D-80538 München
http:// www.stefanschmerbeck.de
E-mail: stefan@stefanschmerbeck.de
Phone: +49 89 21 32 99 94
Fax: +49 89 21 02 47 27

Silvana Sintow-Behrens
Schleibingerstrasse 8
D-81669 Muenchen
http://www.sintow-behrens.com
E-mail: office@sintow-behrens.com
Phone: +49-89-44 21 89 00
Fax: +49-89-44 21 89 03

Theateragentur Heidi Steinhaus
Herzogparkstr. 3
D-81679 München
http://www.heidi-steinhaus.de
E-mail: Steinhaus@heidi-steinhaus.de
Phone: +49 89 93 93 01 10
Fax: +49 89 93 93 01 11

artesystem GmbH *(Thomas Voigt)*
Kurfuerstendamm 157
D-10709 Berlin
http://www.artesystem.com
E-mail: voigt@artesystem.com
Phone: +49 30 3490 21-99
Fax: +49 30 3490 21-45

Theateragentur Neill Thornborrow *(Neill Thornborrow)*
Drakestr. 2
D-40545 Düsseldorf
http://www.thornborrow-agentur.de
E-mail: thornborrow.agent@t-online.de
Phone: +49 211 57 80 51
Fax: +49 211 55 34 98

Künstleragentur Tobias Kade
Ammonstraße 72
D-01067 Dresden
http://www.kuenstleragentur-kade.de
E-mail: tobias-kade@gmx.de
Phone: +49 351 / 490 67 94
Fax: +49 351 / 490 67 93

Konzertdirektion Tobischek *(Dr. Herbert Tobischek)*
Zimmermannstraße 59
D-45239 Essen
http://www.tobconcert.de
E-mail: tobischek@arcor.de
Phone: +49 201 840 51 75
Fax: +49 201 840 51 76

Künstleragentur von Sohl
Mühlweg 34
D-06114 Halle (Saale)
http://www.vonsohl.de
E-mail: office@vonsohl.de
Phone: +49 345 68589960
Fax: +49 345 68589961

Theateragentur Winkler *(Astrid Winkler)*
Grillparzerstr. 46
D-81675 München
http://www.agentur-winkler.com
E-mail: astrid.winkler@agentur-winkler.com
Phone: +49 89 470 58 57
Fax: +49 89 470 71 23

XENIA EVANGELISTA communications *(Xenia Evangelista)*
Merzbacherstraße 32
D-80637 München
http://www.xeniaevangelista.com
E-mail: welcome@xeniaevangelista.com
Phone: +49 89 120 38 28 5

TURNUS Konzert-und Theater-Agentur Zagovec *(Rainer Zagovec)*
Rathaus Strasse 42 http://www.zagovec-artists.de
D-65428 Rüsselsheim E-mail: zagovec.konzert@t-online.de
  Phone: +49 6142 316 81
  Fax: +49 6142 30 11 24

Agents in Austria

Artists Management Vienna *(Bernd Schmickl)*
Rainergasse 35 http://www.artistsmanagementvienna.net
A-1050 Wien E-mail: bschmickl@hotmail.com
  Phone: +43 1 581 62 71
  Fax: +43 1 581 62 71

AVM Artist Vocal Management *(Heinz Felsner, Michael Gangl)*
Eduard Kleingasse 19 http://www.a-v-m.at
A-1130 Wien E-mail: office@a-v-m.at
  Phone: +43 676 421 35 30

Baron & Weingartner International Artists Management
Bösendorferstrasse 4 / 12 http://www.baronartists.com
A-1010 Vienna E-mail: office@baronartists.com
  Phone: +43 1 489 61 54
  Fax: +43 1 489 61 54-44

CA Klug Artists & Management *(Clemens Anton Klug)*
Conrad-von-Hötzendorf- http://www.klug-artists.com/
Strasse 24 E-mail: office@klug-artists.com
A-8010 Graz

Claudia Dickie Artists Management
Josef Kollmannstrasse 35 E-mail: dickie.artists@kabsi.at
A-2500 Baden bei Wien Phone: +43 2252 844 99
  Fax: +43 2252 458 97

Colbert Artists Management Europe
  http://www.colbertartists.com
  E-mail: akkcolbert@netway.at
  Phone: +43 1 877 9328
  Fax: +43 1 879 5396

Laurent Delage Artists Management
Siebensterngasse 46/1/44 http://www.delage.at
A-1070 Wien E-mail: office@delage.at
  Phone: +43 1 403 63 49
  Fax: +43 1 403 63 49

Esther Schollum Artists' Management
Guntramsdorfer Straße http://www.estherschollum.at
12/2 E-mail: es@estherschollum.at
A-2340 Mödling bei Wien Phone: +43 2236 41 004
  Fax: +43 2236 41 00 44

Helmut Fischer Artists International

Obere Donaustraße 45A/14
A 1020 Wien
http://www.fischerartists.com
E-mail: fischerartists@yahoo.co.uk
Phone: +43 699 19250916

Franz Hainzl Artists' Management

Postfach 17
A-1043 Wien
http://www.hainzl.net
E-mail: office@hainzl.net
Phone: +43 1 586 45 36
Fax: +43 1 585 55 51

Künstleragentur Hollaender-Calix

Grinzinger Allee 46
A-1190 Wien
http://www.hollaender-calix.at/
E-mail: office.hollaender-calix@chello.at
Phone: +43 1 320 53 17
Fax: +43 1 328 90 70

IAAC Italartist Austroconcert GmbH

Austroconcert
Gluckgasse 1
A-1010 Vienna
http://www.ia-ac.com
E-mail: austroconcert@ia-ac.com
Phone: +43-1-5132657
Fax: +43-1-5126154

IAAC Italartist Austroconcert GmbH

Italartist
Lothringerstrasse 14
A-3400 Klosterneuburg
http://www.ia-ac.com
E-mail: italartist@ia-ac.com
Phone: +43-2243-32614
Fax: +43-2243-25819

Interclassica Music Management GmbH *(Eleanor Hope)*

Schönburgstrasse 4
A-1040 Vienna
Phone: +43 1 585 3980

K und K Wien *(Petra Rückstätter-Klose, Robert Jan Haitink)*

Skodagasse 28/10
A-1080 Wien
http://www.kundkwien.com/
E-mail: office@kundkwien.com
Phone: +43 1 406 33 65
Fax: +43 1 406 33 65

Mag. Phil. Peter S. Lehner

Barawitzkagasse 8/16
A - 1190 Wien
E-mail: psle@aon.at
Phone: +43 (1) 369 81 89

Maloberti Music Management

Head office
Aussichtsweg 24
A-9241 Wernberg
http://www.maloberti.at
E-mail: mauro.maloberti@maloberti.at
Phone: +43 (664) 232 60 84

MAP Mafara Artist Promotion *(Maria Gabriella Mafara, Giovanna Gatta)*

Kirchengasse 19/14
A-1070 Wien

http://www.mafara.com/
E-mail: office@mafara.com
Phone: +43 1 478 26 49
Fax: +43 1 478 26 49

Künstlermanagement Georg Monitzer

Lonserstraße 2/10
6832 Sulz

http://www.mon-arts.net
E-mail: georg.monitzer@aon.at
Phone: +43 5522 45 545
Fax: +43 5522 45 545

Musikbureau Severin Wilscher *(Severin Wilscher)*

Fernkorngasse 46/17
A-1100 Wien

http://www.musikbureau-wilscher.com
E-mail: office@musikbureau-wilscher.com
Phone: +43 6643 56 87 92

Opera4u.com GmbH *(Kurt-Walther Schober)*

Hermanngasse 3
A-1070 Wien

http://www.opera4u.com
E-mail: agency@opera4u.com
Phone: +43 1 513 75 920
Fax: +43 1 512 93 51

Parnassus Arts Productions

Erzherzog Wilhelm-Ring 13/ 4
A-2500 Baden

E-mail: office@parnassus.at
Phone: +43 2252 82 777
Fax: +43 2252 82 777 50

Primusic Konzert- und Musiktheaterproduktionen GmbH

Herrengasse 6
A-1010 Wien

http://www.primusic.at
E-mail: office@primusic.at
Phone: +43-1-532 71 24
Fax: +43-1-532 71 40

Künstleragentur Dr. Raab & Dr. Böhm GmbH

Plankengasse 7
A-1010 Wien

http://www.rbartists.at
E-mail: office@rbartists.at
Phone: +43-1-512 05 01
Fax: +43-1-512 77 43

Sono Artists Consulting *(Samantha Farber)*

Am Hof 5/15
A-1010 Vienna

http://www.sonoartistsconsulting.com/
E-mail: office@sonoartistsconsulting.com
Fax: +43 1 532 67 58

Brunner-Herrnleben Kunst- und Kulturproduktions und Consulting GmbH *(Susanne Herrnleben)*

Glacisstrasse 57
A-8010 Graz

http://www.werktreue.com
E-mail: Susanne.herrnleben@werktreue.com
Phone: +41 43 344 05 35

Künstlermanagement Till Dönch
Roegergasse 24-26/G2
A-1090 Wien
http://www.doench.at
E-mail: management@doench.at
Phone: +43 1 470 8083
Fax: +43 1 479 6971

Opera Vladarski
Döblinger Hauptstraße 57/18
A-1190 Wien
E-mail: opera@vladarski.com
Phone: +43 1 368 69 60/61
Fax: +43 1 368 69 60

Vienna Music Connection OG *(Iván Paley, Rodrigo Mora)*
Seilerstätte 12/17
A-1010 Wien
http://www.viemuc.com
E-mail: vmc@viemuc.com
Phone: +43 676 757 3098

Mag. Daniel Wolfsbauer, MAS Künstlermanagement
Schröttergasse 50/ 13
A-1100 Wien
http://www.wolfsbauer-artists.com
E-mail: info@wolfsbauer-artists.com
Phone: +43 699 1913 84 96
Fax: +43 1 604 89 28

Agents in Switzerland

Artists Management Zürich *(Rita Schütz)*
Rütistrasse 52
CH-8044 Zürich-Gockhausen
http://www.artistsman.com
E-mail: schuetz@artistsman.com
Phone: +41 44 821 89 57
Fax: +41 44 821 01 27

Arco Artists Management AG *(Aldo Santi)*
Wildbachstrasse 77
CH 8008 Zürich
http://www.arcoartists.ch
E-mail: info@arcoartists.ch
Phone: +41 44 422 08 00
Fax: +41 44 381 12 54

Balmer & Dixon Management AG (Ltd., SA)
Kreuzstrasse 82
CH-8032 Zurich
http://www.badix.ch
E-mail: mail@badix.ch
Phone: +41 43 244 86 44
Fax: +41 43 244 86 49

Caecilia Lyric Department
Rennweg 15
CH-8001 Zürich
http://www.caecilia.ch
E-mail: caecilia@caecilia-lyric.ch
Phone: +41 44 221 33 88
Fax: +41 44 211 71 82

Christoph Boller Artists Management
Magnolienstrasse 3
CH-8008 Zürich
http://www.cbamanagement.ch
E-mail: mail@cbamanagement.ch
Phone: +41 44 422 66 83
Fax: +41 44 422 66 73

Secrétariat Artistique Muriel Denzler *(Muriel Denzler)*
Rue de la Cure 12
CH-2022 Bevaix
http://www.murieldenzler.com
E-mail: secret.art@gmail.com
Phone: +41 32 846 26 12
Fax: +41 32 846 37 87

dieproduktion GmbH *(Björn Jensen)*
Schützenmattstrasse 43
CH-4051 Basel
http://www.dieproduktion.com
E-mail: jensen@dieproduktion.com
Phone: +49 30 868 708 2710

Gerstel International Opera Management *(Teddy Gerstel)*
Stockerstrasse 10
CH-8002 Zürich
E-mail: gerstel@swissonline.ch
Phone: +41 76 391 88 01
Fax: +41 44 253 14 53

image4you Opera management *(Oliver D. Sehmsdorf)*
Turnhallestrasse 16
CH-8357 Guntershausen/Aadorf
http://www.image4you.net
E-mail: success@image4you.net
Phone: +41 52 511 25 38
Fax: +41 52 511 25 39

Lorenzo Fontana Artists Management
Via Adamina 2
CH-6932 Breganzona
http://www.lorenzofontana.ch
E-mail: lorenzofontana77@yahoo.it
Phone: +4176 450 65 44

MAT Opera Genève *(Rajko Markovic)*
60 Boulevard Saint Georges
CH-1205 Genève
http://www.mat-opera.com
E-mail: radomirmarkovic@mat-opera.com
Phone: +33 (0)4 50 37 03 48

OPERA 3000 International Artists Management
Lugano
http://www.opera3000.net
E-mail: liriopera@yahoo.it
Phone: +41 79 730 65 13

Artists Management Verena Keller
Lohwisstrasse 52
CH-8123 Ebmatingen
E-mail: keller.verena@bluewin.ch
Phone: +41 44 980 15 13
Fax: +41 44 980 36 86

Seven Ways to Soak in the Language

1. Join a gym and go to fitness classes. You have no choice but to understand when the instructor is yelling orders *auf Deutsch* into your face.

2. Go to the movies. I found that seeing American movies dubbed into German was the most efficient way.

3. Turn the TV on and leave it on. Watch a lot of TV.

4. Turn the radio on and leave it on. Listen to a lot of radio news.

5. Tell your German-speaking friends and colleagues to correct you every time you make a mistake.

6. Play *Scrabble*™ in German.

7. Get a girlfriend, boyfriend, or both…

Ten Things I Love about Germany and Austria

1. Automatic Stamp machines with the Deutsche Post. The postage is expensive as hell, but you just pump the money in and they print out postage, in any amount.

2. Bank transfers instead of checks; they make life so much easier.

3. Socialized health care

4. Trains

5. Great beer and wine

6. Recycling. It is everywhere. In Germany, you pay a deposit on virtually every bottle (so take your bottles back when they are empty!).

7. Bicycle paths and lanes seemingly everywhere

8. *Kaffee und Kuchen*

9. *Döner*

10. Fresh bread, *Bratwurst* (especially *Thüringerwurst!*), *Maultaschen*, and *Cola-Light* (not to be confused with Diet Coke)

Printed in Poland
by Amazon Fulfillment
Poland Sp. z o.o., Wrocław